Gathering

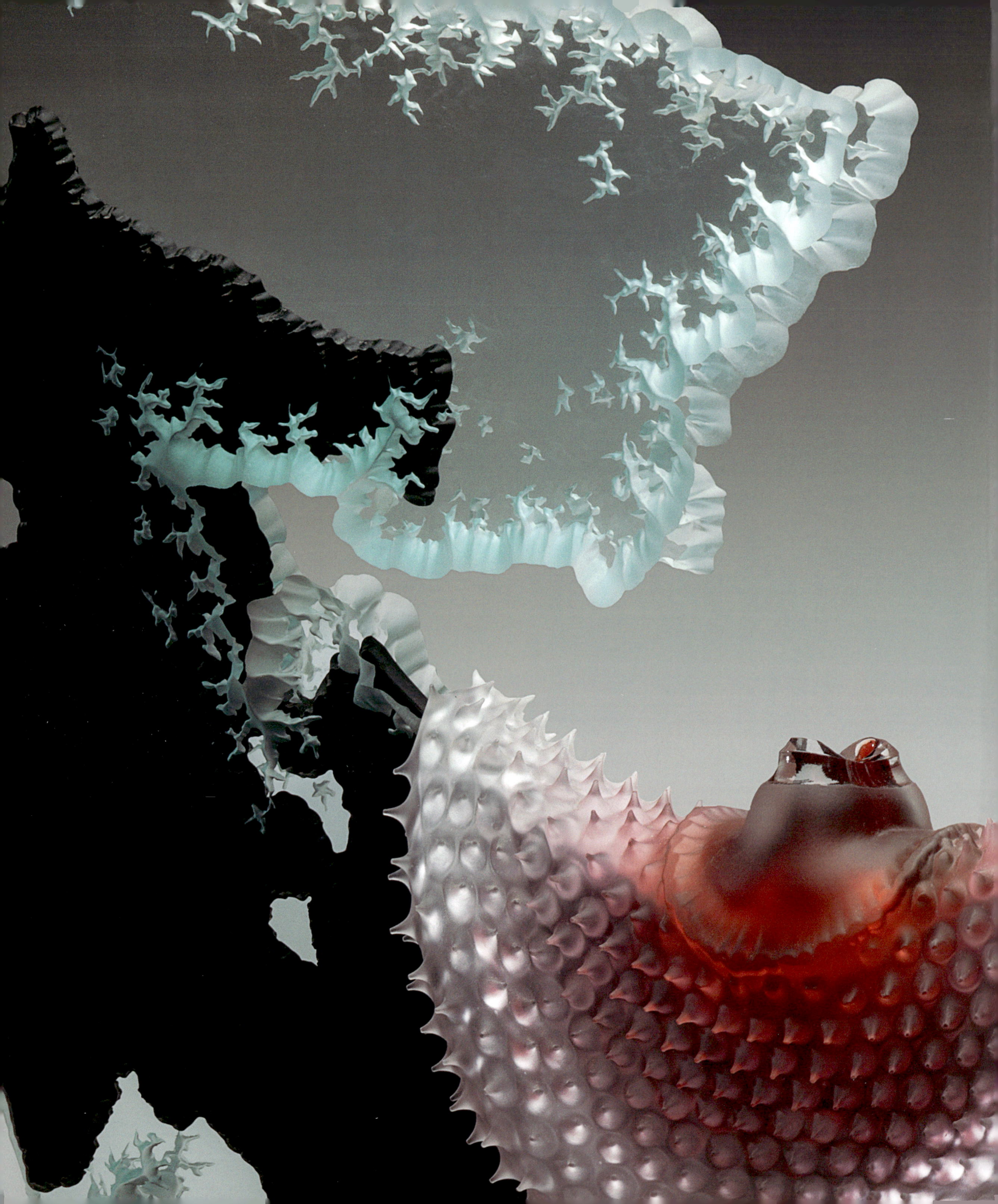

Gathering

The Carl and Betty Pforzheimer
Collection of Studio Glass

Edited by
Sarah N. Chasse
with Lan Morgan

Peabody Essex Museum
Salem, Massachusetts

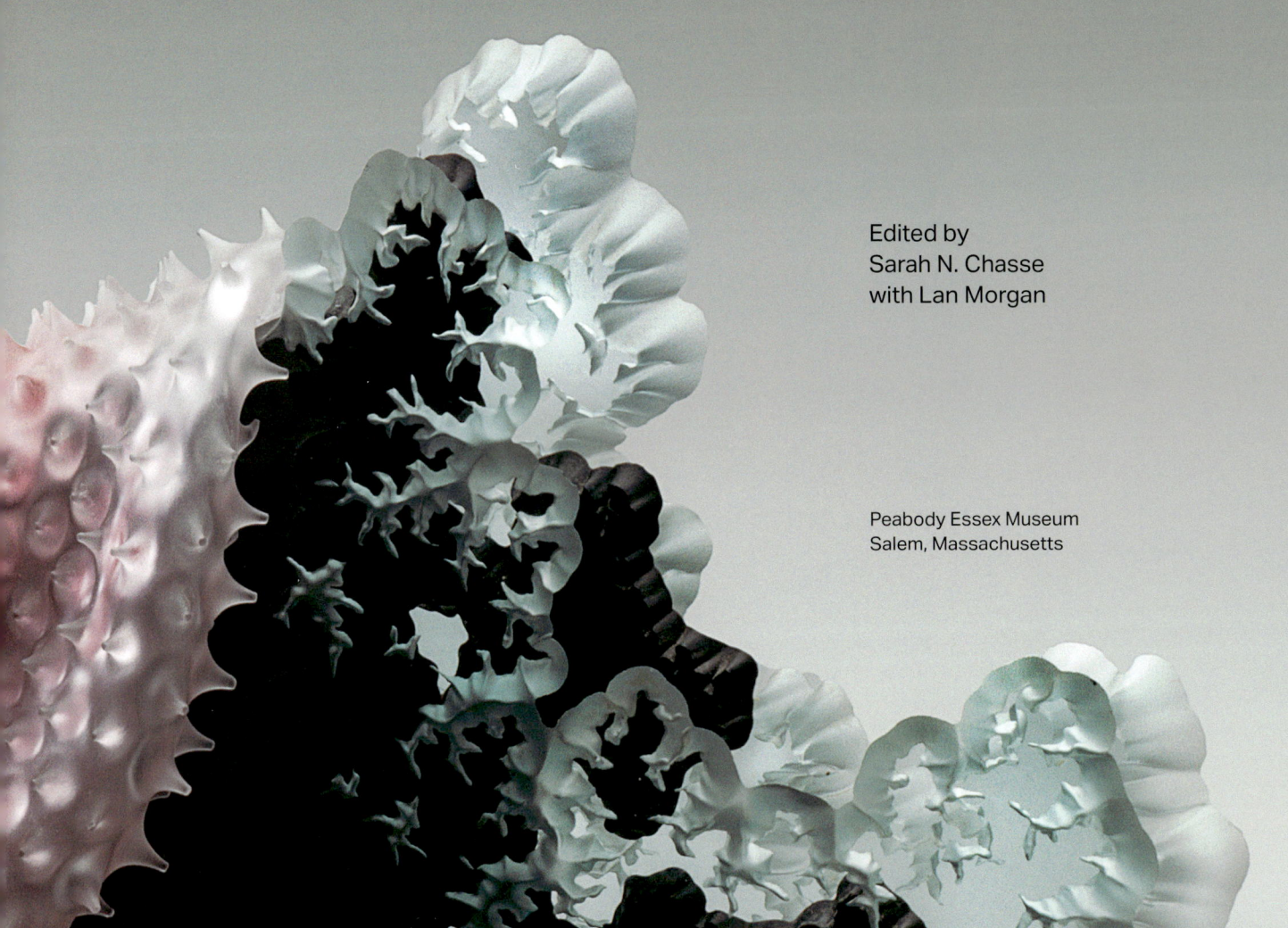

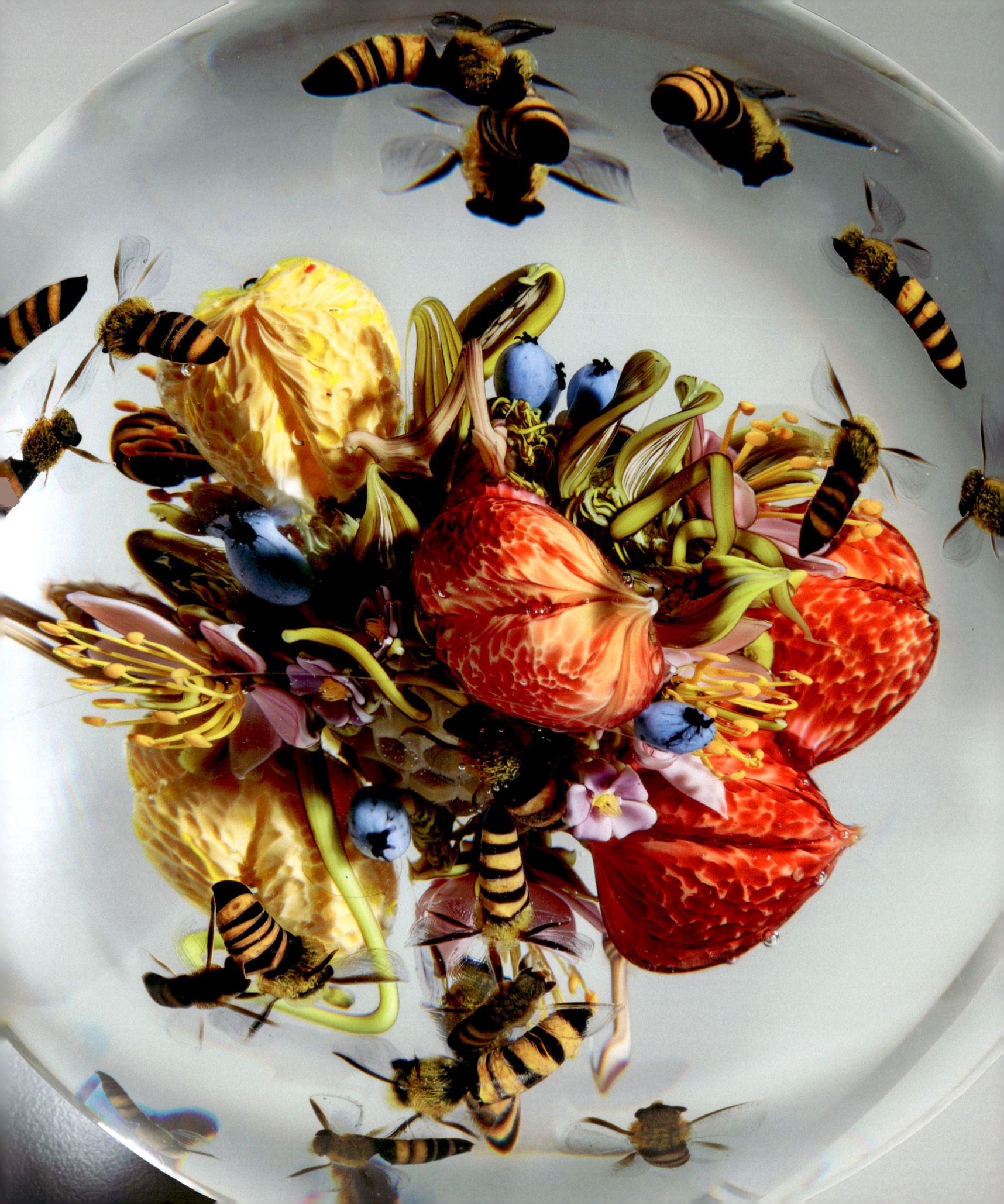

Contents

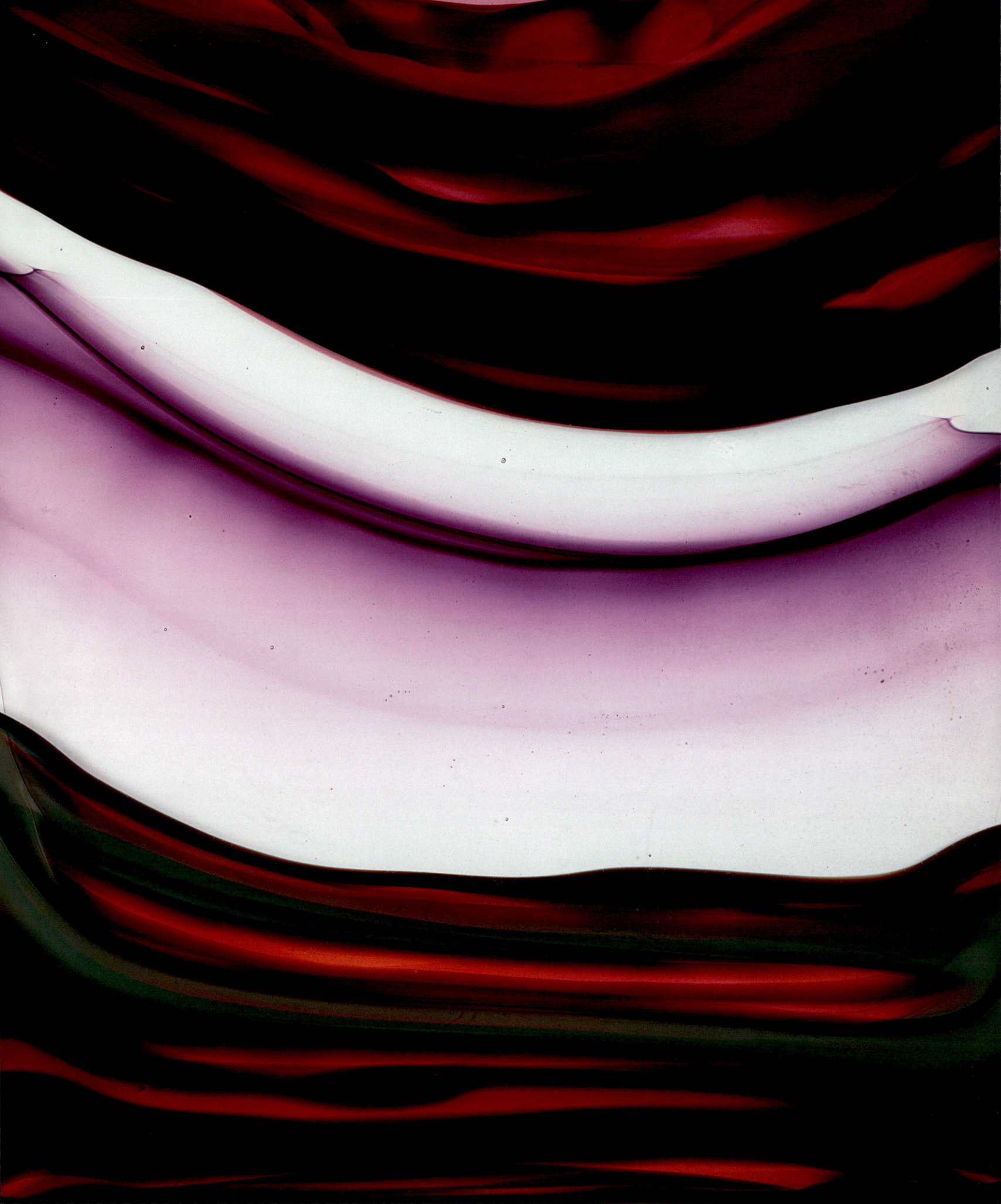

Director's Foreword and Acknowledgments

Glass is performance art . . .
from its fluidity to the way
it scatters light in space.

—Thomas Phifer, architect

As we drink from an everyday glass or look though a glass window, these more mundane versions of the medium may lull us into overlooking glass as a radical expression of human ingenuity. Part matter and energy; part physicality and creativity; part chance and chemistry—these are the dualities that embody glassmaking's remarkable ability to harness and then transform earth, air, and fire. Whether blown, molded, or pressed; twisted or turned; translucent or opaque, glass challenges the balance between fragility and mutability at the hands of glassmaking artists who tease this material into shapes, scales, and colorations that often defy logic or possibility.

This publication honors the superlative collection of works in glass that New York–based collectors Carl and Betty Pforzheimer donated to the Peabody Essex Museum in 2022. The deep personal connections that the couple have forged with artists have imbued this collection with a purposeful character, one dedicated to experimentation, excellence, and the very human act of creativity. Their commitment reminds us of the profound impact that passionately intelligent collecting and philanthropy can have on the creative community, cultural preservation, and education.

This book also celebrates the studio glass gallery, named in the Pforzheimers' honor, that the museum opened in 2024 to showcase selections from the collection's 220 works by 90 international artists. They represent a panoramic view of the evolution and expressive range of glass from the twentieth and twenty-first centuries, with Nancy Callan, Dale Chihuly, Karen LaMonte, Harvey K. Littleton, Richard Marquis, Preston Singletary, Lino Tagliapietra, and Toots Zynsky among the pioneering and influential artists featured in the gallery.

That PEM has acquired the Pforzheimer collection is something of a metaphorical homecoming. Salem, Massachusetts, was home to the first successful glass-producing house in colonial North America between 1639 and 1645, and Massachusetts played a major role in commercial glass production in the eighteenth and nineteenth centuries, with the New England Glass Company—founded in Cambridge in 1818 and moving to Toledo, Ohio, in 1888 to become the Libbey Glass Company—as a prime example. The museum itself has collected glass since 1804, distinguishing it as the first American museum with an international glass collection.

8   Among its over 3,600 examples of historic European and American glass
are a 264-piece set of Irish table glass from 1817 associated with PEM's
historic house, the Ropes Mansion, and over 500 glass works made by
early American firms and donated in 2000 by Massachusetts collector
Gretchen Keuffel Keller. In 1999, the museum began collecting contemporary studio glass and has continued to do so with the generosity of
collectors such as Phyllis and Samuel Rubinovitz and through commissions to artists such as María Magdalena Campos-Pons.

   Gathering: The Carl and Betty Pforzheimer Collection of Studio Glass
attests to our deep appreciation of Carl and Betty Pforzheimer for placing
their trust in the Peabody Essex Museum as the ongoing home for their
lovingly and smartly formed collection. Their desire to share their collection with museum visitors, scholars, and artists for generations to come
underwrites their superlative generosity. They join me in thanking our
Trustee Emeritus Robert N. Shapiro for the timely introduction that led to
this landmark gift to the museum, as well as Amanda Clark MacMullan,
PEM's former Chief Philanthropy Officer, and Sue Kim, PEM's current
Chief Philanthropy Officer, for their respective roles in stewarding our
relationship so thoughtfully. The Pforzheimers and I also wish to acknowl-
edge the seminal counsel of Dean Lahikainen, PEM's Carolyn and Peter
Lynch Curator Emeritus of American Decorative Art, and Dan Lipcan,
Ann C. Pingree Director of the Phillips Library, for his expert handling of
the couple's donation of their glass library to PEM.

   Any medium or process lies dormant until activated by artists who
strive to combine creativity and passion with intelligence and daring, and
so, to the artists represented in the Pforzheimer collection, go our deep
gratitude and admiration.

   Sarah Chasse, PEM's Curator-at-Large, developed the inaugural
Studio Glass installation in the Pforzheimer Gallery and this publication
with an exemplary blend of curatorial rigor and sensitivity. Sarah bene-
fited greatly from the Pforzheimers' graciously shared knowledge, and
the friendship and fun that they have experienced is one of the many
rewards of such projects.

   Together, Sarah and I thank the many people whose talents and
collaboration have contributed to creating our new gallery and this

publication. To Petra Slinkard, Director of Curatorial Affairs, for her unflagging support and finessed oversight of the projects' development and implementation. To Karina Corrigan for her counsel during the acquisition process, and to curatorial intern Isabella Nadeau, who supported Sarah's work throughout the preparation of the gallery and publication. To John Childs, Megan MacNeil, Jacqueline Quint, Don McPhee, and Marta Fodor for their roles in advancing the collection's acquisition, stewardship, and documentation processes; Matthew DelGrosso for leading the gallery's installation implementation; Kelsey Mallet for her expert project management; Dave Seibert and Liandra Charette for an inspiring gallery design; and Chip van Dyke for illuminating media support. To the Corning Museum of Glass for the use of their engaging process and technique videos in the gallery. To Terry Neff for her insightful editorial counsel in the book's formative stages. To Lan Morgan for her excellent texts for the book. To Kathleen Garrett for her astute editing. At Marquand Books, to Gina Broze, Melissa Duffes, and Kestrel Rundle for overseeing the editing, design, and production of this beautiful volume; and Ryan Polich for designing the book's persuasive marriage of text and imagery. To Richard Goodbody for his expert photography of challenging three-dimensional objects, and John Morgan's precise post-production editing. To Kathy Tarantola for her photographic contributions, and to Buck Ennis for his at-home photography of the couple.

Whether you experience these works in person or through this publication, the Pforzheimers' collecting philosophy, perspective on this unique medium, and aspirations for the impact of their gift are a testament to the beauty, complexity, and potential of studio glass. In these pages is also the expression of what we hold dear at the Peabody Essex Museum—that celebrating the many facets of creativity—from art to science—reflects our belief in the potential of the imagination to inspire, challenge, and delight.

Lynda Roscoe Hartigan
The Rose-Marie and Eijk van Otterloo Executive Director and CEO

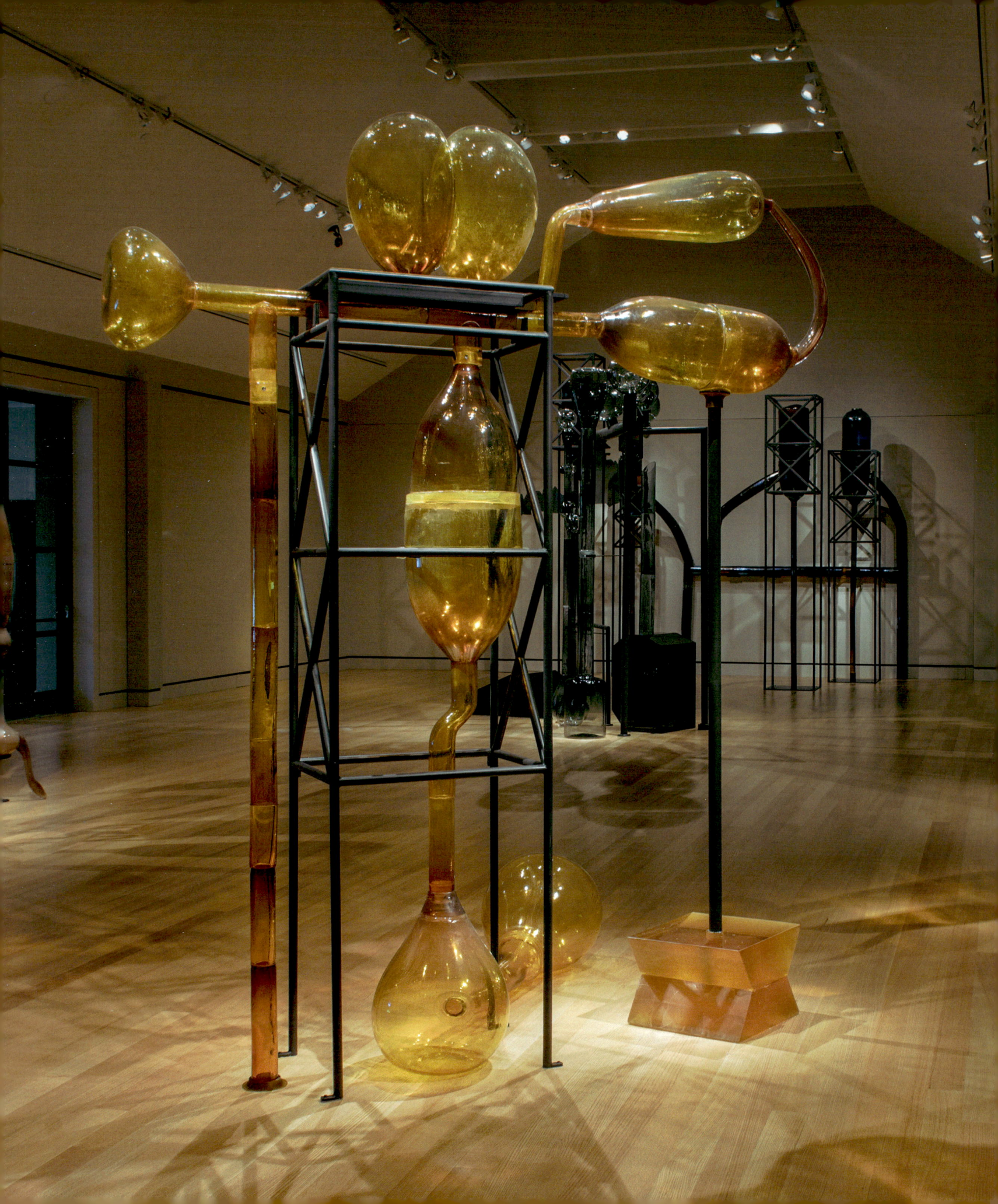

Introduction

225 Years of Collecting Glass at the Peabody Essex Museum

Sarah N. Chasse and Lan Morgan

Glass is everywhere at the Peabody Essex Museum (PEM), in the windows and on the tables of the museum's many historic houses, in the scientific instruments and tools mariners used to navigate the seas, and in the early photographs that commemorate places and people of Salem and around the world. Since its founding as the East India Marine Society (EIMS) in 1799, the museum has been collecting international glass. Beginning as a maritime society, later merging with a local history institution, and finally, evolving into an internationally recognized museum of art and culture, PEM's holdings reflect the development of the institution itself. This has resulted in a unique glass collection that is as geographically diverse as it is eclectic, encompassing both rare and quotidian examples that span centuries.[1]

East India Marine Society

As early as 1800, the first objects containing glass entered the collection of the East India Marine Society. Membership in the society was limited to sea captains and supercargoes who had navigated near or beyond the Cape of Good Hope or Cape Horn. Charged with bringing home objects of natural and artificial curiosity, members returned to Salem with fine art, cultural objects, and natural history specimens acquired while conducting international trade.[2] In January 1800, Captain Nathaniel Silsbee donated the bell-shaped glass base of a water pipe, or hookah, from his travels in India.[3] The pipe constitutes the first glass object recorded in the society logbook, as "Hooker [sic] used in Bengal Smoking Tobacco." In 1804, Captain Benjamin Carpenter, one of the society's founders, donated the museum's first significant glass acquisition, a set of late eighteenth-century English cut-glass chandeliers (fig. 2) and wall sconces. In 1825, they were installed as lighting in the newly opened East India Marine Hall, the first permanent home and exhibition space for the collections. Both chandeliers remain installed in the Hall to this day.

Salem's early mercantile connections with Asia are evident in PEM's significant collection of reverse paintings on glass made for export markets. The collection contains over sixty examples made by Cantonese artists, many with documented histories of purchase by American merchants. The first reverse painting on glass to enter the East India Marine Society collection was in 1825 (fig. 3). Thought to depict Teg Bakht Khān,

Figure 1 María Magdalena Campos-Pons (born 1959, Cuba) and Neil Leonard (born 1959, United States), *Alchemy of the Soul, Elixir for the Spirits*, 2015 (installation view of *Alchemy of the Soul: María Magdalena Campos-Pons*, 2016). Blown glass, cast glass, steel, cast resin, silicone, acrylic, polyvinyl chloride tubing, water, and rum essence, overall: 119½ × 102¼ × 54¾ in. (303.53 × 259.72 × 139.07 cm). Peabody Essex Museum purchase, made possible by the Nancy Tieken Memorial Fund and the Elizabeth Rogers Fund, 2015, 2015.46.8

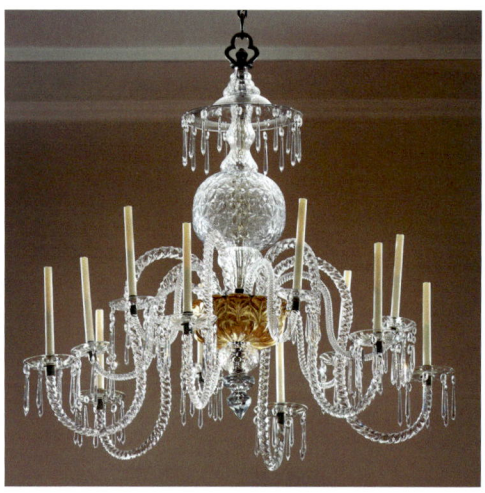

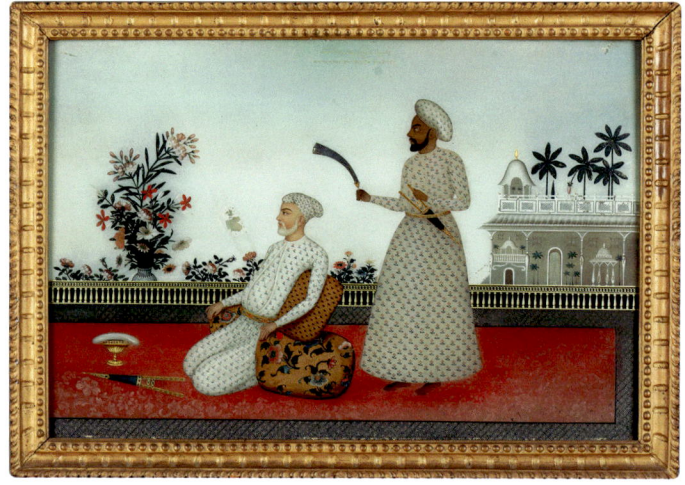

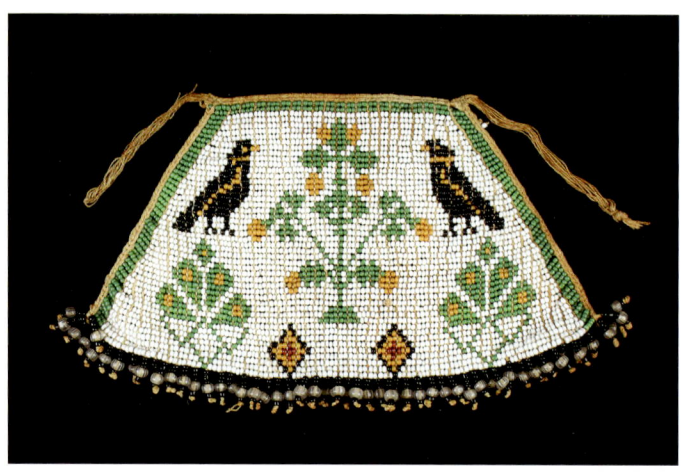

ruler of Surat from 1733 to 1746, the portrait was acquired by Nathan Cook, probably during his time as a ship captain in Asia. Reverse paintings on glass were a popular export item among the many American traders flooding the harbors of China and India, and were usually painted on imported English panes of glass or mirrored glass. While the precise origins of this work remain a mystery, recent analysis of the frame's construction suggests it was produced in China and that the painting is a copy of a miniature Cook acquired while in India.[4] Later acquisitions to the collection have resulted in its diversity of Asian glass holdings, including a Japanese Buddhist bronze reliquary with a glass sphere dating to 1679, and several examples of Chinese imperial glass.

The early members of the East India Marine Society also collected Indigenous artworks widely celebrated for their exceptional aesthetic qualities and provenance. PEM's collection of Native American art spans North, Central, and South America—making it the oldest ongoing collection of its kind in the western hemisphere, representing ten thousand years of Indigenous visual expression. Trade in rubber, lumber, guano, and silver in South America resulted in the donation of rare Amazon Basin featherwork and glass beadwork as well as Peruvian and Bolivian ceramics.[5] One outstanding example of early beadwork, brought into the collection before 1821, is a women's queyu, or apron, composed of glass beads (fig. 4). The apron depicts two naturalistic birds, diamonds, and flowering plants in vivid yellow and green, popular colors held in the highest esteem in the Guianas. The first documentation of these beaded aprons in the region dates as early as 1652.[6] Glass beads have been an important trade commodity from the beginning of European contact, and the examples of the glass beads used in this work likely came from the Netherlands, a major exporter of glass beads from Bavaria and Bohemia.[7]

Essex Institute

The diversity of PEM's glass collections owes thanks to another of its predecessor organizations: the Essex Institute. Founded in 1821 as the

Figure 2 Artists in England, Chandelier in East India Marine Hall, 1760s, with later additions. Cut lead glass, metal, and gold, 44 × 44 in. (111.76 × 111.76 cm). Peabody Essex Museum, gift of Benjamin Carpenter, 1804, M81

Figure 3 Artists in Guangzhou, China, Portrait of Nawab Namdar Teg Bakht Khān Bahadur and a servant, 1790–91, after an Indian miniature. Reverse glass painting, 17½ × 25½ in. (44.5 × 65 cm). Peabody Essex Museum, gift of Nathan Cook, 1825, E9942

Figure 4 Possibly Lokono [Arawak] artist in Guyana, Woman's queyu (apron), ca. 1800–20. Glass beads and cordage, 6 × 10½ × ¼ in. (15.24 × 26.67 × .635 cm). Peabody Essex Museum collection, before 1821, E7433

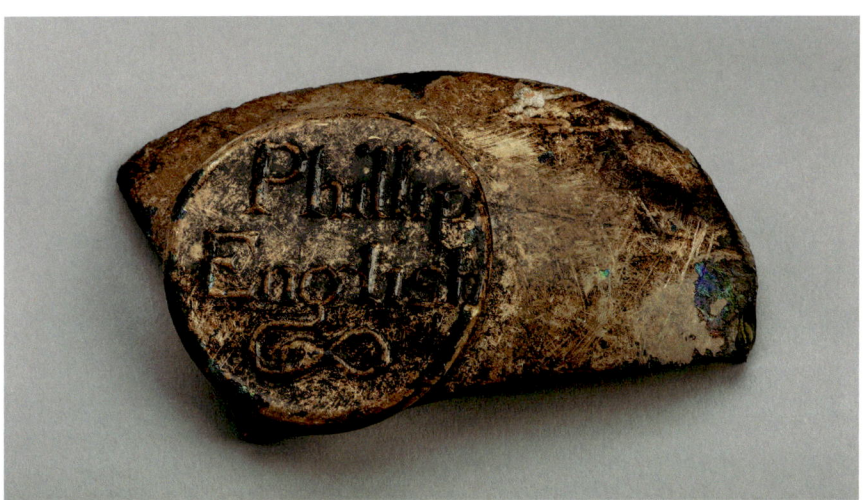

Figure 5 Artists in England, bottle fragment owned by Philip English, late 17th century. Glass, 1¾ × 3 × ⅝ in. (4.45 × 7.62 × 1.59 cm). Peabody Essex Museum purchase, 1946, 126985

Essex Historical Society, the Essex Institute was among the first museums in the country to collect decorative arts. Its collection comprised a wide range of fine and everyday objects, spanning the seventeenth to the twentieth centuries, compiled to reflect the material culture and history of Essex County, Massachusetts and New England.

Many important early seventeenth-century examples of American glass came in through the Essex Institute. They illuminate the significant role glass played in the early British colony. Several even relate to an infamous episode in American history, the Salem Witch Trials of 1692. One of the most evocative examples is a rare leaded window with diamond-shaped panes, typical of the style found in seventeenth-century American and English architecture.

The window was likely once installed in a home in Salem built by Joshua Buffum, a founder of Salem's first Quaker community in the 1660s, who was connected to many of the prominent community members involved in the Witch Trials. Joshua Buffum's surviving account book includes entries for casement windows and hardware, indicating that he likely produced the piece himself and possibly sourced the panes locally. This rare survivor, one of two in PEM's collection associated with the Trials, is significant for its historical association as well as its materiality. The translucence of the panes would have provided a crucial source of light in a dark seventeenth-century home, as well as a vista to the world outside. Two Buffum family homes stood side by side near Proctor's Ledge, the execution site for many innocent people accused of witchcraft. Thus, this window once acted as a portal onto unimaginable scenes of violence.

Another rare glass object connected to the Witch Trials is a bottle-seal fragment originally owned by Philip English, one of the many people accused of witchcraft in the area (fig. 5). English was an immigrant from the Isle of Jersey. He settled in Salem in about 1670 and married Mary Holingworth, the daughter of a wealthy tavern owner. English's success in international maritime trade provided him with great wealth, but his affluence, foreign birth, and increasing influence in local government attracted jealousy and suspicion. In 1692, the Englishes were convicted and imprisoned on charges of witchcraft before fleeing to New York, where they waited for the hysteria to pass. Upon returning to Salem, Philip

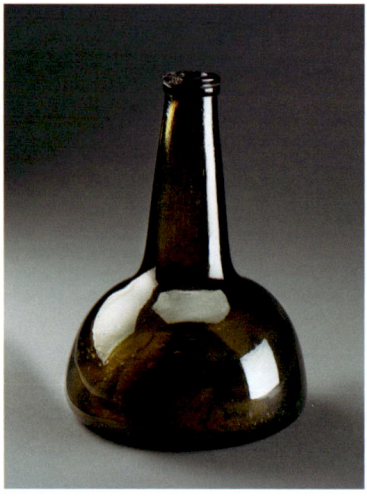

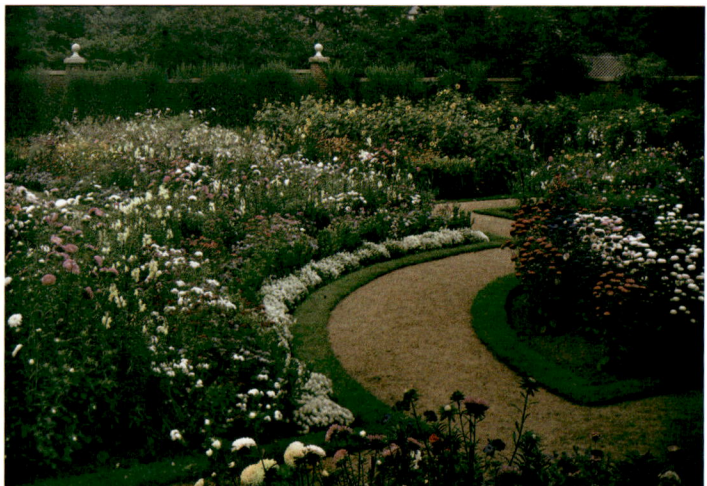

spent the rest of his life seeking recovery of, and compensation for, his valuable lost property. This bottle fragment, likely produced in Britain and branded with English's name, is a poignant marker of his identity.

The majority of the Essex Institute's glass collecting focused on seventeenth- through nineteenth-century American and European examples with a documented history of regional ownership. The most notable donation was given by George Rea Curwen (1823–1900). Curwen began collecting decorative arts from prominent Salem families, including his own, at the age of 25.[8] He was distinctive for assembling a private decorative arts collection before the Civil War. His collection was donated to the Essex Institute after his death and numbers over 350 objects, almost all produced before 1815. Curwen had a particular interest in tableware and amassed a large collection of glass stemware that includes many English and European forms used in Salem in the seventeenth and eighteenth centuries.[9]

Other donations of glass aligned with this pattern. In 1911, Cecelia Remond Babcock gifted an elegantly shaped gin bottle (fig. 6) with a significant family history. The bottle belonged to her father, John Remond. It included a note written by him stating: "Presented to me by my mother the day I sailed on the 25th of July 1798, on the letter of marque, brig Six Brothers." Born in the Dutch colony of Curaçao in 1788, John Remond traveled to Salem at the age of 10. He learned the trades of barbering and catering and married an accomplished baker and cook, Mary Lenox. The couple ran a catering business in Salem's Hamilton Hall for many years and were known and sought after for their dazzling feasts. The Remonds were influential activists championing abolition, women's suffrage, and school desegregation in Salem, as well as raising talented children who also led in these causes.

The Essex Institute also acquired important examples of early photographic processes, in which glass was an essential component, including a rare series of seven autochromes depicting the gardens behind the Ropes Mansion, in Salem (fig. 7). Invented in the early twentieth century, autochromes were the first commercially viable form of color photography. Color was achieved by applying dyed red, blue, and green grains of

Figure 6 Artist in the Netherlands, John Remond's gin bottle, mid-18th century. Blown glass, 8¼ × Diam. 5¾ in. (20.96 × 14.61 cm). Peabody Essex Museum, gift of Cecelia Remond Babcock, 1911, 102810

Figure 7 Artist in Salem, view of the garden of the Ropes Mansion, 1915. Autochrome, 5 × 7 × ⅛ in. (12.7 × 17.78 × 0.32 cm). Peabody Essex Museum, gift of the Trustees of the Ropes Memorial, 1989, R2083

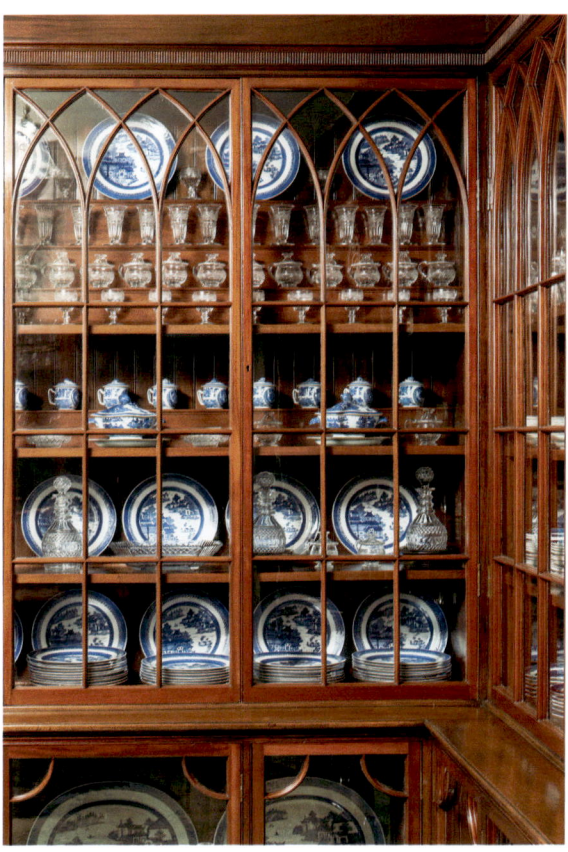

Figure 8 Ceramics and glass on view in the 1893 China Room in the Ropes Mansion, 2015

potato starch onto glass, followed by a layer of silver gelatin. The photographs of the garden were taken to help winter visitors to the house visualize the garden in bloom.[10]

Indeed, the Essex Institute was also a pioneer in the preservation of historic houses and architecture, and acquired many notable Salem buildings and their contents. In doing so, significant domestic glass objects entered the collection with a documented history of ownership and use. A near complete set of Anglo-Irish table glass survives in the Ropes Mansion, one of several historic homes preserved by the Essex Institute and still under PEM's care. Joseph and Sally Orne purchased the 197-piece set, including water tumblers, stemmed wine glasses, lemonade cups, custard cups, conical jelly glasses for serving dessert, and three decanters of different sizes to hold water, wine, and sherry, from Nathan Hastings & Co. Boston in 1817. Today, the set resides in the home's glass-doored pantry, specially built around 1894 to showcase the family's ceramic and glass collections (fig. 8).

Peabody Essex Museum and the Twenty-First Century

After a series of mergers that absorbed several local cultural and scientific institutions, the Peabody Museum (a later iteration of the East India Marine Society) and Essex Institute merged to form the Peabody Essex Museum in 1992, reenvisioned as an international art museum focused on art and culture. PEM's approach to collecting glass has reflected the museum's expanded definition of art, which embraces fine and decorative art traditions, vernacular art, studio craft, and design. In 2000, the museum acquired over 500 important examples of glass from the Gretchen Keller Glass Collection from Bradford College. Gretchen Keuffel Keller (1885–1974) of New Jersey assembled the collection by focusing on American glass made prior to 1885, favoring works from major glassmaking centers, such as the Boston and Sandwich Glass Company (1826–1888). She had an exquisite eye for rare forms and colors, as exemplified in an unusual pitcher, one of a pair, from New Jersey embellished with a looped opaque white-and-blue body and a dimensional applied clear glass layer in a

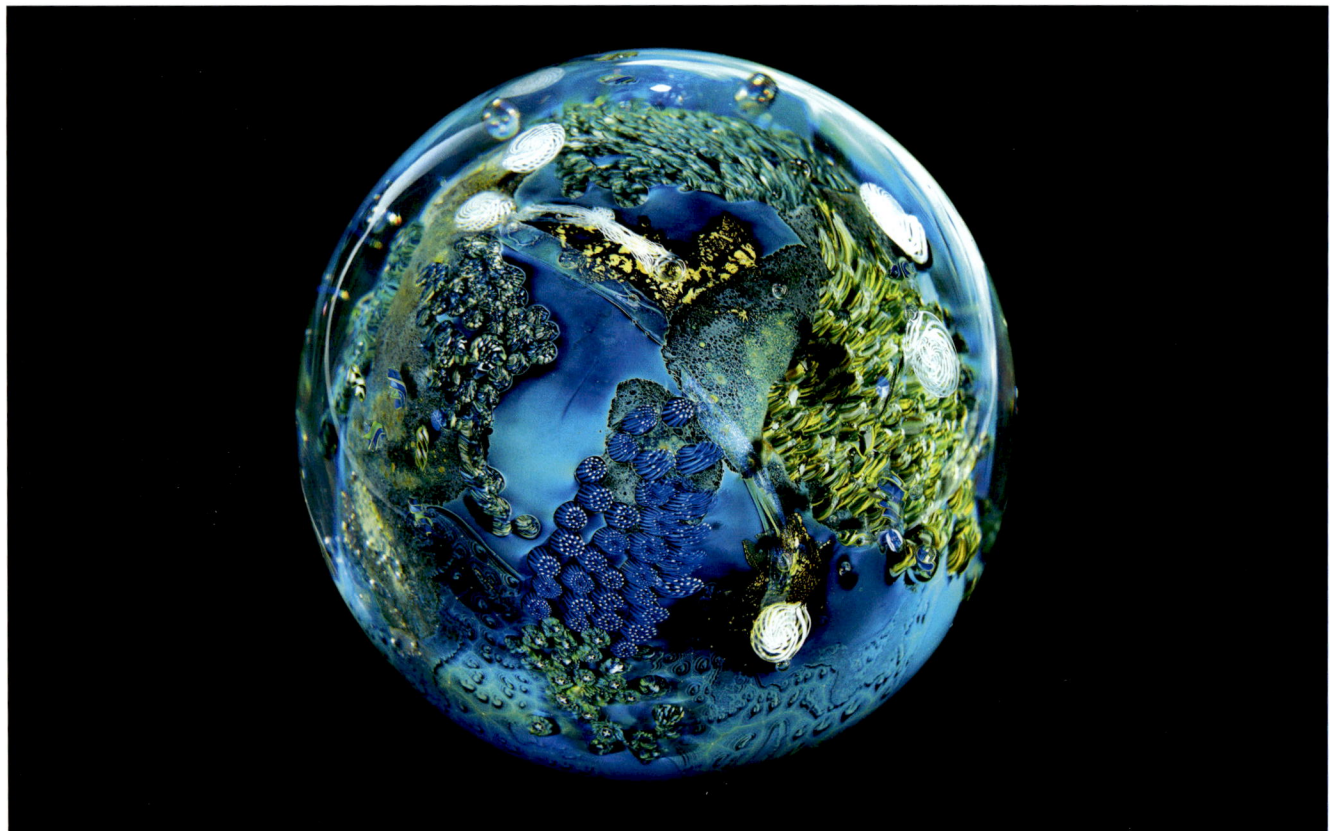

Figure 9 Josh Simpson (born 1949, United States), *Mega Megaplanet*, 1999. Flameworked glass, 11 × Diam. 11 in. (27.94 cm). Peabody Essex Museum purchase, 1999, 137968

gadroon pattern. These masterpieces of nineteenth-century glassmaking also each feature a 1853 U.S. silver half dime enclosed in a hollow knop at the base, possibly included to commemorate an event or simply to mark their date of production.

More recently, PEM has sought out works of studio and contemporary craft that explore technical and creative innovations in glass. In 1999, PEM acquired its first pieces of American studio glass directly from Massachusetts artists Sidney Hutter and Josh Simpson. Simpson's *Mega Megaplanet* (fig. 9), a monumental orb embedded with a sea of intricate *millefiori* forms, is now an iconic work in PEM's collection.

In 2014, the museum commissioned María Magdalena Campos-Pons to create a series of works for a major exhibition, *Alchemy of the Soul: María Magdalena Campos-Pons*, which opened in 2016 (fig. 1). Campos-Pons conceived of seven massive sculptures in glass that evoke the ghostlike forms of abandoned sugar factories dotting the countryside near her childhood home in Matanzas, Cuba. She collaborated with glassmakers in Boston and California to realize the sculptures. The ambitious project connected the brutal history of the Cuban sugar industry to trade between New England and the Caribbean in the eighteenth and nineteenth centuries. The installation offered visitors a visceral experience that ignited the senses and stimulated an awareness of place, memory, identity, and labor. Campos-Pons's project also prompted the curatorial team to explore PEM's own collection in search of objects related to the manufacture of rum. This led to the discovery of a nineteenth-century blown-glass bottle preserving raw sugar from

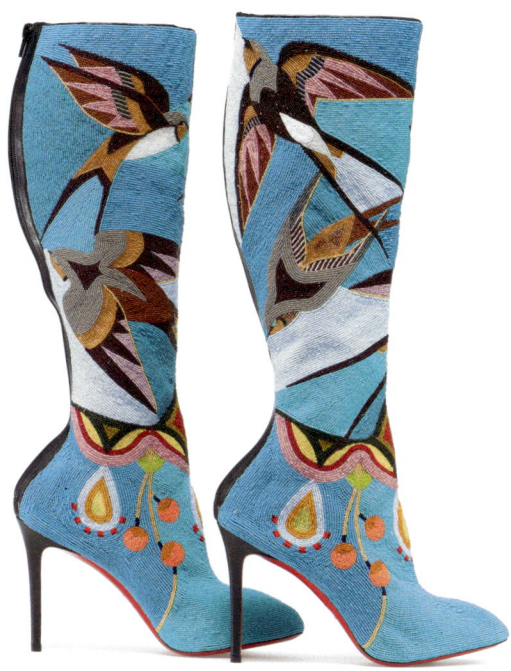

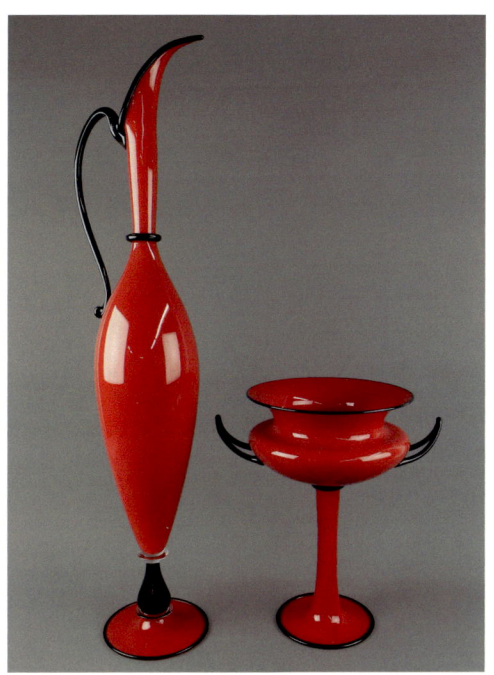

Figure 10 Jamie Okuma (born 1980, United States, Luiseño and Shoshone-Bannock), *Boots*, 2014. Glass beads on boots designed by Christian Louboutin, 19½ × 9⅛ × 3½ in. (49.53 × 23.114 × 8.89 cm). Peabody Essex Museum commission with support from Katrina M. Carye, John Curuby, Karen Keane and Dan Elias, Cynthia Gardner, Merry Glosband, and Steve and Ellen Hoffman and the Willoughby Stuart Memorial Fund, 2014.44.1AB

Figure 11 Dante Marioni (born 1964, United States), *Red Pair*, 1995. Blown glass, 33½ × 7¾ × 6½ in. (85.09 × 19.69 × 16.51 cm). Peabody Essex Museum, gift of Phyllis and Samuel Rubinovitz, 2016.35.5AB

Matanzas, likely from the factories near Campos-Pons's home, and a rum bottle from a Salem distillery that represents the transformation of Caribbean sugar into spirits in New England.[11]

In the same year, PEM commissioned a pair of beaded boots by Jamie Okuma for inclusion in the major traveling exhibition *Native Fashion Now* (fig. 10). Okuma is known for her intricately detailed and sumptuous beadwork that adorns garments, footwear, accessories, and dolls. By hand-stitching thousands of antique glass beads onto a pair of luxury Christian Louboutin boots, Okuma depicts graceful swallows swirling over abstract floral motifs. The scene evokes childhood memories of summers spent rescuing swallows from their nests in a waterslide on her homelands. Akin to the bird and floral motifs on the nineteenth-century queyu from Guyana, both examples of women's glass beadwork telegraph that Native concepts of dress and beauty are inextricably bound to identity.

In 2016, PEM was presented with an extraordinary opportunity to acquire fifty-eight pieces of contemporary glass from Massachusetts–based collectors Phyllis and Samuel Rubinovitz. This landmark gift marked the first substantial donation of studio glass to PEM. With works by many of the central figures in the movement, including Stephen Rolfe Powell, Dante Marioni (fig. 11), Clare Belfrage, Lino Tagliapietra, and Dale Chihuly, the Rubinovitz collection serves as a foundational acquisition that shaped the direction of PEM's contemporary glass projects for the years that followed.

In 2024, the Asian glass collection at PEM was substantially enhanced by a transformative gift of Japanese cloisonné enamels from scholar and collector Fredric T. Schneider that traces four centuries of cloisonné enamel production. First practiced in Japan in the seventeenth century, the labor-intensive technique of decorating metal forms with colored-glass paste reached a pinnacle of technical and artistic excellence during the late nineteenth and early twentieth centuries. The Schneider collection

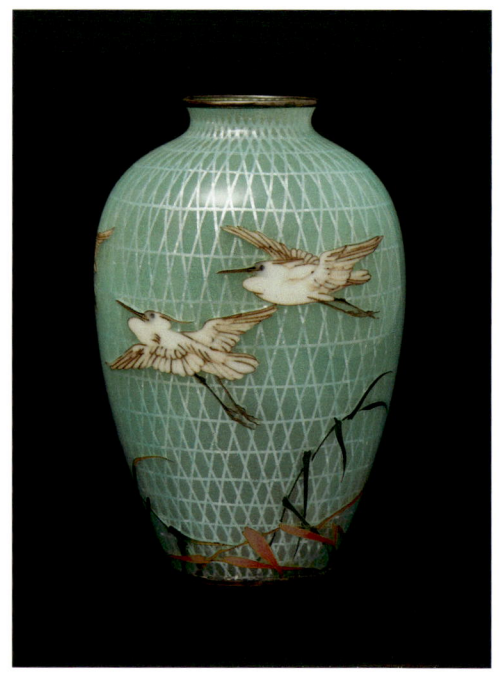

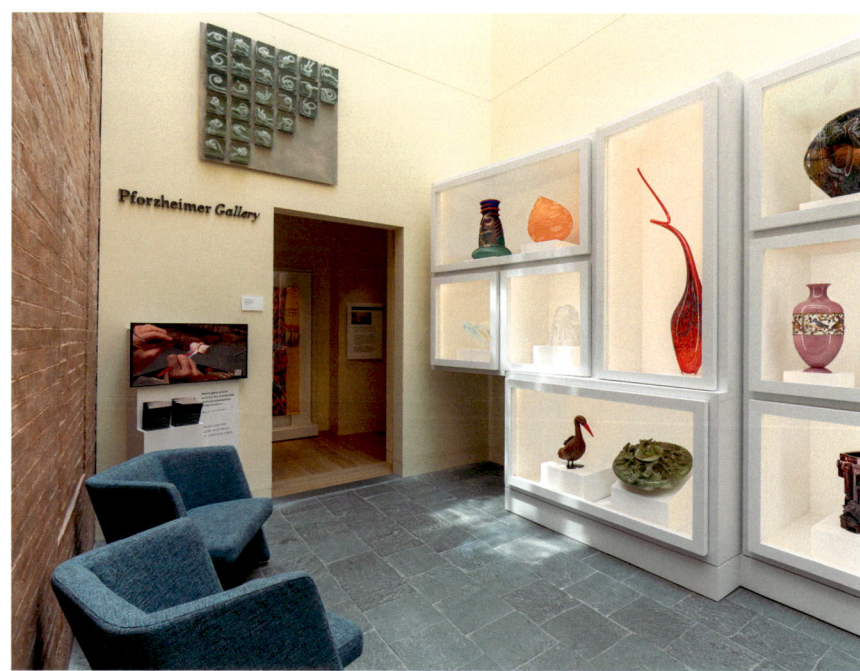

includes commissions for the Japanese imperial family, pieces for export—among them masterworks exhibited at many international fairs—as well as a group of important cloisonné enamel pieces by contemporary master practitioners (fig. 12).

In 2021, Carl and Betty Pforzheimer, of Scarsdale, New York, were looking for a museum that could become a home for their collection of historic and studio glass. Compelled by PEM's history and holdings in glass, they decided to donate 268 objects to the museum and over 100 books, journals, and glass-collecting ephemera to PEM's Phillips Library. The Pforzheimers augmented the donation with generous companion funding to support its continued care, cataloguing, documentation, and publication. Their foresight guarantees the longevity of this transformative gift to PEM's collection. Endowed funds for future acquisitions will also enable the Pforzheimer collection to grow in depth and represent future generations of glass artists.

With their gift, a new chapter in PEM's glass-collecting history began. In May 2024, the museum opened the newly named Pforzheimer Gallery, as a long-term space designated for the display of studio and contemporary glass (figs. 13 and 14). PEM is now an essential destination for researching and experiencing international studio glass. With these recent major gifts, the stage is set for future ambitious projects at PEM that tell the story of the history of glass, glassmaking, and human expression.

Figure 12 Attributed to Ōta Toshirō (1869–1940, Japan), Vase with designs of egrets flying above reeds, 1910–20. *Plique-à-jour* enamel, 5 × Diam. 10⅛ in. (12.7 × 27.7 cm). Peabody Essex Museum, Fredric T. Schneider Collection, gift of Fredric T. Schneider and Lynn Whisnant Reiser, 2024.6.1

Figure 13 View of the inaugural installation *Studio Glass*, in the Pforzheimer Gallery, Peabody Essex Museum, May 2024

Figure 14 (following spread) View of the inaugural installation *Studio Glass*, in the Pforzheimer Gallery, Peabody Essex Museum, May 2024

Notes

1. Connections to early American glassmaking date back even further than the museum's founding, to the seventeenth century, as Salem was home to one of the first successful glasshouses in the American colonies, which operated between 1638–1645. The first book of the town records notes that Obadiah Hullme, with his wife Catharine, was granted one acre of land for a house near to the "glasse house" in 1638. Subsequent entries show grants made to the other "glass men" and their wives: Ananias Concklin, Lawrence and Cassandra Southwick, and John Concklin. The location of the glasshouse was between present day Boston and Aborn Streets. Thought to have primarily produced window glass and bottles, no documented examples of finished pieces from the glasshouse survive, although some examples of slag recovered by a later owner of the property were donated to the Essex Institute. James Kimball, "The First Glass Factory—Where?", *Essex Institute Historical Collections*, January 1879, Vol XVI, No. 1 (January 1879): 1–7. John A. Wells, *The Peabody Story: Events in Peabody's History, 1626–1972* (Salem: Essex Institute, 1972), 148–49, 152–54.

2. East India Marine Society, *The East-India Marine Society of Salem*, (Salem: Palfray, 1821), 4, cited in George H. Schwartz, *Collecting the Globe: The Salem East India Marine Society Museum* (Amherst: University of Massachusetts Press, 2020), 10.

3. Smoking devices such as water pipes, known as hookahs, were often collected by society members as objects of great curiosity. PEM has many full examples of these smoking devices that were made in a variety of materials and shapes. Bases could be made of silver, glass, metal, or coconut. It is likely that Silsbee found this example most intriguing as a part of a hookah, but perhaps the sculptural, delicately fluted glass was appealing for its material as well. Susan S. Bean, *Yankee India: American Commercial and Cultural Encounters with India in the Age of Sail, 1784–1860* (Salem: Peabody Essex Museum and Ahmedabad, India: Mapin Publishing Pvt. Ltd., 2001), 85.

4. Karina Corrigan, "The Governor of Surat and the Apotheosis of Washington: Cantonese Reverse Glass Paintings for Early Nineteenth Century American Market," in *China and the West: Reconsidering Chinese Reverse Glass Painting* (Berlin: De Gruyter and Romont: Vitrocentre Romont, 2023): 98–100.

5. John R. Grimes, "Curiosity, Cabinets, and Knowledge—A Perspective on the Native American Collection of the Peabody Essex Museum," in *Uncommon Legacies: Native American Art from the Peabody Essex Museum*, ed. John R. Grimes, Christian F. Feest, and Mary Lou Curran (New York: American Federation of Arts in association with University of Washington Press, 2002), 19.

6. Michael Oehrl, "Beaded Aprons of the Coastal Peoples of the Guianas," *BEADS: Journal of the Society of Bead Researchers*, 31 (2019): 21–38. Available at: https://surface.syr.edu/beads/vol31/iss1/6.

7. Oehrl, 34.

8. Dean Lahikainen, "Collecting American Decorative Arts a Century Ago . . . The Curwen Collection," in *Antiques Show Catalog* (Salem: Peabody Essex Museum, 1993), 24.

9. Lahikainen, 24.

10. Trustees of the Ropes Memorial Records, MSS 191. Courtesy of Phillips Library, Peabody Essex Museum, Rowley, MA.

11. For bottle of sugar, see Josh Basseches, "Transforming Pain into Beauty: The Alchemy of María Magdelena Campos-Pons," in Josh Basseches, ed., *Alchemy of the Soul: María Magdelena Campos-Pons* (Salem, MA: Peabody Essex Museum, 2016), fig. 19, p. 46, and for both bottles, see "In the PEM Collection," (Peabody Essex Museum digital publication, 2016) http://alchemy.pem.org/in_pem_collection/.

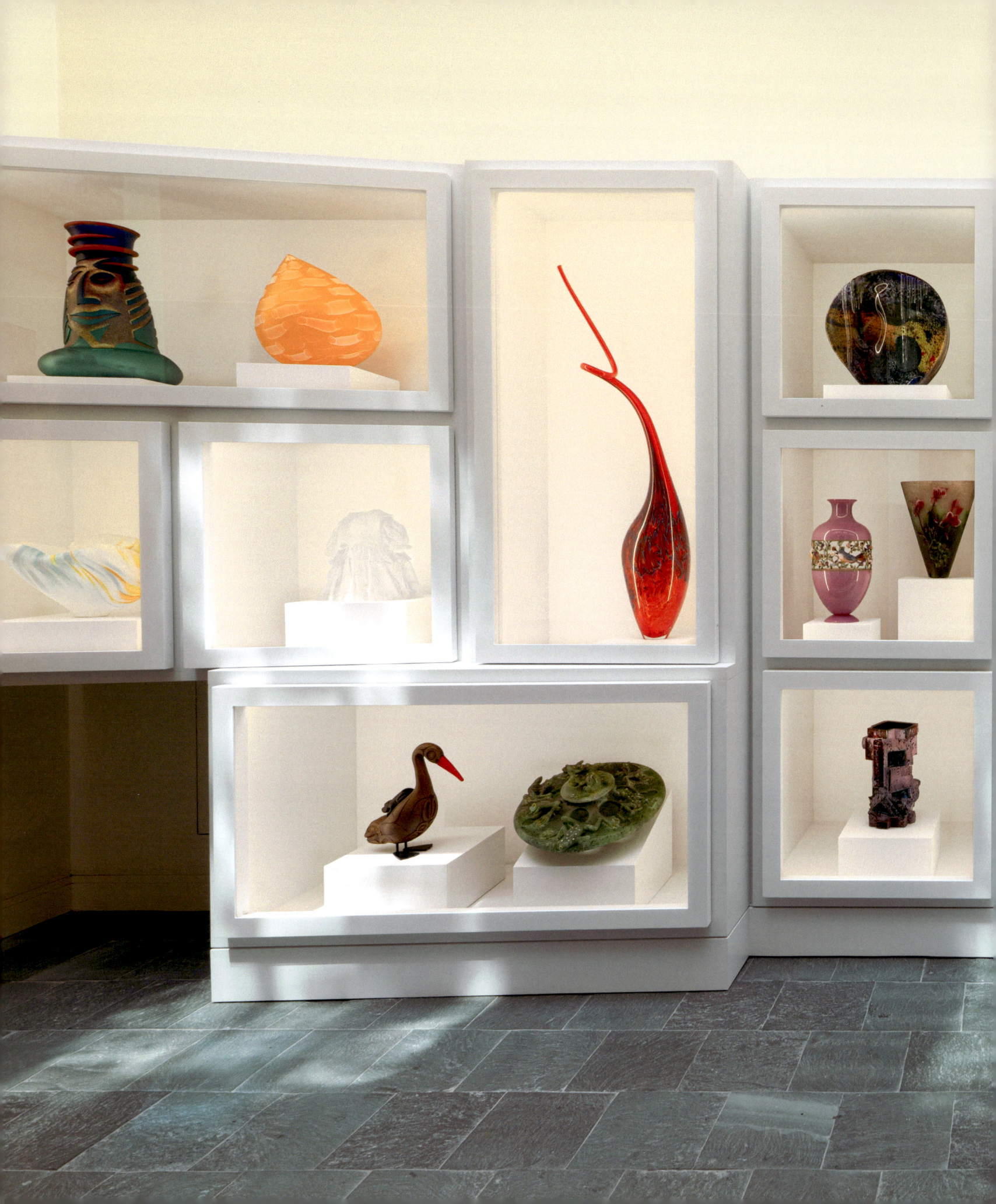

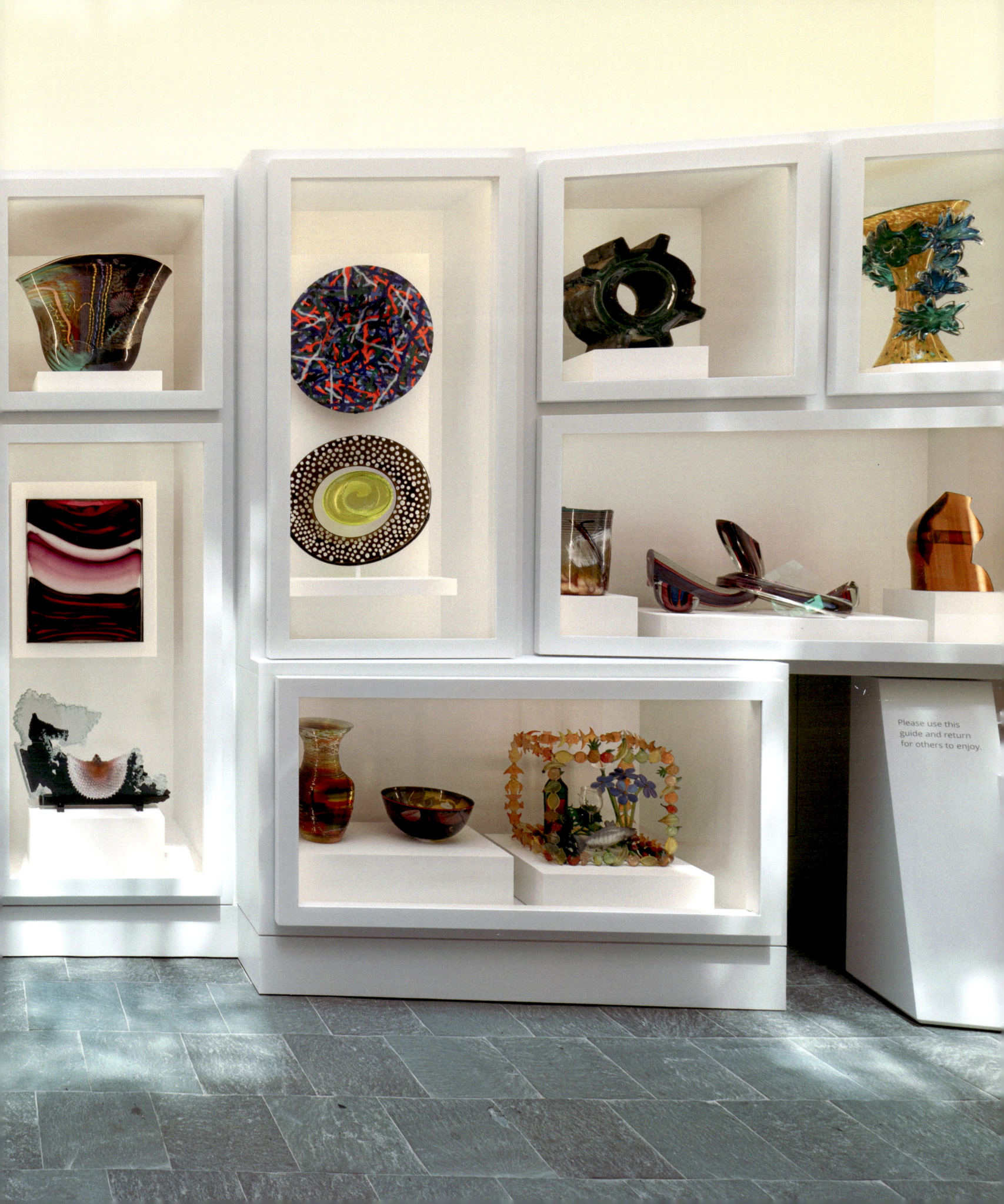

Please use this
guide and return
for others to enjoy.

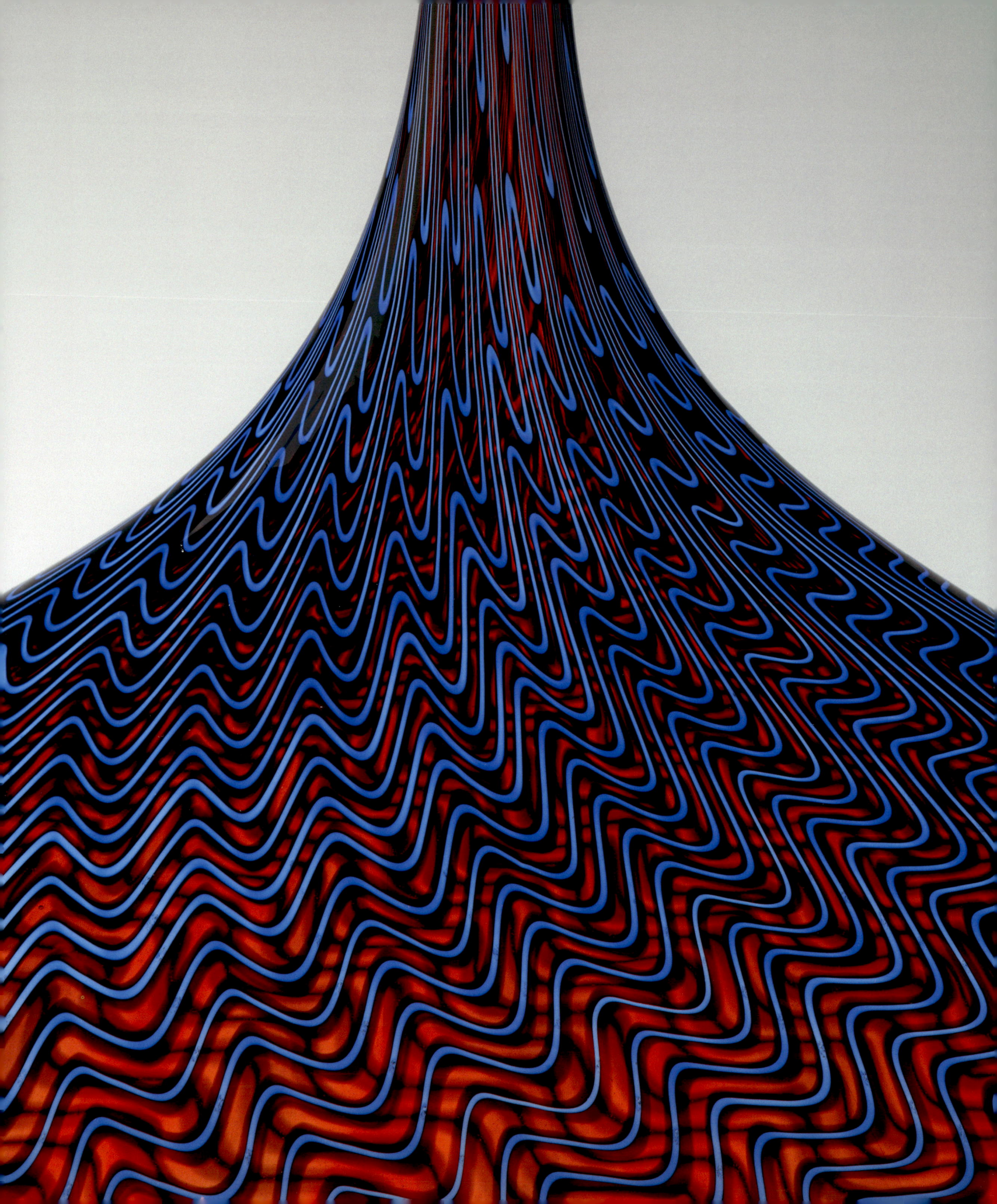

Crafting a Legacy

The Carl and Betty Pforzheimer Collection of Glass

Sarah N. Chasse

Collecting at its best is very far from mere acquisitiveness; it may become one of the most humanistic of occupations, seeking to illustrate by the assembling of significant *reliques*, the march of the human spirit in its quest of beauty and the aspirations that were its guide.

—Arthur Davison Ficke[1]

In 1979, Carl and Betty Pforzheimer, of Scarsdale, New York, walked into a contemporary art glass gallery in New York City and fell in love with a small paperweight vase by the artist Mark Peiser (fig. 1). They bought it on the spot. Although they might not have guessed it at the time, this purchase began their journey of collecting exemplary glass art for more than forty years. The scope of their collecting demonstrates their passion for these extraordinary objects and the limitless potential of the medium. However, perhaps even more significantly, the collection they have built stands as a testament to their admiration for the artists they collected and forged deep connections with over four decades.

The Collectors

The collection that Carl and Betty Pforzheimer built was a collaborative effort driven by their passion for an art form they discovered together. They found studio glass twenty years after marrying, with already full lives and three mostly grown children. While they may not have set out to be art collectors, there were precedents in both of their families for a life dedicated to philanthropy and to fostering learning, as well as a model for a collector's life (fig. 2).

Carl H. Pforzheimer 3rd was born in 1937 to Carl H. Pforzheimer Jr. (1907–1996) and Carol Koehler Pforzheimer (1910–2010). The Pforzheimers were a notable New York family. Carl 3rd's grandfather, Carl H. Pforzheimer (1879–1957), a noted financier, founded Carl H. Pforzheimer & Company in 1901, an investment banking house specializing in oil investments. Carl 3rd grew up across the street from his grandfather's house in Purchase, New York, and was influenced early on by his grandfather's true passion in life besides his business: his renowned library collection of books and papers related to the British Romantic poet Percy Bysshe Shelley (1792–1822). Carl remembers his grandfather's collection well and especially recalls that Carl Sr. was a fastidious record keeper of his collection, a skill, Carl notes, that was passed down to his father and to him. Three generations of his family stewarded the voluminous library collection of eight thousand original manuscripts and thirteen thousand printed volumes related to Shelley and his circle. Following his grandfather's death, the family-run Carl and Lily Pforzheimer Foundation oversaw the care of the collection,

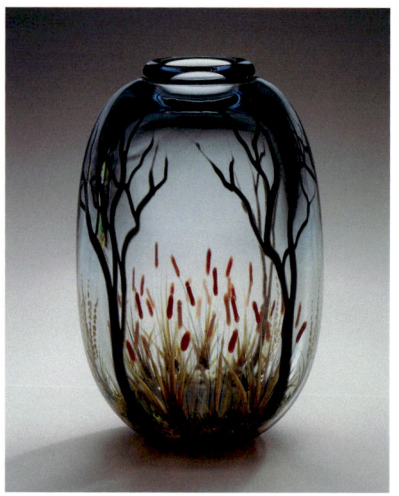

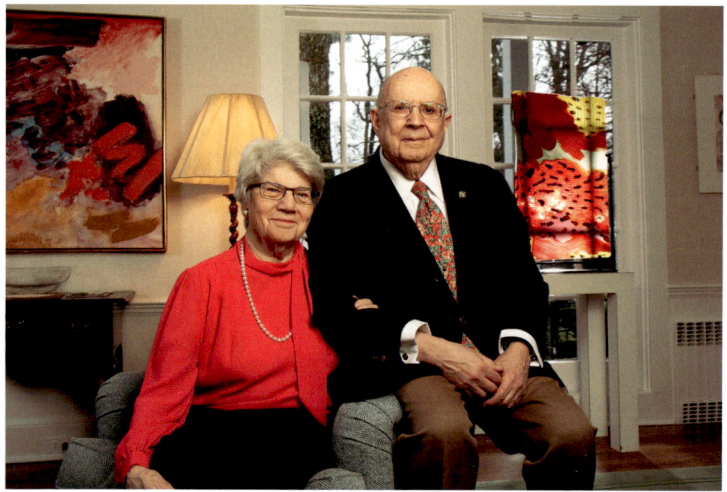

ultimately donating it to the New York Public Library in 1987.[2] After attending the Horace Mann School, followed by Harvard University, Carl 3rd continued in the family business, eventually running Carl H. Pforzheimer & Co. LLC after his father's passing, and later CHIPCO Asset Management LLC. Following the examples set by his grandparents and parents, Carl took philanthropy seriously from a young age, ultimately chairing the boards of the National Humanities Center, Visiting Nurse Service of New York, Pace University, Horace Mann-Barnard School, and serving as president of the Scarsdale Public Schools. His support has always been focused on education, health, and the humanities. Carl also continued his involvement with his family's legacy at the New York Public Library, becoming a life trustee at 72 and a foundation trustee in 2023, an esteemed role to which only three people have been appointed.

Elizabeth (Betty) Jane Strauss enjoyed a happy childhood as the daughter of Burton and Mildred Kaufman Strauss of Manhattan. Her father was a Wall Street stockbroker for six decades, and both of her parents were dedicated philanthropists, as their parents had been. Although her family members were not dedicated collectors, Betty remembers having an eye for objects from a young age, which she believes informs her preference for three-dimensional art over two-dimensional works. She adored her grandparents' collection of miniatures, several pieces of which she inherited, and her grandfather's curio cabinet of Meissen porcelain. Betty later attended Wellesley College, graduating in the same class as Madeleine Albright. Her maternal grandmother was one of six women who founded an organization now called Visions: Services for the Blind and Visually Impaired in New York in the 1920s. The family's commitment to philanthropy was passed on to her parents, eventually inspiring Betty's lifelong charitable work focused on disabled children and education. In 2024, Betty celebrated forty years of service on the Bank Street College of Education Board of Trustees. She was a founder of New Alternatives for Children in Manhattan, and still serves on the board and is a trustee emerita of Blythedale Children's Hospital. Betty served on the board of Wellesley College for fifteen years and remains closely connected to the college and her network of friends. Equally involved at a local level,

Figure 1 Mark Peiser (born 1938, United States), *Cattail Swamp*, 1979. Flame-worked and blown glass. Collection of Carl and Betty Pforzheimer

Figure 2 Carl and Betty at home in Scarsdale, New York, 2024

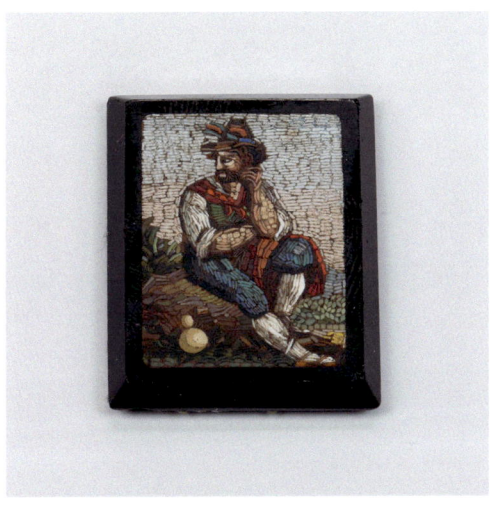

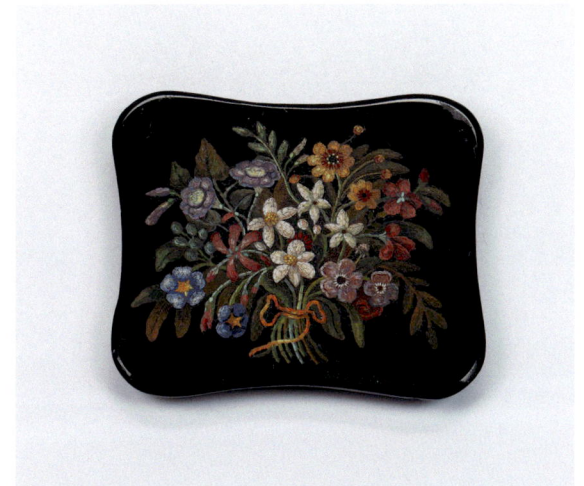

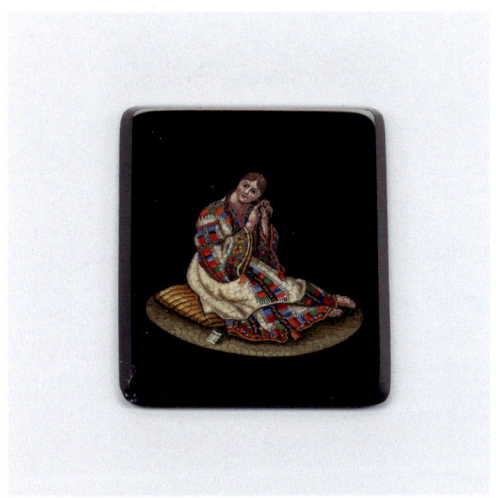

Figure 3 (clockwise from top left)

Artist in Italy, Micromosaic [man], 18th–19th century. Glass and felt, 1¼ × 1 × ⅛ in. (3.18 × 2.54 × 0.32 cm). Peabody Essex Museum, gift of Carl and Betty Pforzheimer, 2022.6.78

Artist in Italy, Micromosaic [flowers], 18th–19th century. Glass and stone, 1½ × 1¾ × ⅛ in. (3.81 × 4.45 × 0.32 cm). Peabody Essex Museum, gift of Carl and Betty Pforzheimer, 2022.6.70

Artist in Italy, Micromosaic [woman], 18th–19th century. Glass and stone, 1½ × 1¼ × ¼ in. (3.81 × 3.18 × 0.64 cm). Peabody Essex Museum, gift of Carl and Betty Pforzheimer, 2022.6.75

she is a longtime supporter of Scarsdale Public Library (recently serving on the committee for the complete renovation of the library), the Westchester Community Foundation, and Literacy Volunteers of Westchester County.

Collecting Historic Glass

Carl Pforzheimer 3rd and Betty Strauss first met at a mutual friend's graduation party in New York. Carl was bound for Harvard College and Betty was a rising senior in high school. When Betty attended Wellesley the following year, Carl reached out. Married in 1959, following Betty's graduation, the young newlyweds moved to London for Carl's first job and soon after collected their first artwork together. While exploring on Portobello Road, they found and fell in love with a nineteenth-century Italian micromosaic of a man (fig. 3). A family friend in London learned of their interest and gave them a couple of micromosaics, starting them on a path of collecting. Carl and Betty continued to collect these intricate glassworks over the decades as they traveled, eventually building a collection of nearly twenty works.

Another precedent in Carl and Betty's interest in glass collecting had deeper roots in the family. Carl was gifted about ten paperweights from his grandmother in the late 1960s; she gave them while she was still alive so "she could enjoy his enjoyment of them."[3] A few paperweights in their early collection were gifted to Betty from the mother of her oldest friend. These gifted collections inspired Carl and Betty to seek out more paperweights in the 1990s, a decade recognized as the height of the market for paperweight collecting. They sought professional counsel from Lauren Tarshis, then director of the Paperweight Department at Sotheby's, who advised them on purchases including notable works from famous sales such as the Henry Stern Collection of Antique Glass Paperweights and the 1998 sale of the Homer Perkins Collection of Glass Paperweights, both at Christie's. With the family paperweights and the works Carl and Betty later collected, the couple built a rich collection of outstanding works of paperweight art from the best production houses of France in the nineteenth century, including superlative examples from the houses of Clichy, Baccarat, and Saint-Louis (fig. 4).

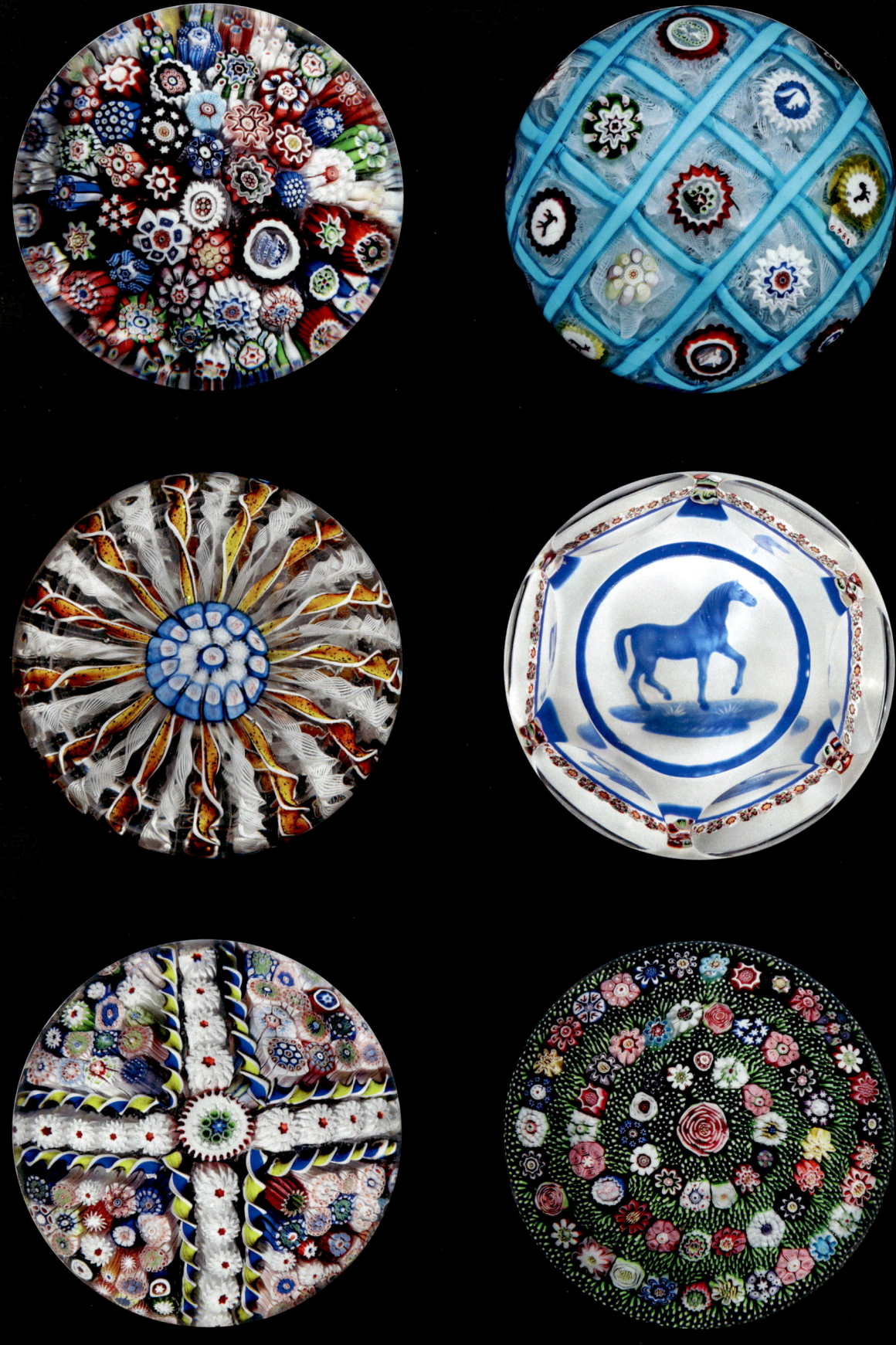

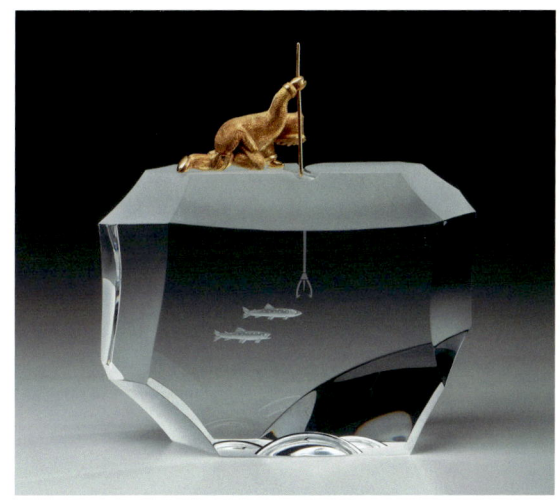

Figure 4 (clockwise from top left)

Baccarat (France), Commemorative signed and dated paperweight, 1858. *Millefiori* glass, 2 × Diam. 2¾ in. (5.08 × 6.99 cm). Peabody Essex Museum, gift of Carl and Betty Pforzheimer, 2022.6.235

Baccarat (France), Paperweight, 1849. *Millefiori* glass, 2¼ × Diam. 3 in. (5.72 × 7.62 cm). Peabody Essex Museum, gift of Carl and Betty Pforzheimer, 2022.6.244

Baccarat (France), Prancing horse paperweight, ca. 1845–1855. *Millefiori* and engraved lead glass, 2⅛ × Diam. 3¼ in. (5.4 × 8.26 cm). Peabody Essex Museum, gift of Carl and Betty Pforzheimer, 2022.6.241

Clichy Glasshouse (France), Paperweight, 19th century. *Millefiori* glass, 1¾ × Diam. 2½ in. (4.45 × 6.35 cm). Peabody Essex Museum, gift of Carl and Betty Pforzheimer, 2022.6.245

Cristalleries de Saint-Louis (France), Paperweight, 19th century. *Millefiori* glass, 1¾ × Diam. 2¾ in. (4.45 × 6.99 cm). Peabody Essex Museum, gift of Carl and Betty Pforzheimer, 2022.6.246

Cristalleries de Saint-Louis (France), Paperweight, 19th century. *Millefiori* and aventurine glass, 2 × Diam. 3 in. (5.08 × 7.62 cm). Peabody Essex Museum, gift of Carl and Betty Pforzheimer, 2022.6.247

Figure 5 James A. Houston (1921–2005, Canada, worked in United States), for Steuben Glass Works (United States), *Arctic Fisherman*, 1970. Sag cast, cut, and wheel-engraved lead glass, and 18k gold, overall: 8½ × 8 × 3¾ in. (21.59 × 20.32 × 9.53 cm). Peabody Essex Museum, gift of Carl and Betty Pforzheimer, 2022.6.163AB

Carl and Betty eventually also collected works from significant American glass companies such as Steuben Glass Inc. and Tiffany & Company. Steuben opened a new Madison Avenue flagship store in Manhattan in 2000. In the early 2000s, the couple bought several historic pieces designed by Frederick Carder, including a bowl, a goblet, and an *Aurene* perfume bottle from the store (Checklist, p. 161). Additionally, although contemporary production glass largely fell out of the scope of their interest in collecting, they also acquired two twentieth-century Steuben works by significant artists working for the firm. They became enamored with an *Arctic Fisherman* sculpture by James Houston, buying the limited-edition version with gold details, which soon became a family favorite (fig. 5).[4] They later also acquired Eric Hilton's *Infinite Journey* from the store (pl. 24).[5]

The most significant historic glass works in the Pforzheimers' collection are two Tiffany & Company lamps. Carl always remembers loving Tiffany lamps for their beauty, but also for their allure as iconic examples of American glass artistry. He remembers walking into Macklowe Gallery in Manhattan one day with Betty, meeting Ben Macklowe and Lary Matlick, and falling for their charm and expert salesmanship. Carl and Betty first bought a lamp with a *Dogwood* pattern shade that they later exchanged for a *Poppy* shade lamp, which Betty reads by in their home office daily (fig. 6). They also acquired a lamp with a *Dragonfly* shade with an outstanding turtleback mosaic base that provides a glowing welcome to visitors in the entry to their home (fig. 7).[6]

Early Collecting of Studio Glass

In November of 1979, the Pforzheimers were at the Contemporary Art Glass Gallery on Madison Avenue in New York City, predecessor to today's Heller Gallery, talking to dealer Doug Heller when a consignor brought in Mark Peiser's *Cattail Swamp* paperweight vase (fig. 1). Carl and Betty loved it and bought it on the spot. Betty loved "how painterly it was." The vase was from Peiser's *Paperweight* series (1975–1981), which drew on the techniques and concepts of historic nineteenth-century paperweight traditions in a new, inventive, and contemporary mode. Drawing with melted glass canes of various colors on molten glass, the artist would

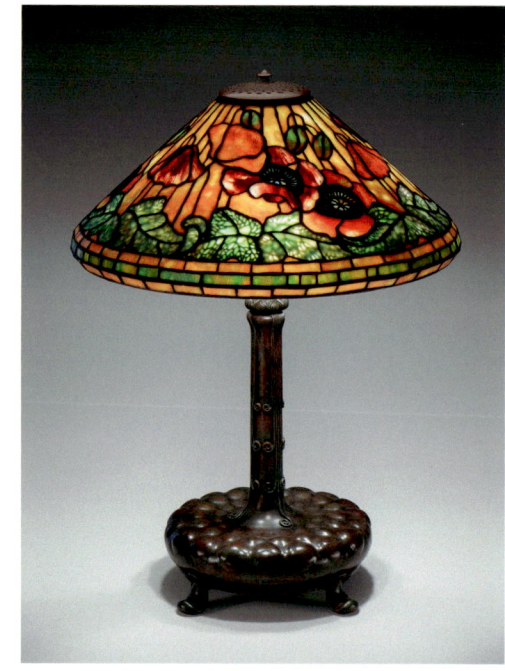

then encapsulate the "drawn" images, most frequently landscape imagery, between layers of glass to create a three-dimensional vase form. From that first acquisition, Doug Heller became a clear influence informing their collecting. "Doug was a superb mentor and salesman and taught us the basics of appreciating the emerging art glass movement. A fair amount of our collection was inspired by what Heller Gallery carried and by Doug's and his brother Michael's patient descriptions of why they were carrying it." Within two years of purchasing Peiser's vase, the Pforzheimers purchased six more works from the Hellers' Contemporary Art Glass Gallery by many of the early leaders of the Studio Glass movement including Tom Patti, Dominick Labino, and Harvey Littleton.[7]

Carl and Betty's early purchases established a pattern of collecting works through direct connections with artists and relationships with key dealers. In addition to purchases from Doug Heller, they made several early acquisitions through the Craftsman Gallery in Scarsdale, run by Rosanne Raab, including a work by Howard Ben Tré in 1981. When it came time for delivery, the artist brought it to their house himself and placed it in their sunroom, where it stayed for over forty years (pl. 2).

New York Experimental Glass Workshop and Toots Zynsky
Early in their collecting days, Carl's passion for glass extended to learning the techniques involved in creating the glass he loved. Doug Heller shared a flyer with Carl about classes at the New York Experimental Glass Workshop (the Workshop), an organization founded in 1977 by then-recent art school graduates Erik Erikson, Richard Yelle, and Joe Upham. The motivation for the workshop was to provide studio space for artists and a public glassmaking education program. Carl recognized the name Tina Yelle (Richard's sister, whom he enlisted to help run the administration of the organization) on the flyer as the sister of Mary Yelle, their son Gary's girlfriend.[8] Carl signed up for a weekend workshop with the artist Toots Zynsky in May 1982. Zynsky was based at the Workshop from 1980 to 1983. The class was supposed to consist of Carl and a woman, but it was so hot in the studio, 110°, that the woman dropped out and only Carl remained. He remembers making his first piece with Zynsky, something he describes as "a blob," but regardless of the success of his first piece, Carl was hooked.

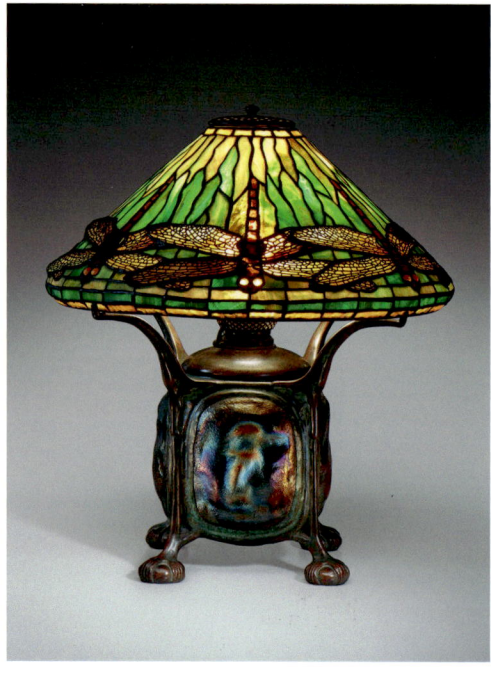

Figure 6 Attributed to Clara Driscoll (1861–1944) for Tiffany Studios (United States), *Poppy* Table Lamp, ca. 1900. Leaded glass and patinated bronze. Collection of Carl and Betty Pforzheimer

Figure 7 Attributed to Clara Driscoll (1861–1944) for Tiffany Studios (United States), *Dragonfly* Table Lamp, ca. 1910. Leaded glass and patinated bronze. Collection of Carl and Betty Pforzheimer

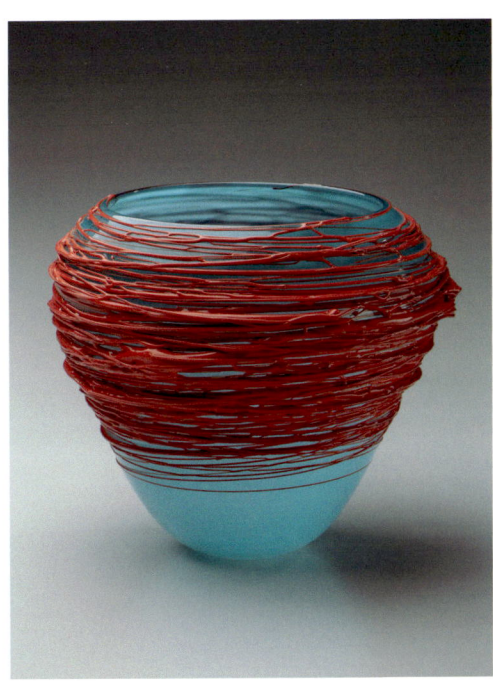

Figure 8 Toots Zynsky (born 1951, United States), Untitled, 1982. Blown glass with hot-spun opaque glass thread wrap, 6⅜ × Diam. 7 in. (16.19 × 17.78 cm). Peabody Essex Museum, gift of Carl and Betty Pforzheimer, 2022.6.229

The weekend of his first class, Carl went with Zynsky to her apartment and studio in the Bowery to see more of her work and ended up buying an early work directly from the artist (fig. 8).[9] The untitled sculpture, described as "hot mouth-blown blue glass with hot spun red glass thread wrap around the top," is an early marker of Zynsky's exploration with glass threads.[10] It was made before she moved to the Netherlands in 1983, where she developed her iconic *filet-de-verre* (fused and thermo-formed glass threads) process in collaboration with the Dutch inventor Mathijs Teunissen van Manen, a technique that would define her work and her identity in glass throughout her career.[11] One weekend workshop had already provided so much more than hands-on learning for Carl. In addition to learning from and connecting personally with a pioneering artist in the Studio Glass movement, the experience provided access to early and now rare work directly from the artist. Opportunities like this make the Pforzheimer collection significant for the depth and breadth of the artists and the range of their works represented.

In the case of Toots Zynsky, Carl and Betty maintained a continued connection and friendship with her over three decades, ultimately acquiring five additional works through various sources. In 2016, they acquired a significant early example of her *filet-de-verre* work at auction (Checklist, p. 161, Sculptural vessel). The artist described it as an experimental piece, noting, "I made it in my first studio in Amsterdam, after moving there in early 1983. It's the only one of its kind and was an extension of my earlier blown works with torched-on threads, which led to the evolution of working exclusively with fused and thermo-formed glass threads."[12]

UrbanGlass and Bill Gudenrath
Following the success of his first workshop, Carl asked Tina Yelle if he could take regular classes with someone, emphasizing that he did not aspire to be an artist, but wanted to learn techniques and understand the intricacies of how glass was made. Tina connected Carl to Bill Gudenrath (fig. 9), a master glass artist working out of the New York Experimental Glass Workshop, and Carl took classes with him on Saturday mornings for twenty years, spanning the time when the organization moved to Brooklyn and expanded, becoming UrbanGlass in 1991. Carl and Betty's

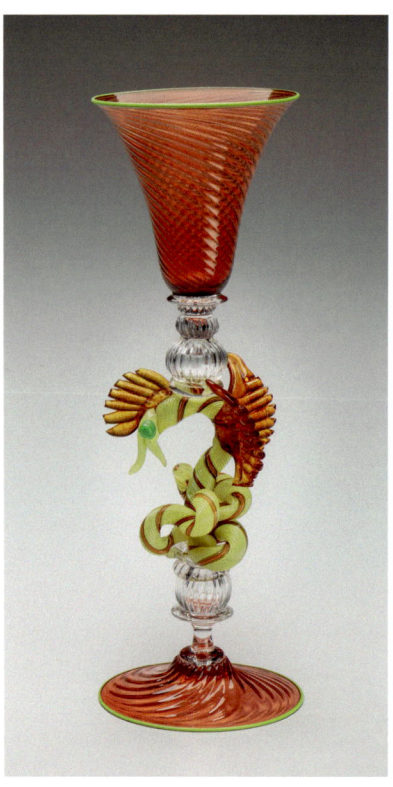

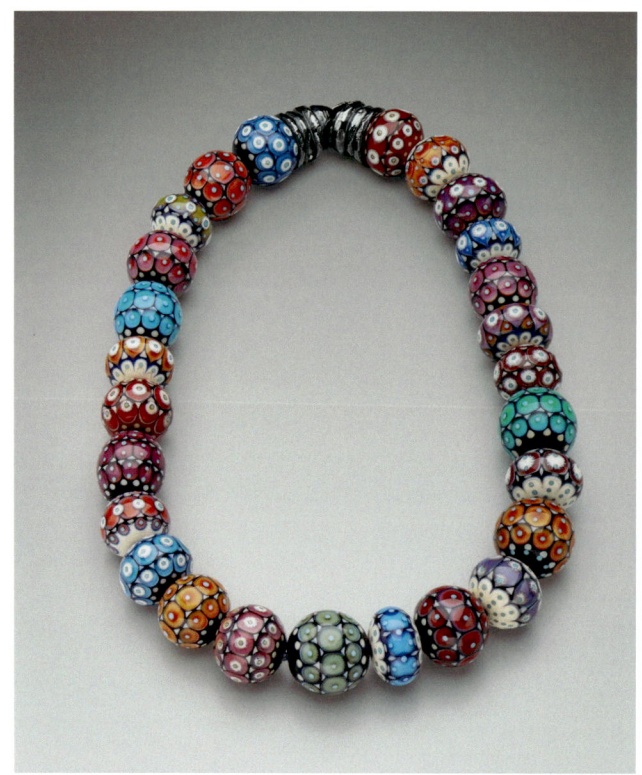

cupboards are filled with small blown-glass works, vases, drinking glasses, and pitchers that Carl made over the years, which they continue to use daily. At the height of Carl's interest in making glass, he installed a flame-working bench in the basement of their home for his experimentation in that technique.

With the three Pforzheimer children grown and out of the house, Betty would tag along on these Saturday sessions as a self-described groupie. After the hot shop, the three would go out for pizza together, developing a deep camaraderie and friendship that continues to this day. Carl's initial involvement at the Workshop as an eager student would prove fruitful for the Pforzheimers and for the organization now known as UrbanGlass. Carl joined the board in 1986, serving as treasurer until 2000, secretary until 2005, and chairman from 2005 until 2011. Following his chairmanship, he has continued to lead on the board and, since 2014, has served on the audit committee. For Carl and Betty, UrbanGlass was central to making connections with many influential artists who often also became close friends, as stated by many of the artists connected to them through this organization. Kristina Logan is one of many artists who cite Carl's passion for understanding glass techniques as significant. "I was first introduced to Carl through UrbanGlass with the help of Amy Schwartz and Bill Gudenrath. Carl took several flameworking classes with me and we became friends over the years. His love of glass art and desire to understand how it is created was always a special part of knowing him."[13] The Pforzheimers collected a few early pieces of Logan's directly from the artist: in 1991, a pair of beaded candlesticks (Checklist, p. 157) and in 2002, a red *pâte-de-verre* teapot (pl. 35), as well as several pieces remaining in the family collection. Most recently, Carl commissioned a Kristina Logan

Figure 9 William Gudenrath (born 1950, United States), Dragon-stem goblet, 1995. Blown glass, 12¼ × Diam. 4 in. (31.12 × 10.16 cm). Peabody Essex Museum, gift of Carl and Betty Pforzheimer, 2022.6.51

Figure 10 Kristina Logan (born 1964, United States), *Grand Sophia Necklace*, 2022. Flameworked glass, nylon thread, and sterling silver clasp. Collection of Carl and Betty Pforzheimer

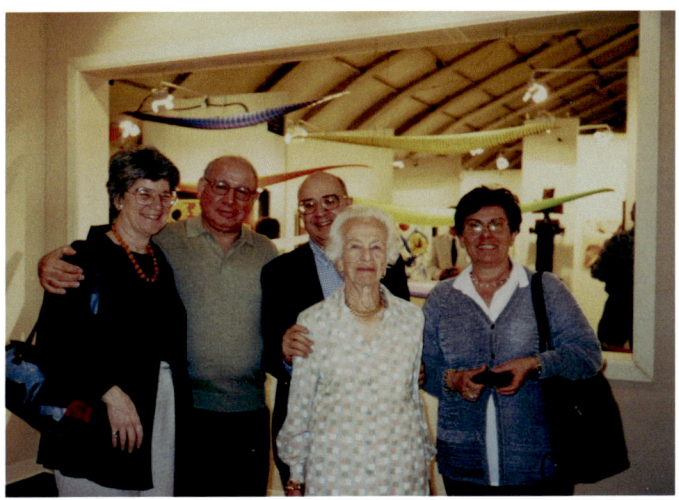

Figure 11 The Pforzheimers and the Tagliapietras with the Holsten Galleries display of the *Endeavor* series at the Palm Beach International Art & Antique Fair, Palm Beach, Florida, March 1999. L to R: Betty Pforzheimer, Lino Tagliapietra, Carl Pforzheimer, Carol K. Pforzheimer, and Lina Tagliapietra

beaded necklace, ostensibly as a gift for Betty, but with the intention that it eventually be gifted to PEM to join the rest of their collection and round out their coverage of Logan's work with an iconic piece of her jewelry (fig. 10).

Lino Tagliapietra

Around 1989, Carl and Betty traveled to Venice with Bill Gudenrath. Through Bill's connections, they visited several studios in Murano. One evening, Bill took them for dinner with the artist Lino Tagliapietra and his wife Lina. The visit happened at a pivotal moment in the master glassblower's career, when he was breaking away from the very traditional, heavily guarded factory glass system in Murano to do his own independent work. After a dinner, Carl discreetly asked Bill if it would be inappropriate to ask if he could buy a piece from Tagliapietra, and Bill encouraged him. The artist was storing his independent work at home at that time; the Pforzheimers remember looking at works stored in a large cupboard. Carl and Betty chose a vase and carried it home to New York (pl. 53). The piece they acquired that night, from the artist's *Notte del Redentore* series, is a significant marker of the artist's early independent work and demonstrates his skillful marriage of form and pattern in a vessel. *Notte del Redentore*, the Night of the Redeemer, is a beloved religious holiday celebrated in Venice that originally marked the end of a seventeenth-century plague in the city. The colors and patterns in this series evoke the fireworks over the water that end the lively holiday. The work is a harbinger of the prolific and consistently innovative work Lino would create in the decades to come.

Theirs was more than just an artist-and-patron relationship: that first visit between the Pforzheimers and Tagliapietras cemented a close friendship between the couples that has lasted for over thirty years (fig. 11). In the words of Carl, "Lino's work has become more than just pieces of glass to us. His friendship has endowed us with an extra appreciation of his work ethic, his boundless creativity, his desire to work longer and better than most artists are able to. We respect him for his legendary generosity to young glass artists in sharing his mastery of the medium."[14] This relationship also fostered privileged access to Lino's work throughout all the

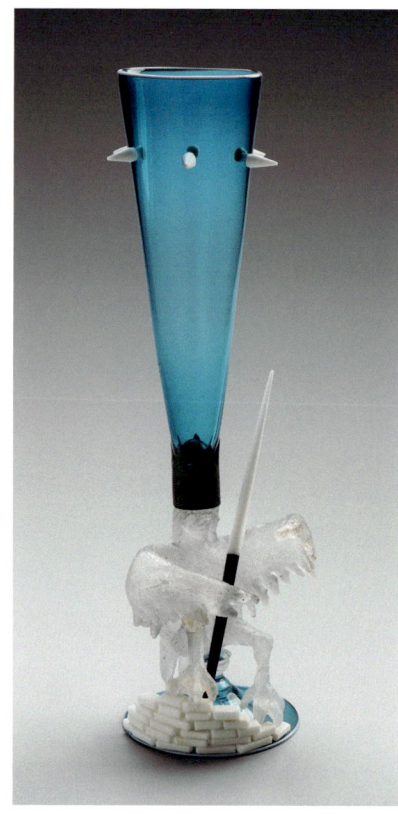

stages of his development as an independent artist. In addition to buying work directly from the artist when opportunities presented themselves, Carl and Betty continued to acquire works through the primary market via the artist's studio and specialized dealers like Heller Gallery and Schantz Galleries, as well as the secondary market through auction. The Pforzheimers' passion for acquiring Tagliapietra's work has made their collection one of the largest representations of his work in North America. Beyond a numerical evaluation, their collection captures the full range of the artist's work from 1983 to 2019, encompassing early pieces done in collaboration with Marina Angelin at Effetre International to masterworks such as *Dinosaur* (pl. 61), created in the years before his retirement in 2023.

Figure 12 Nancy Callan (born 1964, United States), *Ice Princess*, 1995. Blown glass and metal, 13½ × 4⅞ × 4½ in. (34.29 × 12.38 × 11.43 cm). Peabody Essex Museum, gift of Carl and Betty Pforzheimer, 2022.6.19AB

Figure 13 (and following page) Toby Ruth Schwartz (1954–2017, United States), *The Pforzheimer Family*, 1987. Engraved glass. Collection of Carl and Betty Pforzheimer

Nancy Callan

Glassmakers are by necessity a collaborative and close-knit community. As Carl and Betty met more artists and became increasingly involved in supporting organizations like UrbanGlass and later the Corning Museum of Glass (CMOG), they became connected with young artists coming up in the field. In early 1996, Carl and Betty met the aspiring glass artist Nancy Callan at CMOG, when she was student at Massachusetts College of Art (Mass Art). On her first trip to CMOG, Callan had ended up taking an advanced glassblowing class with Lino Tagliapietra in 1995.[15] By the end of the weekend, the *maestro* liked the young, eager student so much that he entrusted her to carry his tools to Boston for a program he was leading at Mass Art.[16] She was in awe of the artist and the responsibility entrusted to her, carefully driving Lino's tools back to Boston in her father's old El Dorado. Carl and Betty continued their connection with Callan after meeting her at the Corning, and later that summer, they bought one of her early student works, *Ice Princess* (fig. 12). In a letter she wrote to Carl and Betty thanking them for their purchase of this piece in August 1996, Callan mentions how "it is the last of a series of five bird/self-portrait goblets" she had made while a student.[17] That summer, Callan exhibited several of her student works at a small show at the Clark Gallery in Lincoln, Massachusetts. Callan remembers how transformative the Pforzheimers' purchase and the sale of another, larger work at the Clark were to her

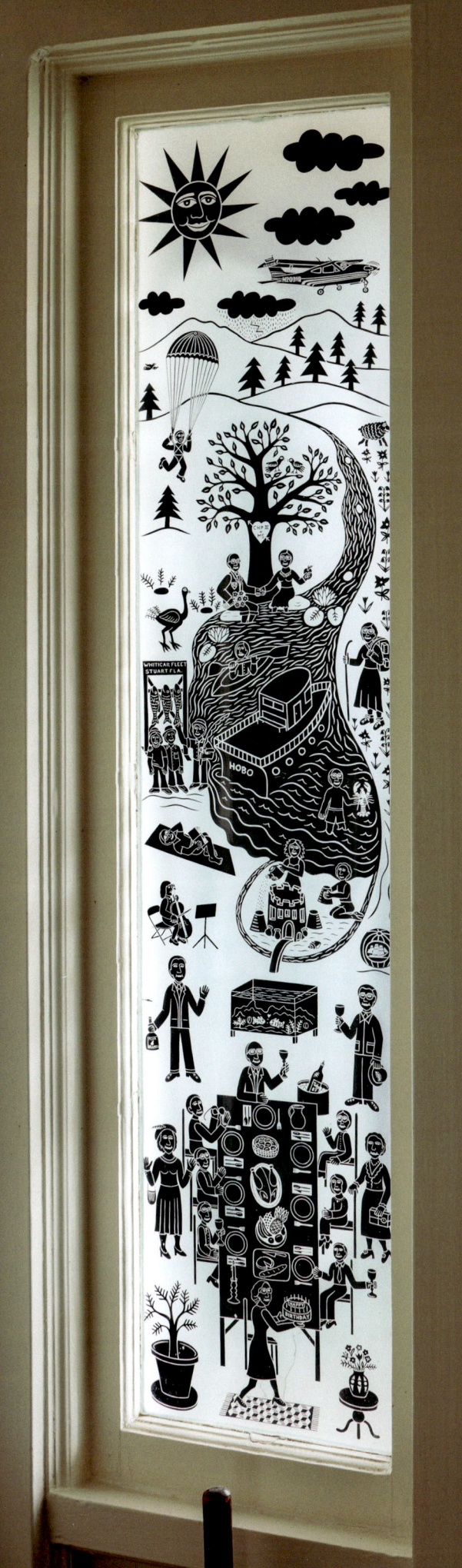

at that transitional moment in her life following her graduation from Mass Art. When the Clark's director Meredyth Moses called Callan to say a collector had just bought her larger *Last Supper* piece, Nancy knew that the money from that sale was what she needed to make the move to Seattle at the invitation of Lino Tagliapietra. She was able to seize that incredible opportunity to move across the country to work with one of the greatest glass artists in the world, becoming a central part of his team for over twenty years.

Conclusion

Artist relationships are central to the Pforzheimer collection, but on a more intimate level, glass was central to Carl and Betty's daily life at home. They displayed their collection throughout their home in Scarsdale, Carl's Manhattan office, their New York City apartment, and their weekend lake house in New Jersey. They enjoyed living with their collection and sharing it with friends and family in all of their spaces every day, and still keep many treasured works at home. Perhaps no work demonstrates the centrality of glass to their lives and their collecting story more than a work they commissioned from Toby Ruth Schwartz in 1987 (fig. 13). The artist, celebrated for her work engraving glass, created two panels for the sidelights of the front door in Carl and Betty's Scarsdale home, where they have lived since 1965. Carl and Betty stumbled upon Schwartz's studio on a long weekend in Vermont, after following a sign for "Hot Glass." Once they met the artist, they realized they had two small vases by her in their collection and struck up a conversation that led to the commission. Schwartz came to visit them in Scarsdale, studied family photo albums, and listened to stories. The etched clear glass panels depict stories of their family life, family members, special events, and hobbies in delightful and intricate details: a family Thanksgiving dinner; Carl's love of fishing and glassblowing; a family academic procession with the schools of each family member; Betty pushing a pram with a baby and two busy toddlers. Commissioned about eight years after they collected their first piece of studio glass, the panels honor Carl and Betty's most important joy in life—their family—but also their deep passion for life, for finding joy in pursuing their passions, and for collecting studio glass and supporting artists.

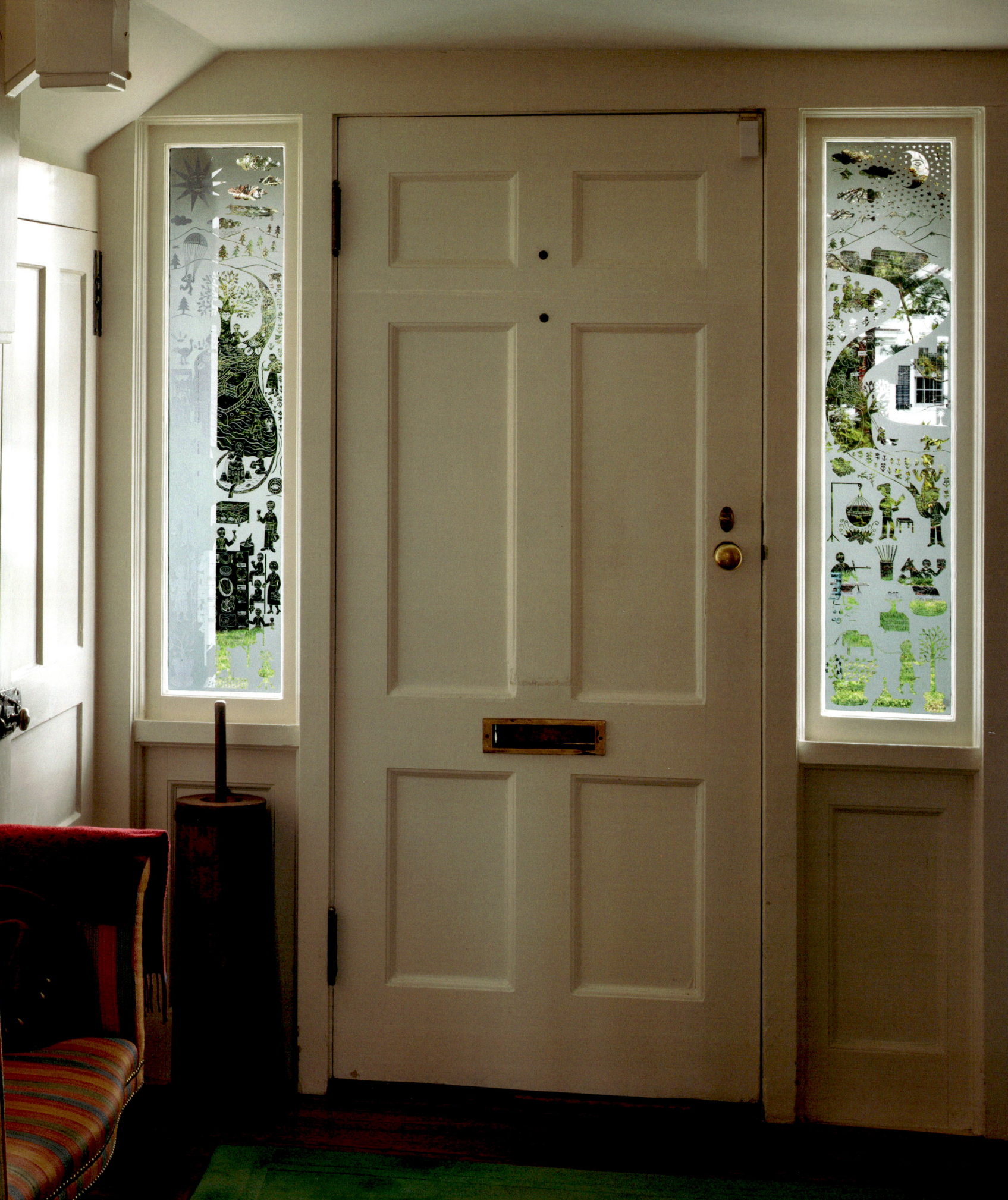

The Pforzheimers' studio glass collection, built over four decades, includes 268 objects to date by over 90 international artists, representing major glass artists and centers in Australia, the Czech Republic, Germany, France, Japan, Sweden, New Zealand, and the United States. With objects dating from 1966 to 2020, the collection encapsulates the range and depth of the Studio Glass movement and features many of the pioneering makers who defined the field, including Harvey K. Littleton, Marvin Lipofsky, Mark Peiser, Toots Zynsky, Dale Chihuly, Ann Wolff, and others. Rather than just focusing on earlier leaders of the movement, Carl and Betty continue to collect leading contemporary makers who shape the field today, like Nancy Callan, Jamie Harris, Preston Singletary, and Thaddeus Wolfe, all represented in the collection by strong examples of their still-evolving careers. Multiple works represent many of the significant artists, some with outstanding examples of major series from their career, like Mark Peiser, or in the case of Toots Zynsky and Lino Tagliapietra, in-depth representations of works over the course of their careers. Proving their expertise at philanthropy, Carl and Betty ensured the future success and impact of their collection with generous companion funding for its continued care. Their foresight guarantees the longevity of this transformative gift to PEM's collection, enabling its potential to delight future visitors to the museum and undoubtedly inspire new generations of artists. Endowed funds for future acquisitions will also enable the Pforzheimer collection to grow in depth and representation of the next generations of glassmakers.

Notes

1. Arthur Davison Ficke, *Chats on Japanese Prints* (New York: Frederick A. Stokes Company, 1917), 409.

2. Stephen Wagner and Doucet Devin Fischer, *The Carl H. Pforzheimer Collection of Shelley and His Circle: A History, a Biography, and a Guide* (New York: New York Public Library, 1996). Lynne Ames, "A Family's Legacy Spans 3 Generations," *New York Times*, February 1, 1987, https://www.nytimes.com/1987/02/01/nyregion/a-familys-legacy-spans-3-generations.html. "Carl H. Pforzheimer Jr., 89, Leading Investment Banker," *New York Times*, November 6, 1996, https://www.nytimes.com/1996/11/06/nyregion/carl-h-pforzheimer-jr-89-leading-investment-banker.html?searchResultPosition=1.

3. Conversation with the collectors and author, Scarsdale, April 12, 2024. Carl's grandmother, Lily Pforzheimer, died in 1970.

4. In 2011, the 108-year-old business shut down, closing both Steuben's factory in Corning, NY, and the Manhattan flagship store, marking the end of an era for a major American glassmaker. Patrick McGeehan, "Steuben Glass Factory and Store to Close," *New York Times*, September 15, 2011, https://archive.nytimes.com/cityroom.blogs.nytimes.com/2011/09/15/steuben-glass-factory-and-store-to-close/.

5. *Infinite Journey* relates closely to Hilton's masterwork, *Innerspace*, at the Corning Museum of Glass, although a quarter of the size. The works were inspired by the landscapes of the artist's native Scotland as well as the landscape of the inner mind.

6. Collectors' email to the author, May 13, 2024.

7. Harvey Littleton, *Geometric Sculpture #15*, 2/9/1980, (Checklist, p. 157) and *Crested Form*, 2/15/1980 (pl. 33); Tom Patti, *Solar Gray Soltex Riser*, 5/20/1980 (pl. 43); Dominick Labino, *Red Festoons*, 11/25/1980 (Checklist, p. 156); William Morris, *Black Soft Form*, 11/25/1980 (Checklist, p. 157); Paul Stankard, *Loosestrife Botanical*, 10/24/1981 (Checklist, p. 159); Jon Kuhn, Sculptured vessel, 12/18/1981 (Checklist, p. 156).

8. Gary Pforzheimer and Mary Yelle married in 1987. Tina Yelle became executive director of the Workshop in 1985. She led the organization for ten years, overseeing their move to Brooklyn in 1991 as well as its rebranding as UrbanGlass. "UrbanGlass (New York Experimental Glass Workshop: Early Years (1977–1981)," Voices in Studio Glass History, Bard Graduate Center, https://exhibitions.bgc.bard.edu/studioglasshistory/artists/tina-yelle/.

9. Soon after that visit, Carl remembers bringing his daughter Annie, an aspiring artist at the time, to visit Zynsky's studio.

10. Toots Zynsky, email to the author, November 28, 2023.

11. The artist notes that she intended to make a black blown piece wrapped with hot-spun red glass threads, but the black glass was incompatible with the red glass, so she used blue instead. Email to the author, November 28, 2023.

12. Toots Zynsky, email to the author, December 16, 2022.

13. Kristina Logan, email to the author, April 29, 2024.

14. Carl Pforzheimer 3rd, email to the author, January 7, 2022.

15. Nancy Callan in Andrew Page, "What I Learned from Lino," *Glass: The UrbanGlass Quarterly* (Winter 2021): 14–19, 15.

16. Conversation with the artist at PEM, May 5, 2024.

17. Carl and Betty Pforzheimer Glass Art Ephemera, MSS 1875. Phillips Library, Peabody Essex Museum, Rowley, MA.

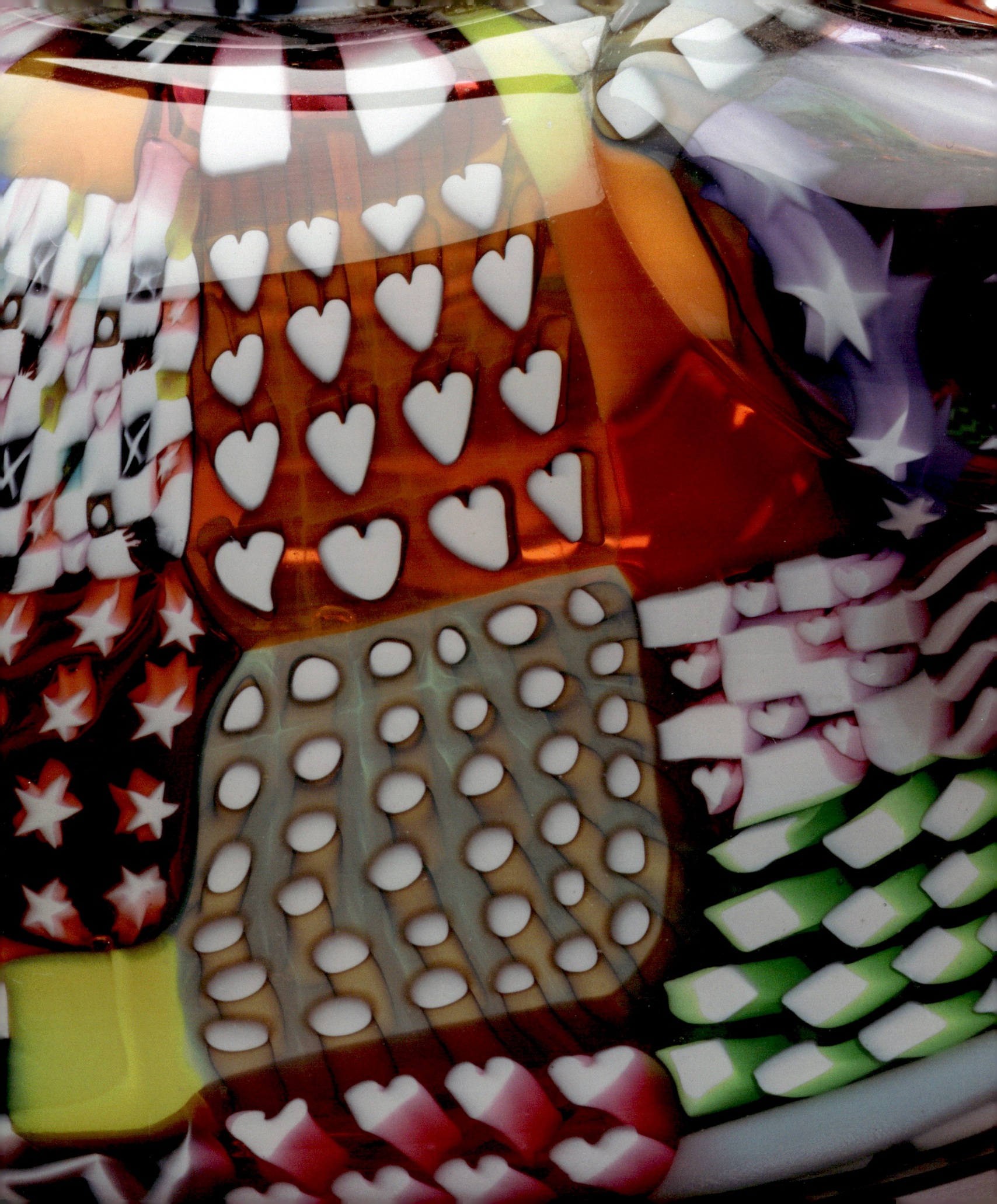

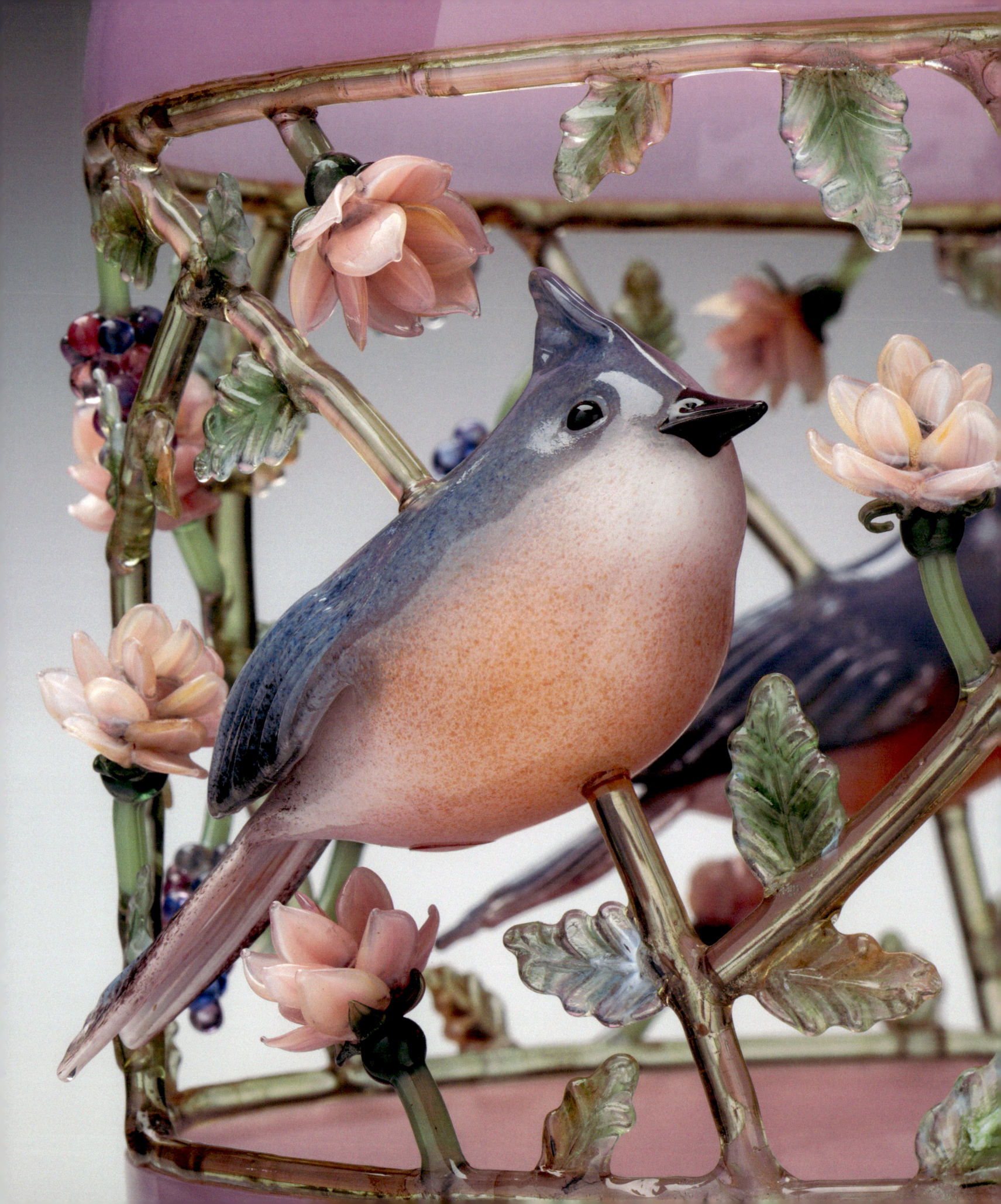

Plates and Entries

All works are in the collection of the Peabody Essex Museum, gift of Carl and Betty Pforzheimer

Oben Abright

born 1980, United States

Market Street Series VIII, 2007, from the *Market Street* series, 2004–14. Cast glass, oil paint, and mold-blown glass, 16¼ × 10½ × 7½ in. (41.28 × 26.67 × 19.05 cm)

"Human emotion is a subject often hidden under our skin and behind our eyes. This desire to reveal the internal landscape of the human mind has led me to pursue the transparency of glass. A glass figure conveys the fragility of life and the luminous presence of a living being by trapping light and color refracted through the body of the subject."
—Oben Abright

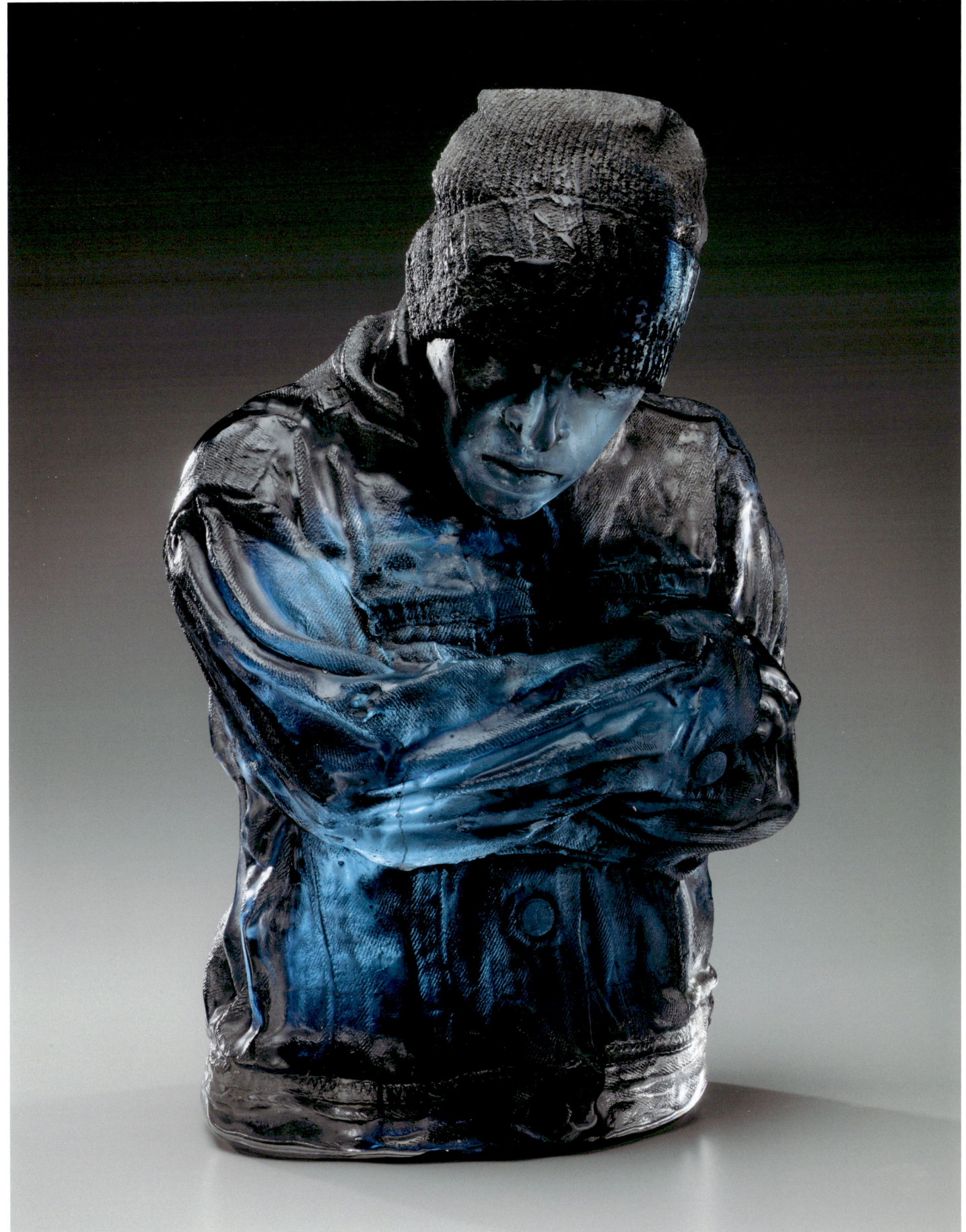

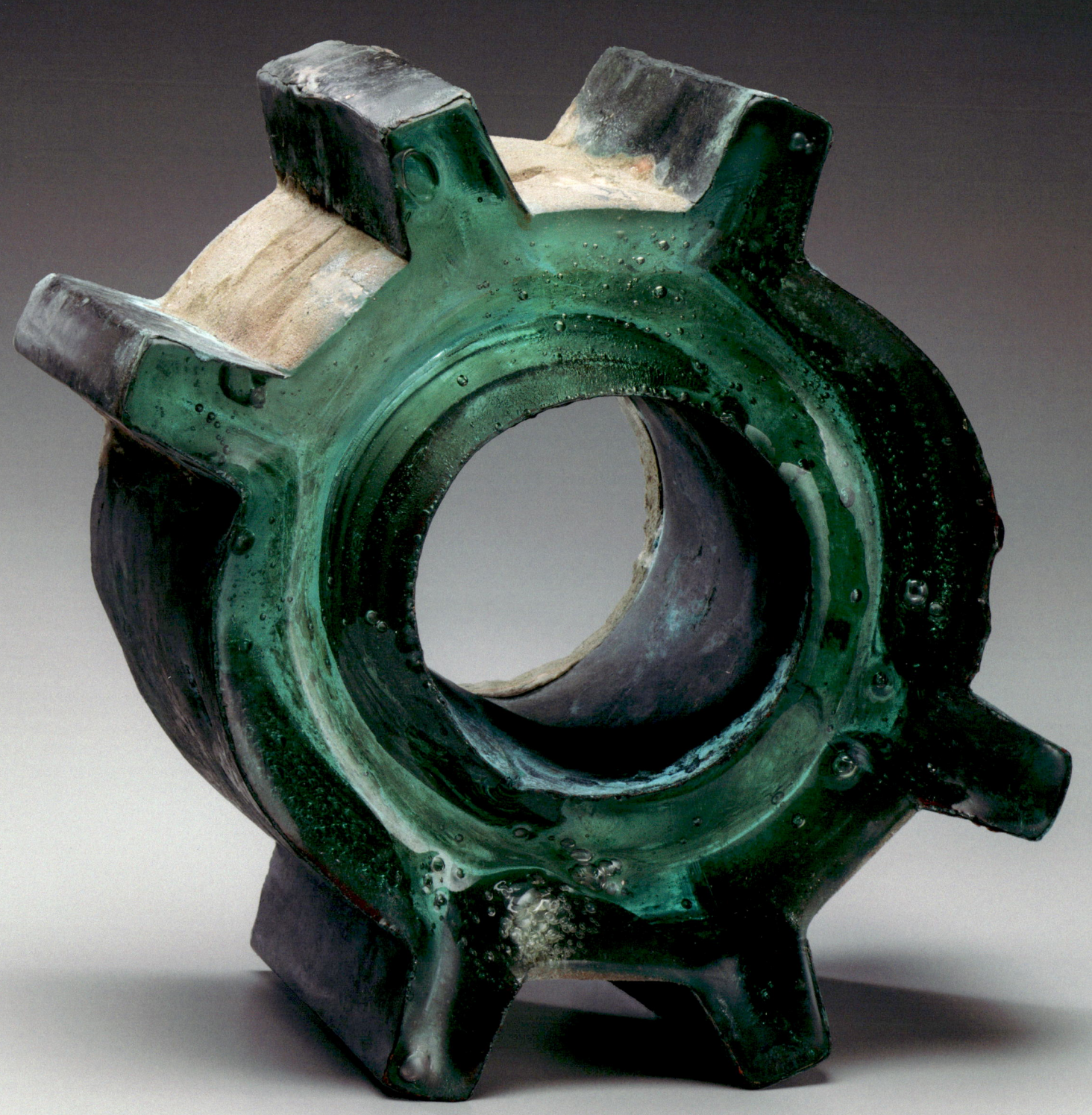

2

Howard Ben Tré

1949–2020, United States

From Benjamin G., 1980.
Cast glass with copper, Diam. 17 ×
9 in. (43.18 × 22.86 cm)

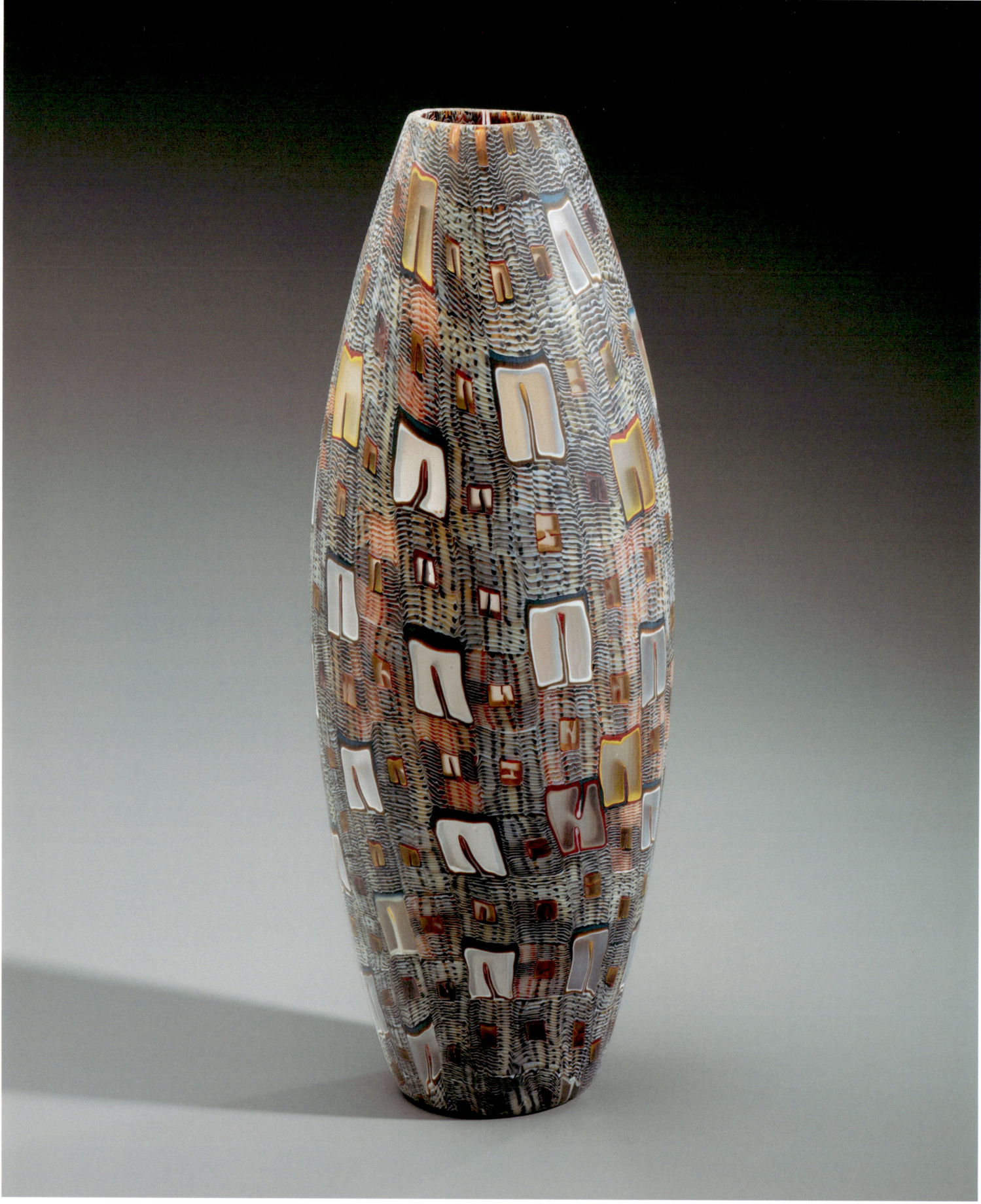

3

Giles Bettison

born 1966, Australia

Paddock Series #52, 1999, from the
Paddock series.
Blown glass, cold-assembled and
hotworked *murrine,* 15½ × Diam.
4¾ in. (39.37 × 12.07 cm)

4

Sonja Blomdahl

born 1952, United States

Vase, 1990.
Blown glass, 10½ × Diam. 9 in.
(26.67 × 22.86 cm)

"I have never followed trends in glass or art. But I feel my work has content that is communicated through color, light, reflection, and the vessel form itself. . . . these pieces have their own voice."
—Sonja Blomdahl

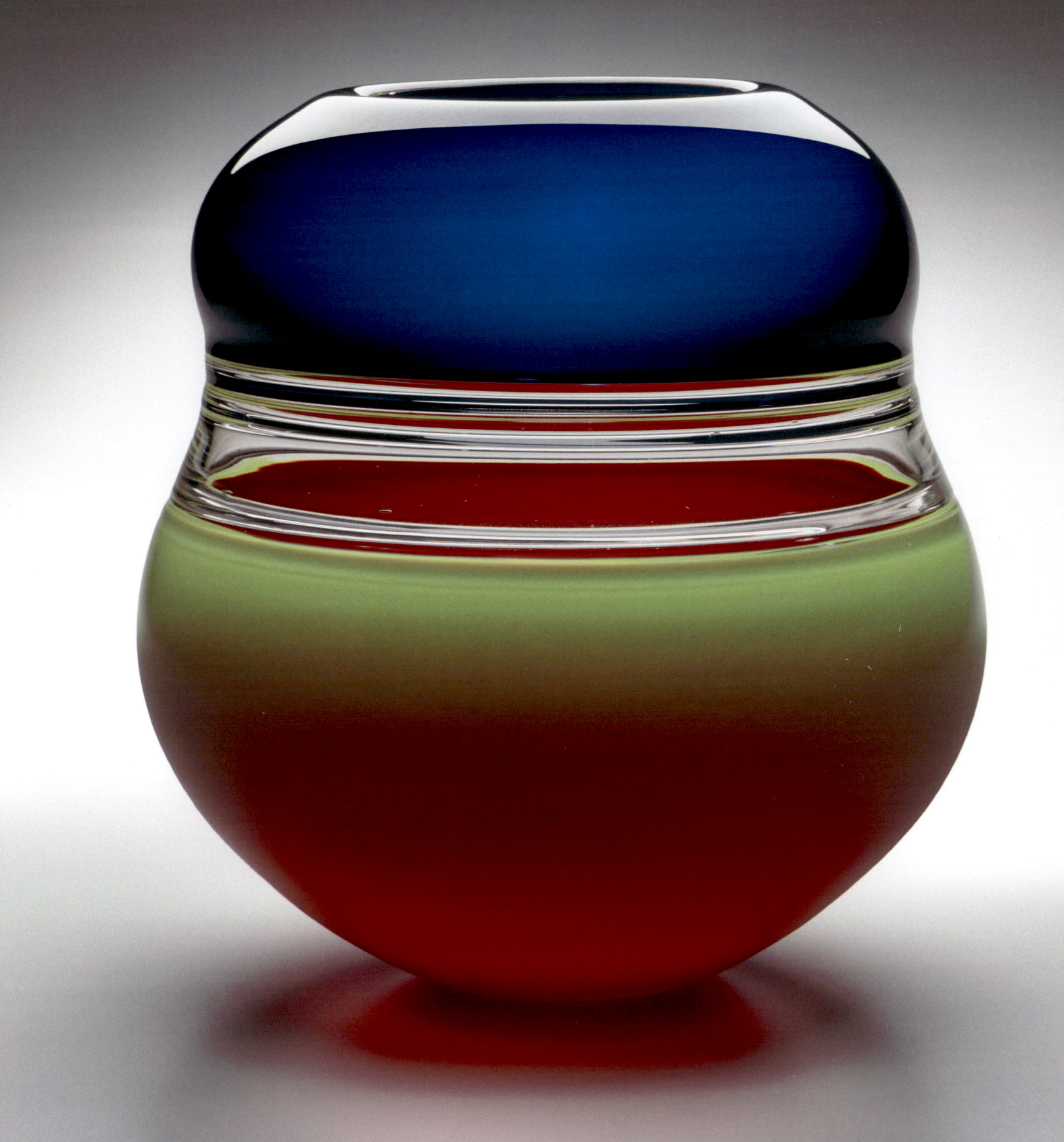

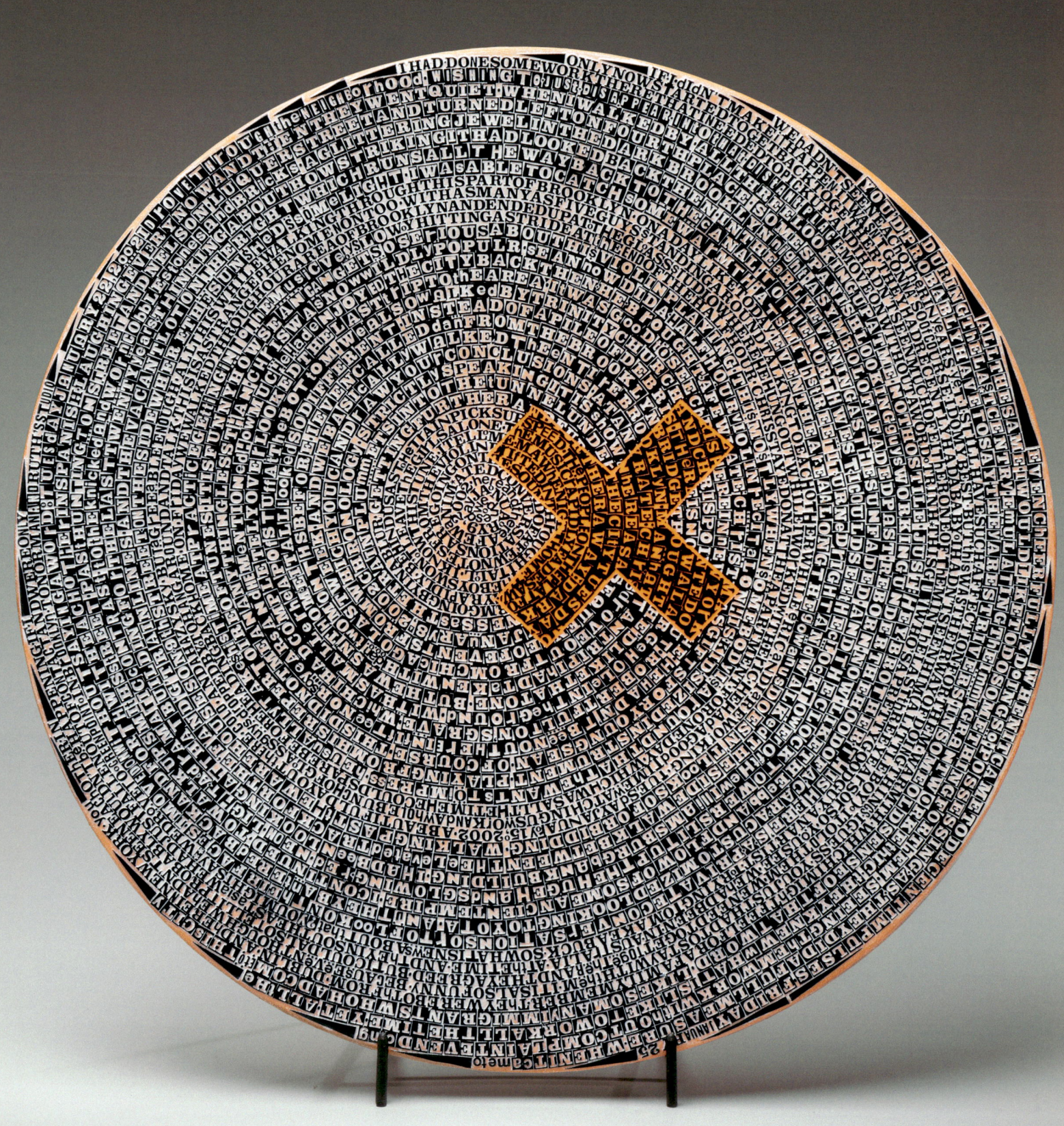

John Brekke

born 1955, United States

Yellow X, 2004.
Blown and carved glass, Diam.
23½ × ½ in. (59.69 × 1.27 cm)

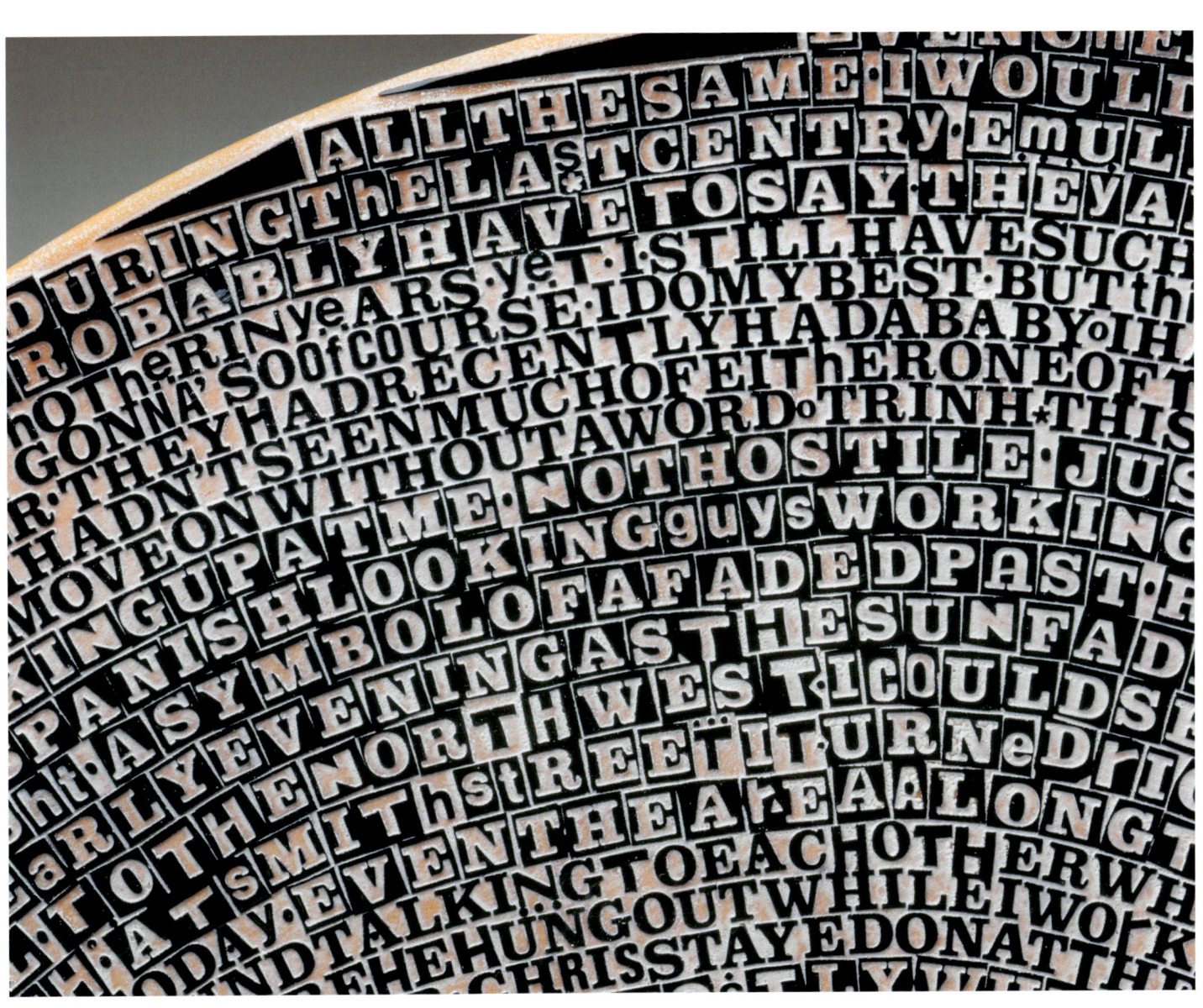

Emily Brock

born 1945, United States

Rare Books, 1990.
Flameworked, blown, and cast glass,
13⅝ × 14½ × 14½ in. (34.61 × 36.83 × 36.83 cm)

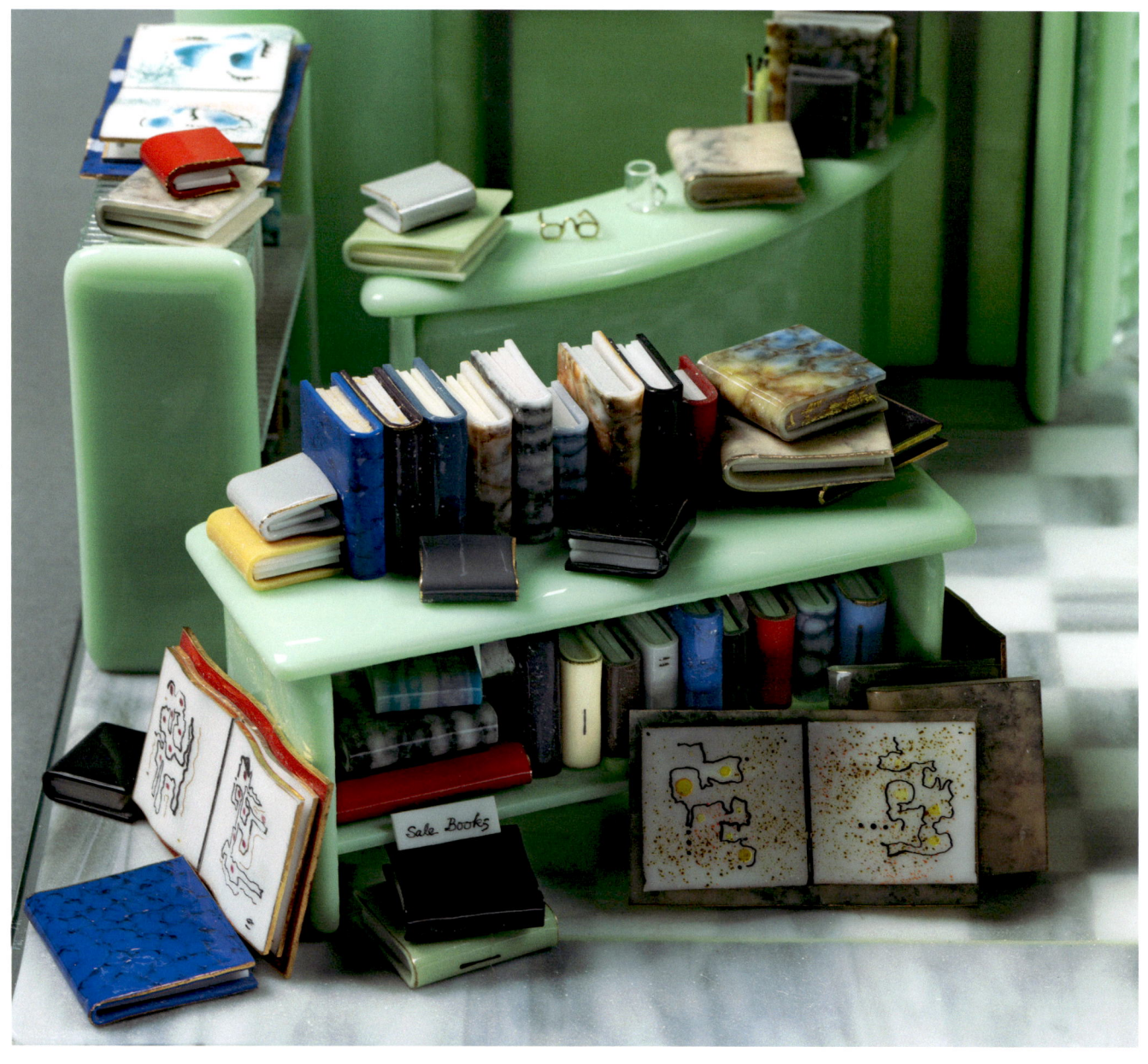

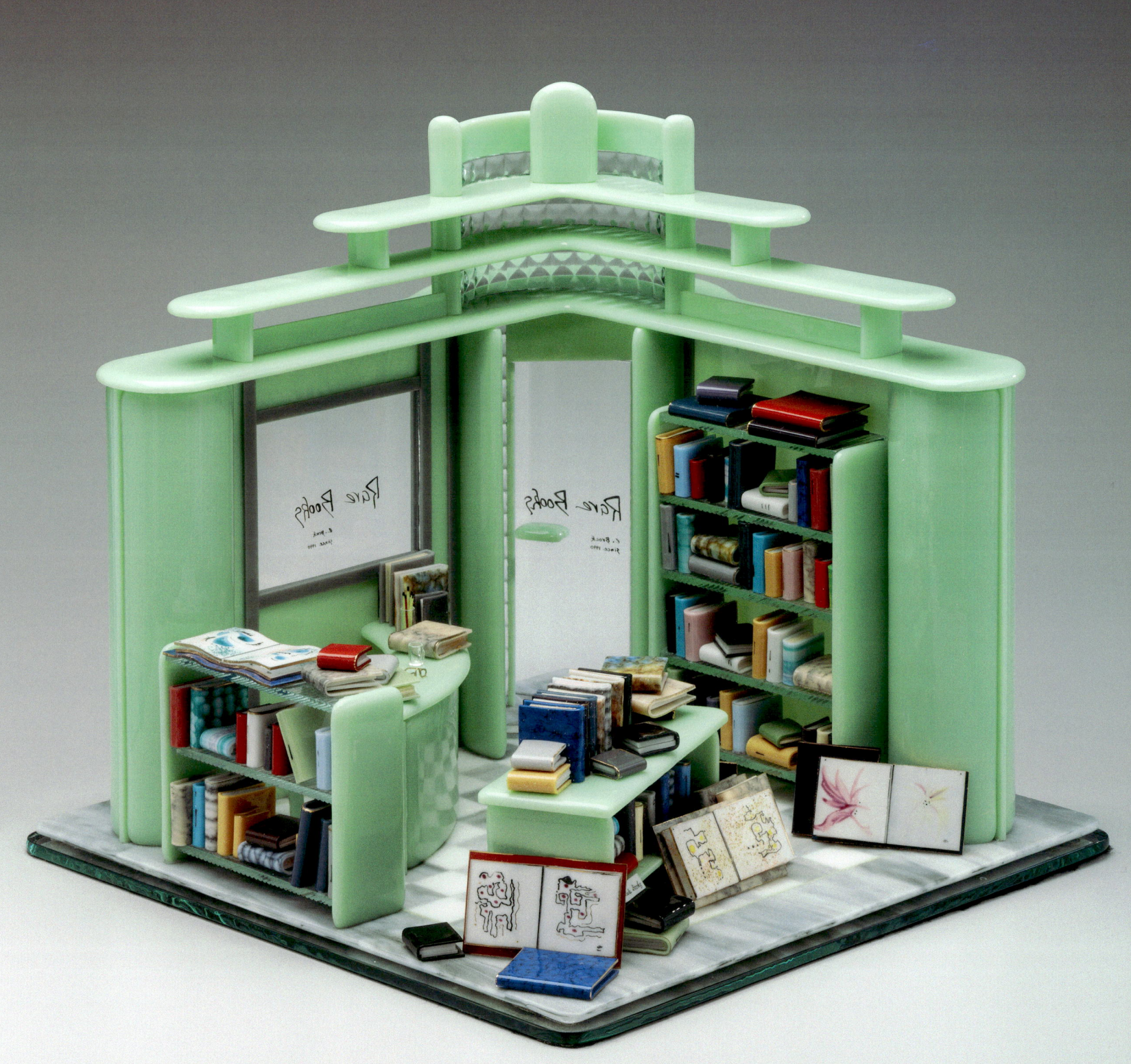

7

Jane Bruce

born 1947, United Kingdom

Bullseye Ball, 2004.
Wheel-cut, kilnformed, and blown
Bullseye glass, 6¾ × Diam. 6¼ in.
(17.15 × 15.89 cm)

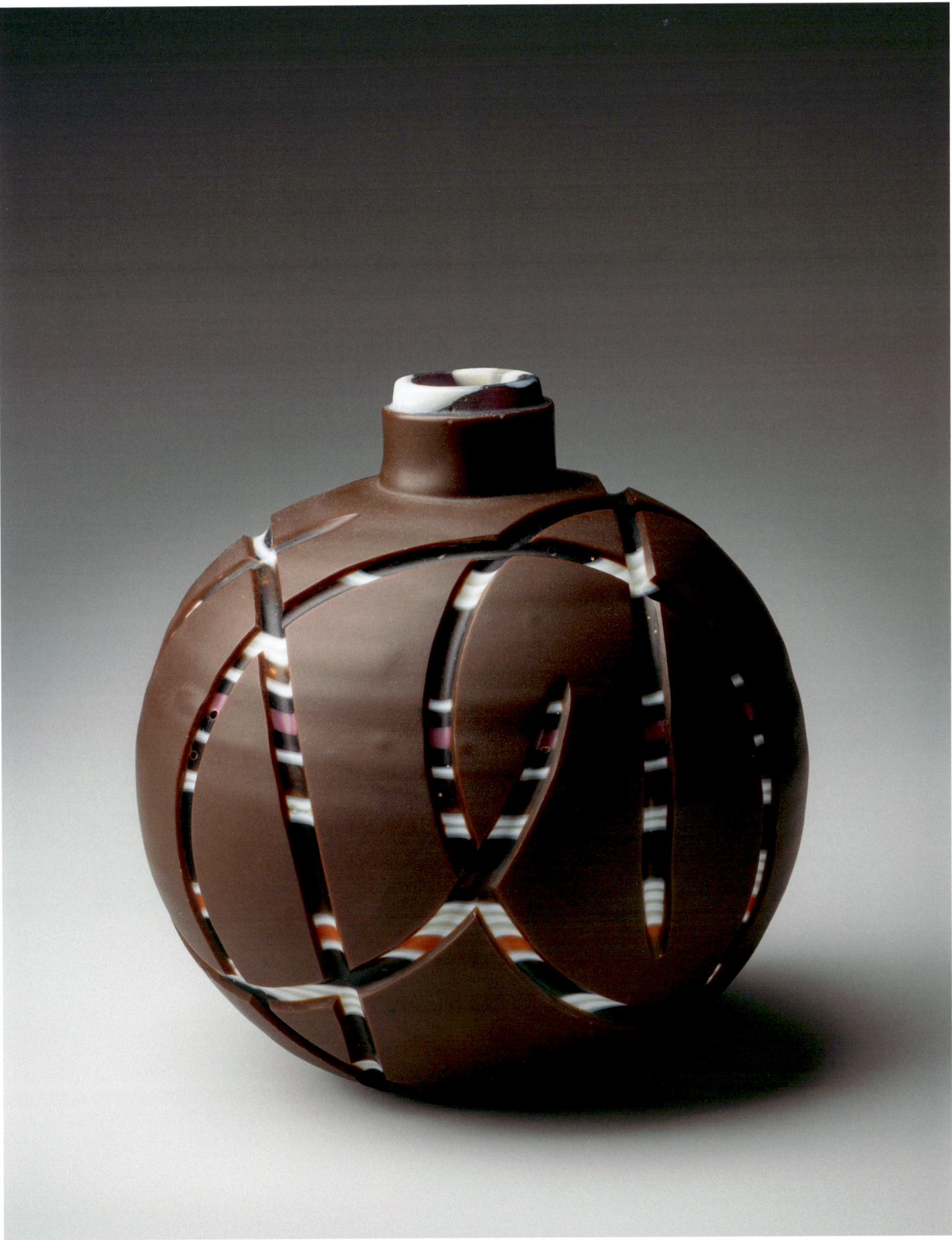

8

Jaroslava Brychtová
1924–2020, Czech Republic

Stanislav Libenský
1921–2002, Czech Republic

Head VI (Queen), 1987.
Cast glass, 13¾ × 7¾ × 5 in. (34.93 × 19.69 × 12.7 cm)

Through the course of fifty years of life and artistic partnership, world-renowned Czech artists Stanislav Libenský and Jaroslava Brychtová created some of the most memorable glass art of the twentieth century.[1] *Head VI (Queen)* is a radiant, small-scale example of their work, notable for the richness and depth of its amber color and its intriguing abstract allusion to the female form.[2]

Through the artists' expertise and deep focus on form, light, and color achieved through cast glass, Libenský and Brychtová demonstrated and celebrated the optical possibilities of the medium in their abstract and figural sculptures. They achieved these effects through a casting process called mold melting, in which solid chunks of glass are placed in a mold and allowed to melt in a large kiln over time. When cooled, a work would be cut and ground to achieve the desired finish. Inspired by cubist principles, Libenský and Brychtová thought of glass as a fourth dimension of "light-space."[3]

Beyond its aesthetic and technical accomplishments, *Head VI (Queen)* held personal significance for the artists. Inscribed on the base: "For Harvey - Stanislav and Jaroslava 1987," Libenský and Brychtová gave the sculpture as a gift to Harvey Littleton, the recognized founder of the American Studio Glass movement, as a thank you after a 1987 visit to Littleton's North Carolina studio. While the gift spoke to their own personal connection with Littleton, it also underscores the strong relationships that developed between international glass artists in the late twentieth century. SNC

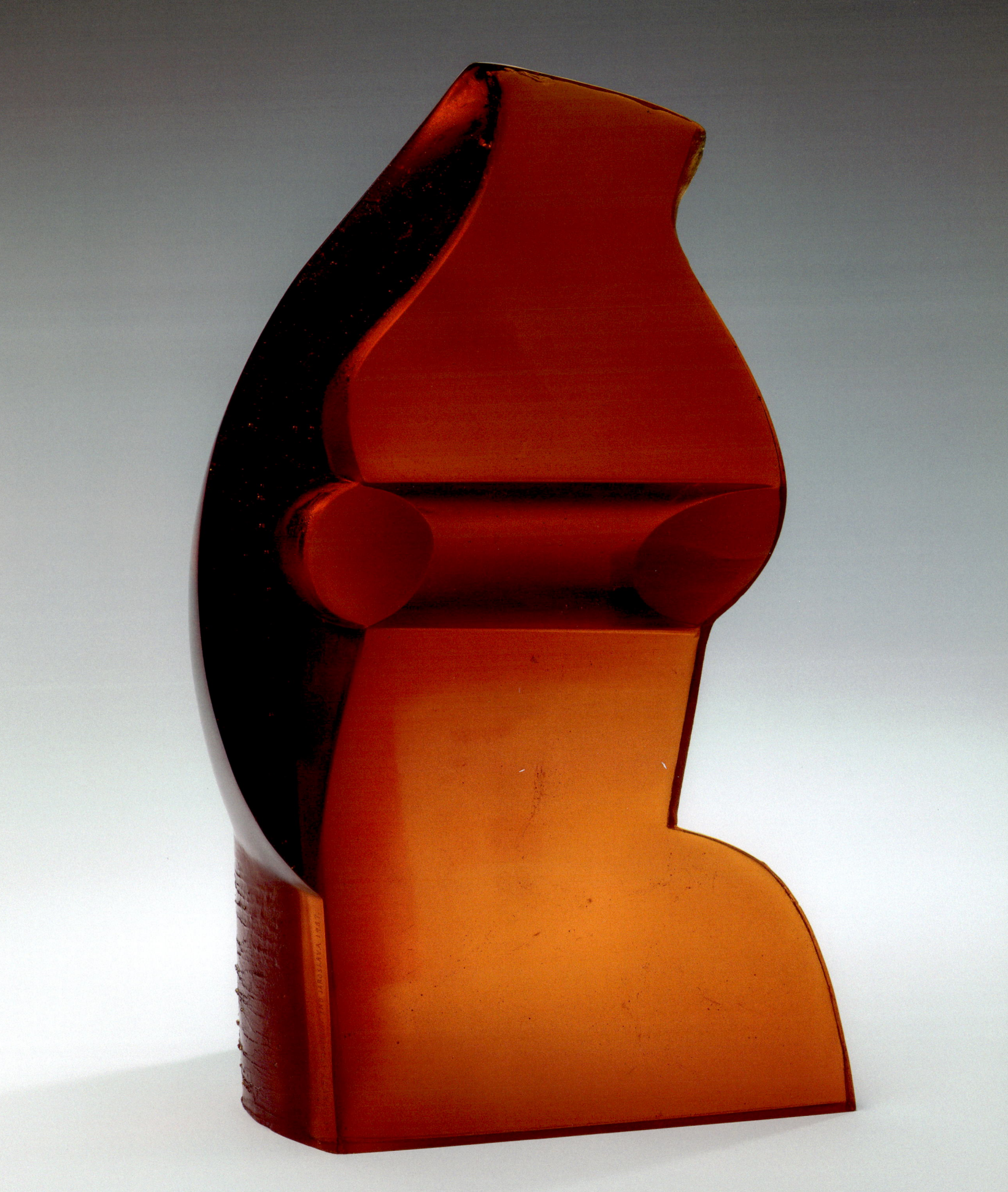

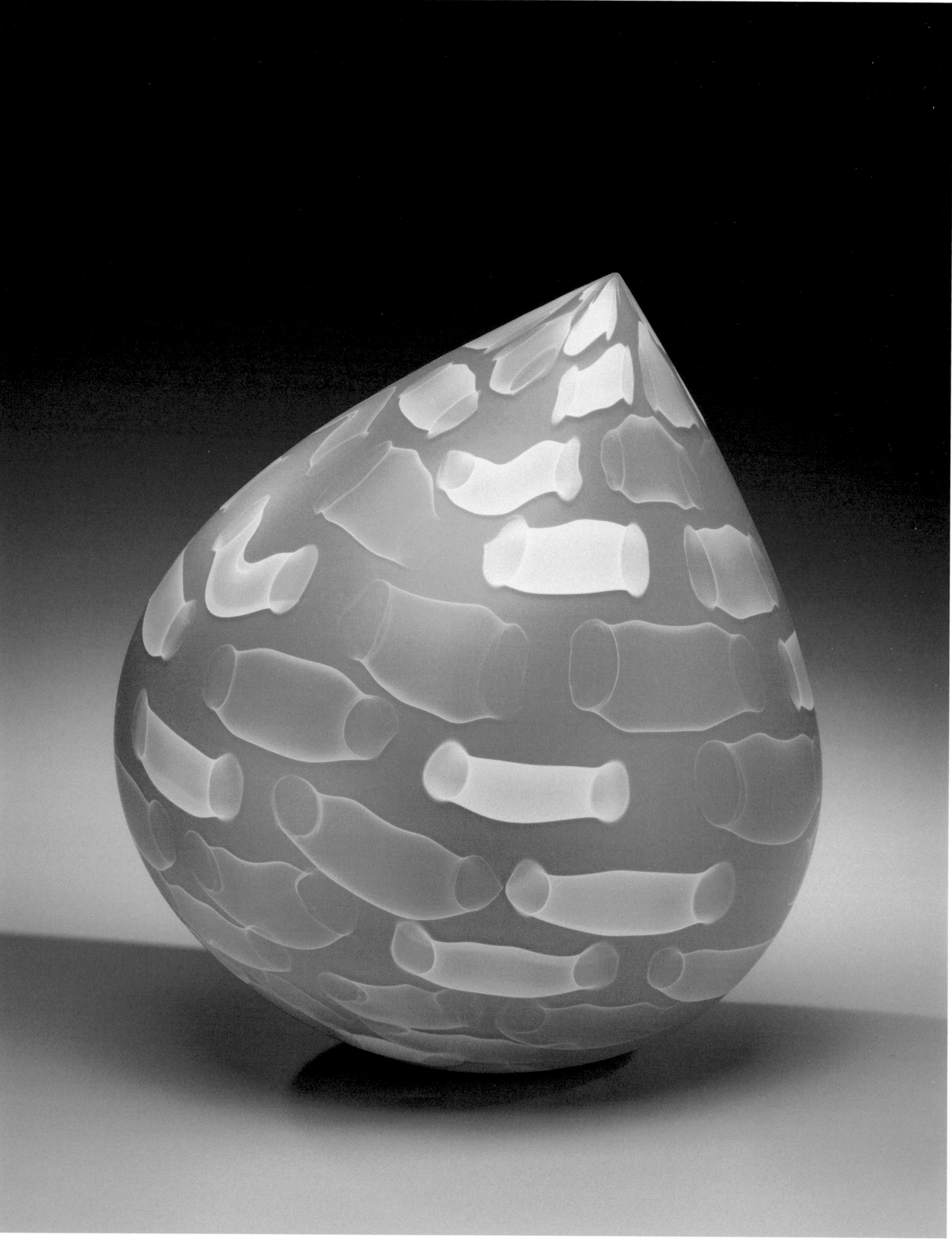

Nancy Callan

born 1964, United States

Melon Droplet, 2019.
Blown and etched glass, 16½ × Diam.
14½ in. (41.91 × 36.83 cm)

"I've always been interested in layering effects in glass and this aspect has become even more important to my current work. The material of glass has magical qualities—there are things that I don't even understand, the way certain colors react, etc., and I love that element of mystery. I want the viewer to be drawn in to take a closer look, and maybe lose themselves for a moment."

—Nancy Callan

William Carlson

born 1950, United States

Concursatio, 2002.
Cast glass on steel plate, cubes: 5 ×
5 × 2½ in. each (12.7 × 12.7 ×
6.35 cm), overall: 39⅝ × 39¾ × 2¾ in.
(100.65 × 100.97 × 6.99 cm)

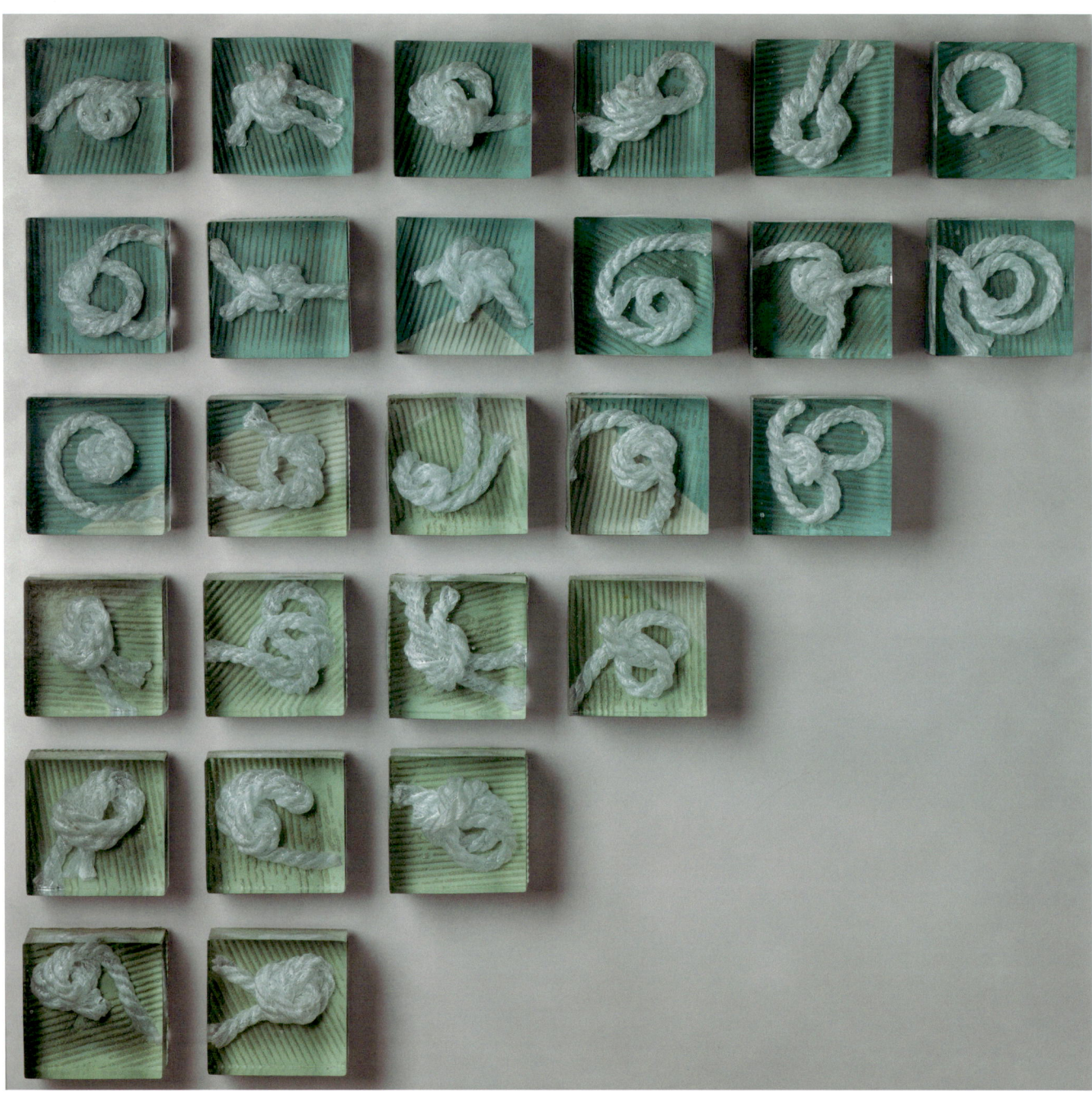

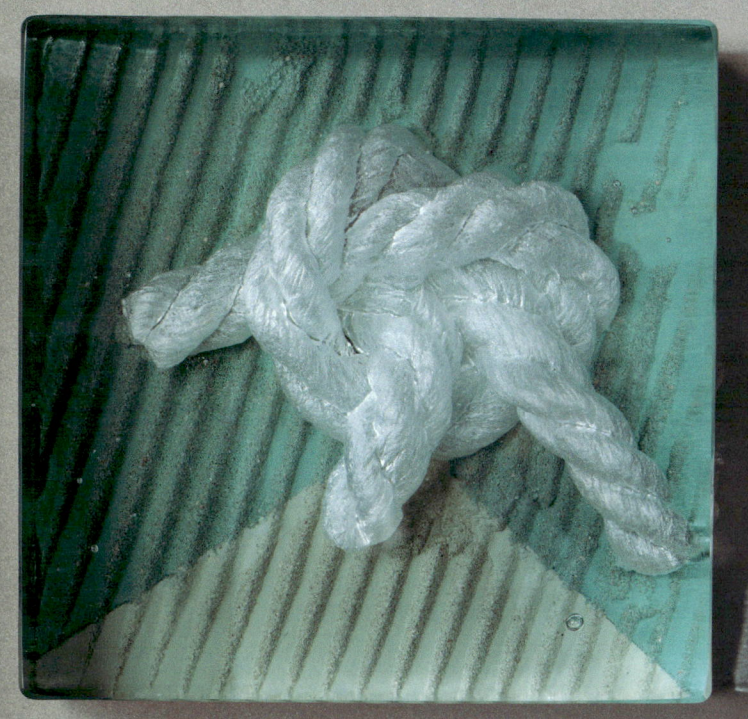
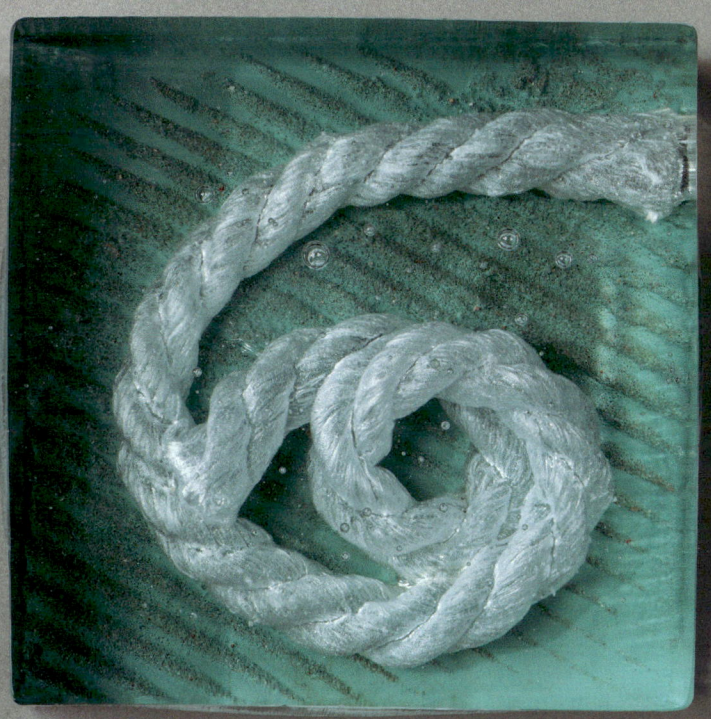
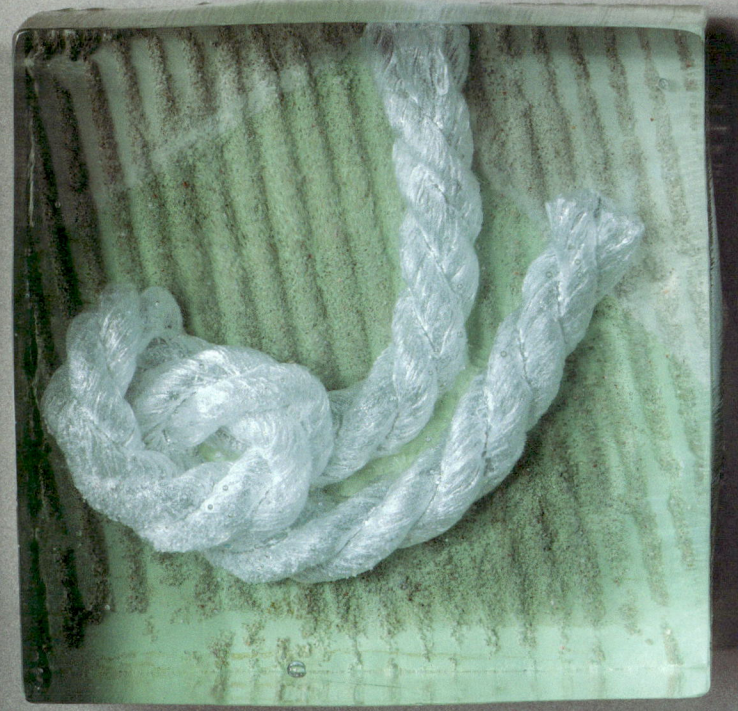
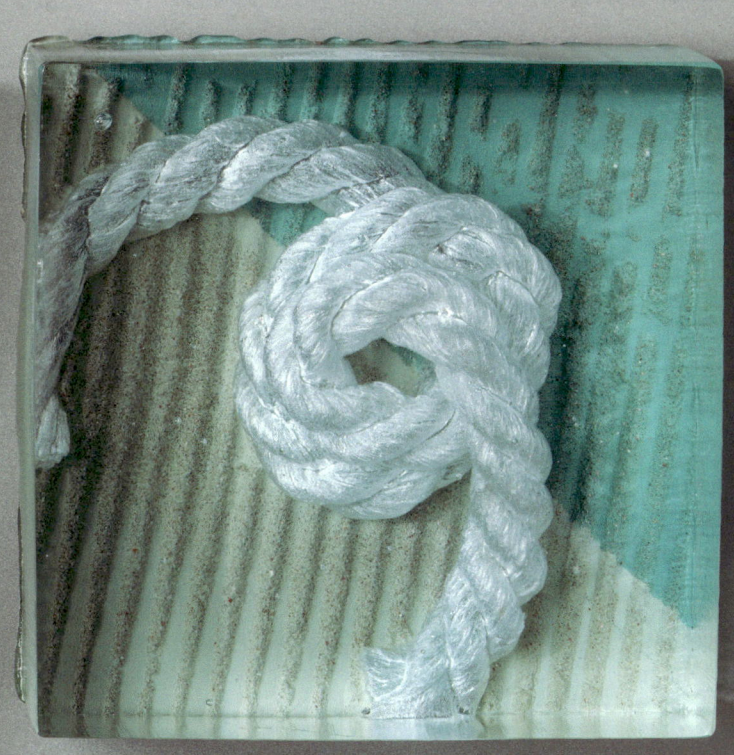

11

Sydney Cash

born 1941, United States

Sculpture, 1981.
Slumped glass, 8¼ × 4⅝ × 4 in.
(20.96 × 11.75 × 10.16 cm)

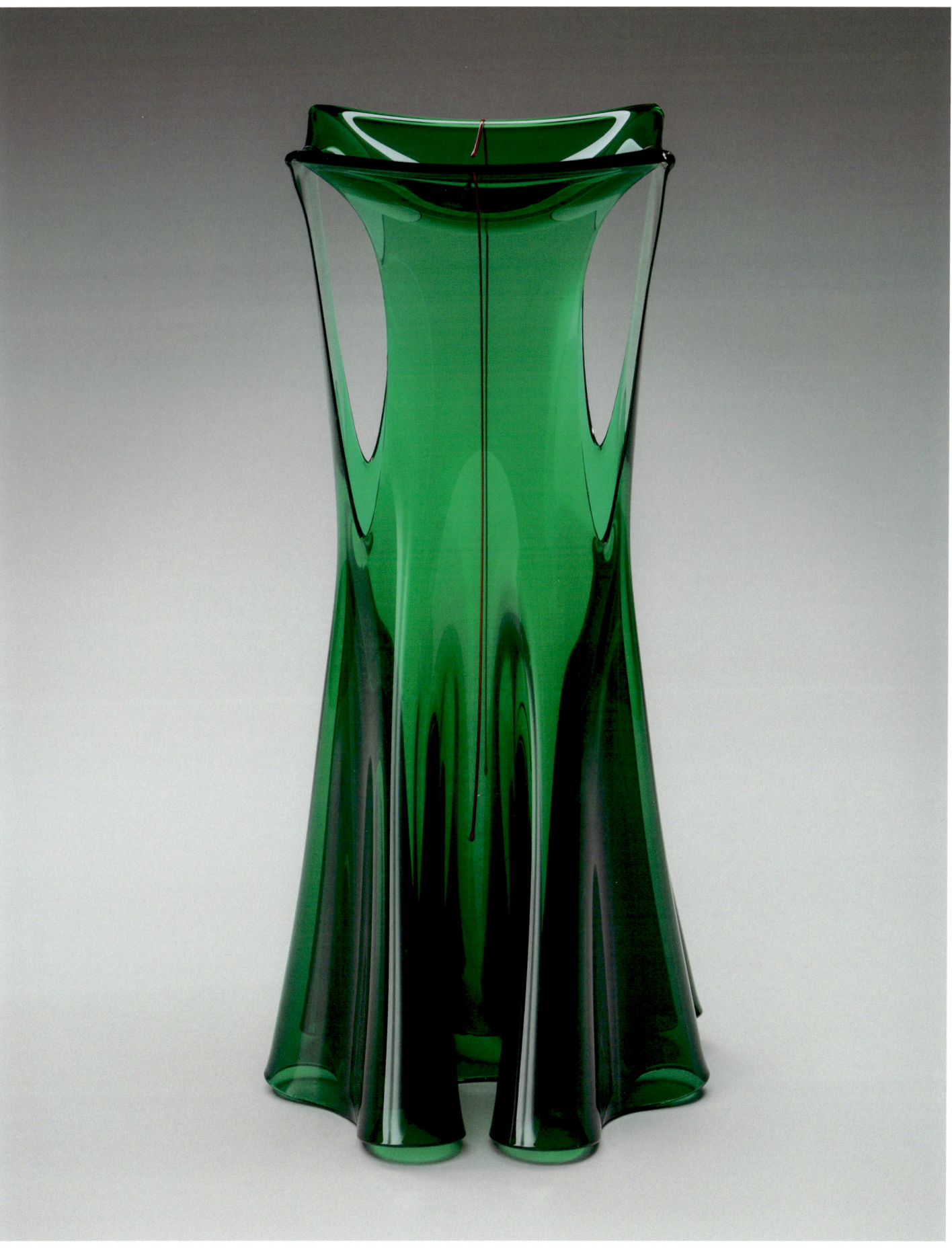

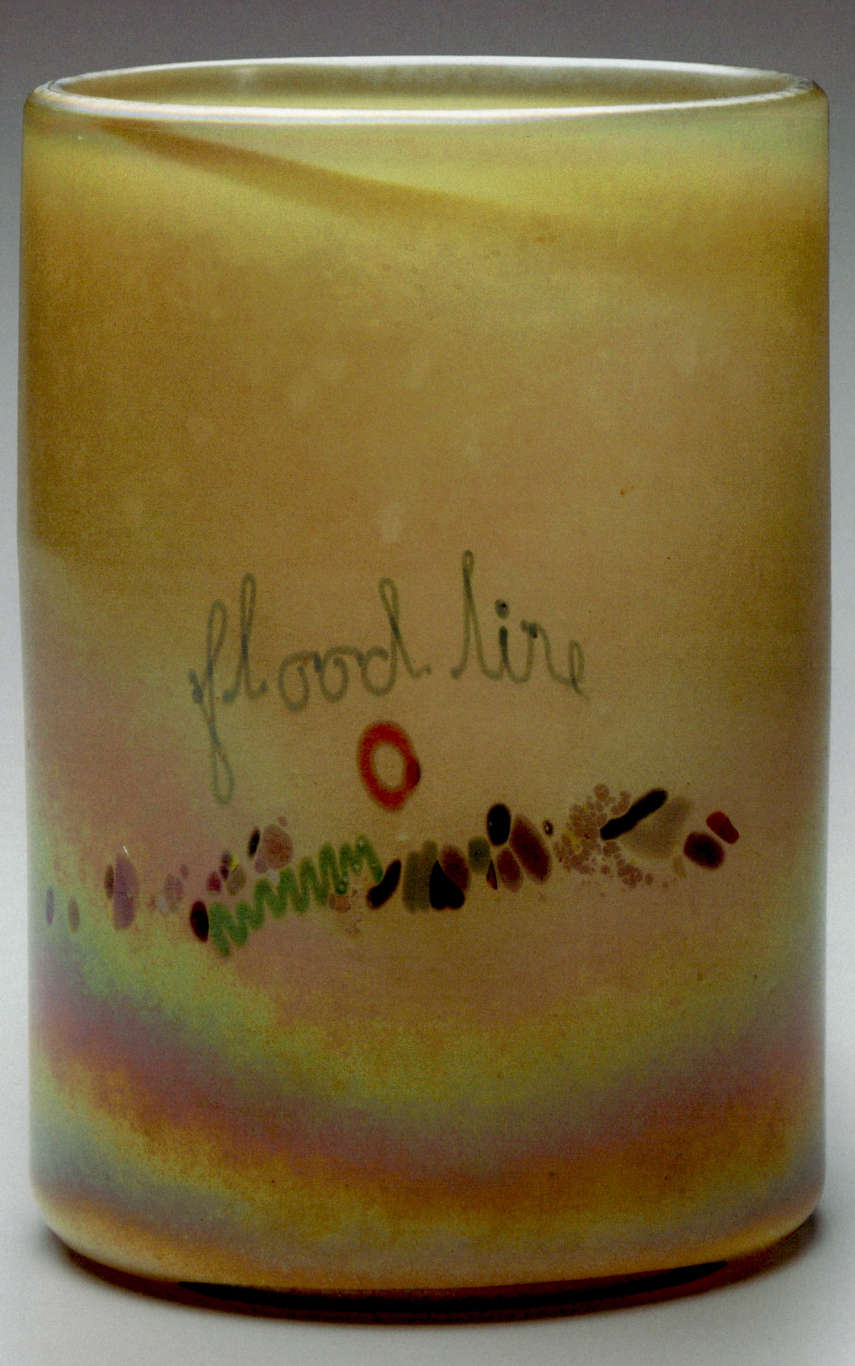

Dale Chihuly
born 1941, United States

Floodline Cylinder, 1974.
Applied and blown glass, 8¾ ×
Diam. 6 in. (22.23 × 15.24 cm)

Dale Chihuly
born 1941, United States

Blanket Cylinder, 1984.
Applied and blown glass, 12⅞ ×
Diam. 8⅛ in. (32.7 × 20.64 cm)

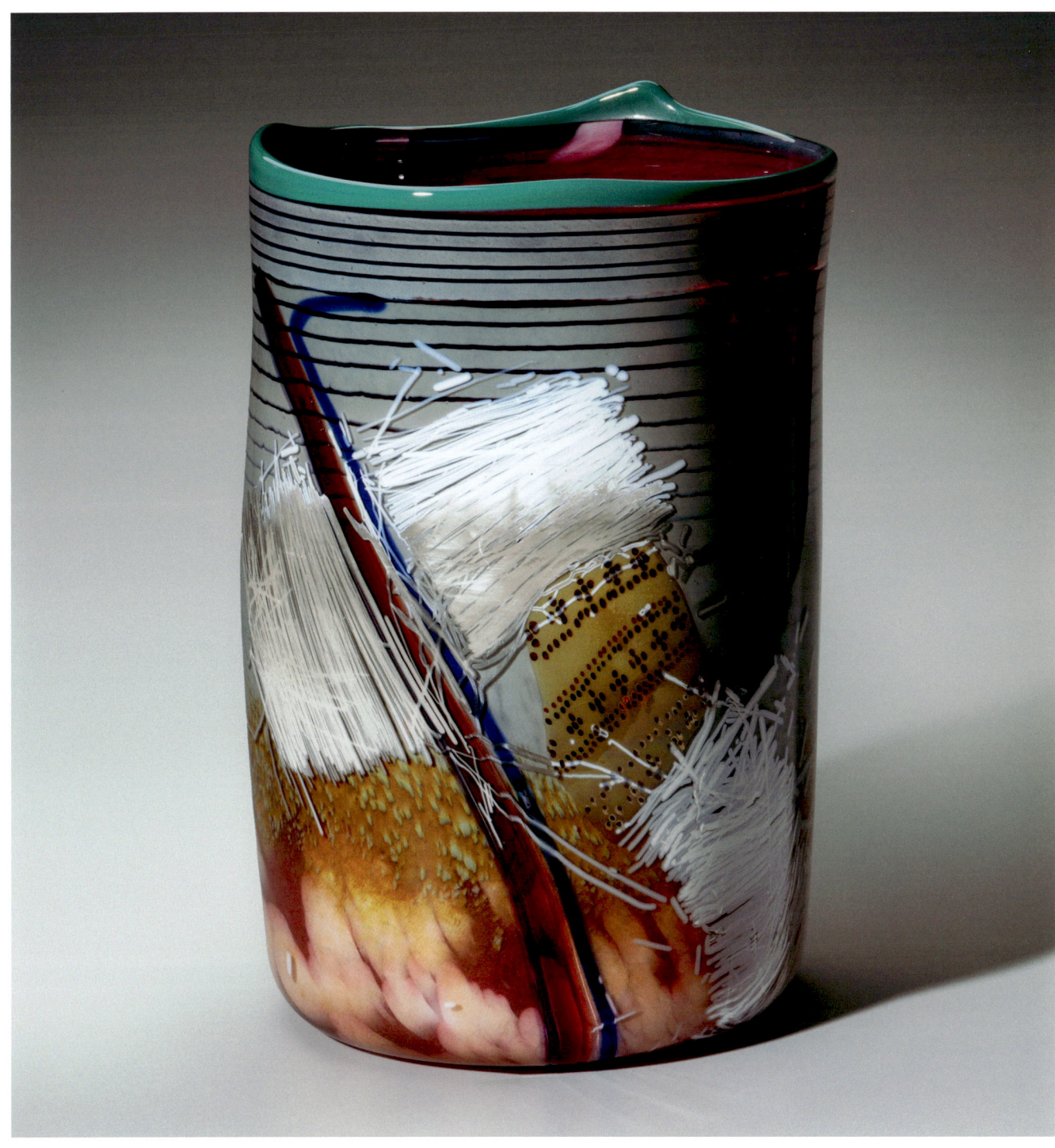

14

Dale Chihuly

born 1941, United States

Lino Tagliapietra

(*assistant*), born 1934, Italy

Vessel, 1993, from the *Venetians*
series.
Blown glass, 21⅛ × 13½ × 13 in.
(53.66 × 34.29 × 33.02 cm)

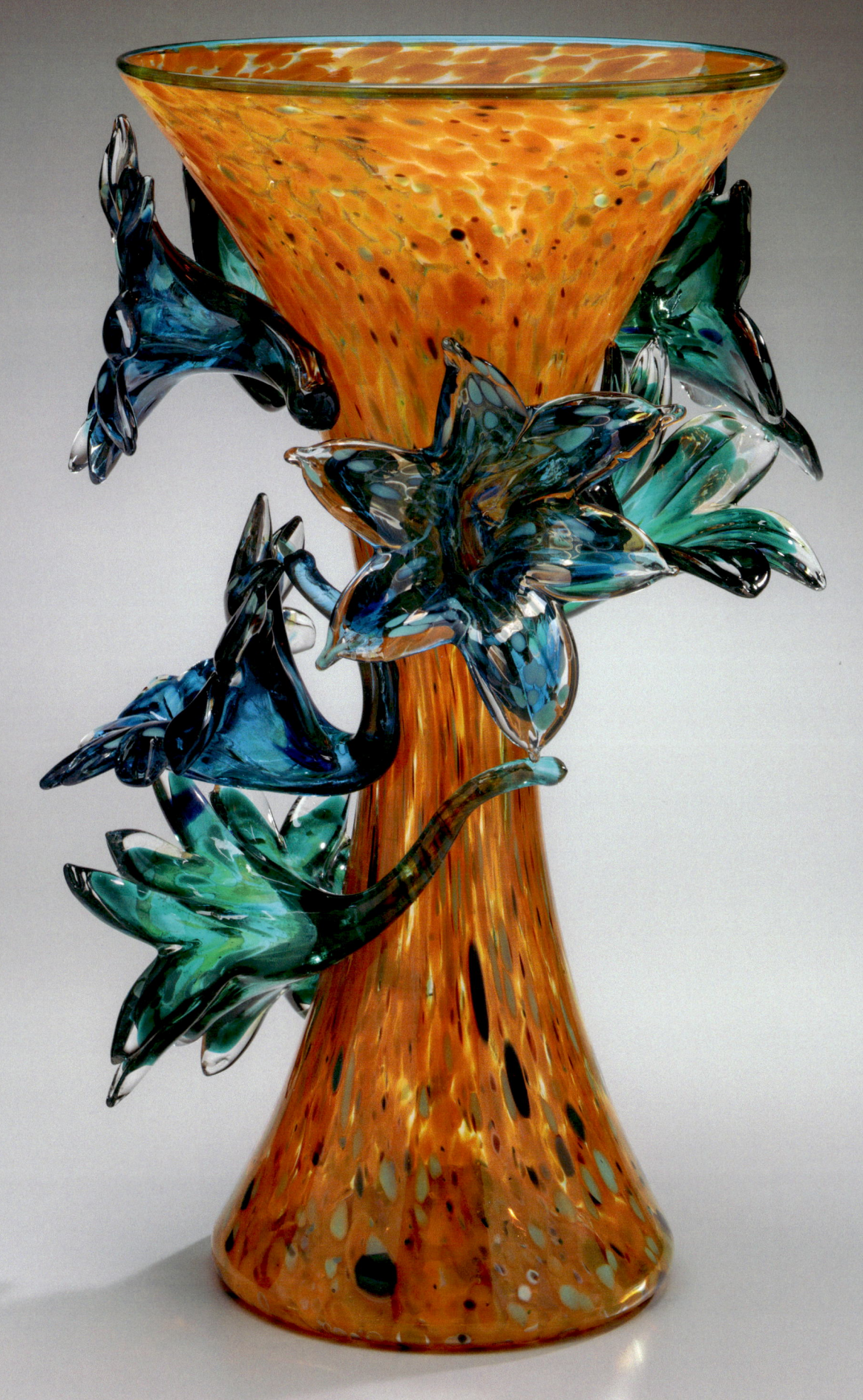

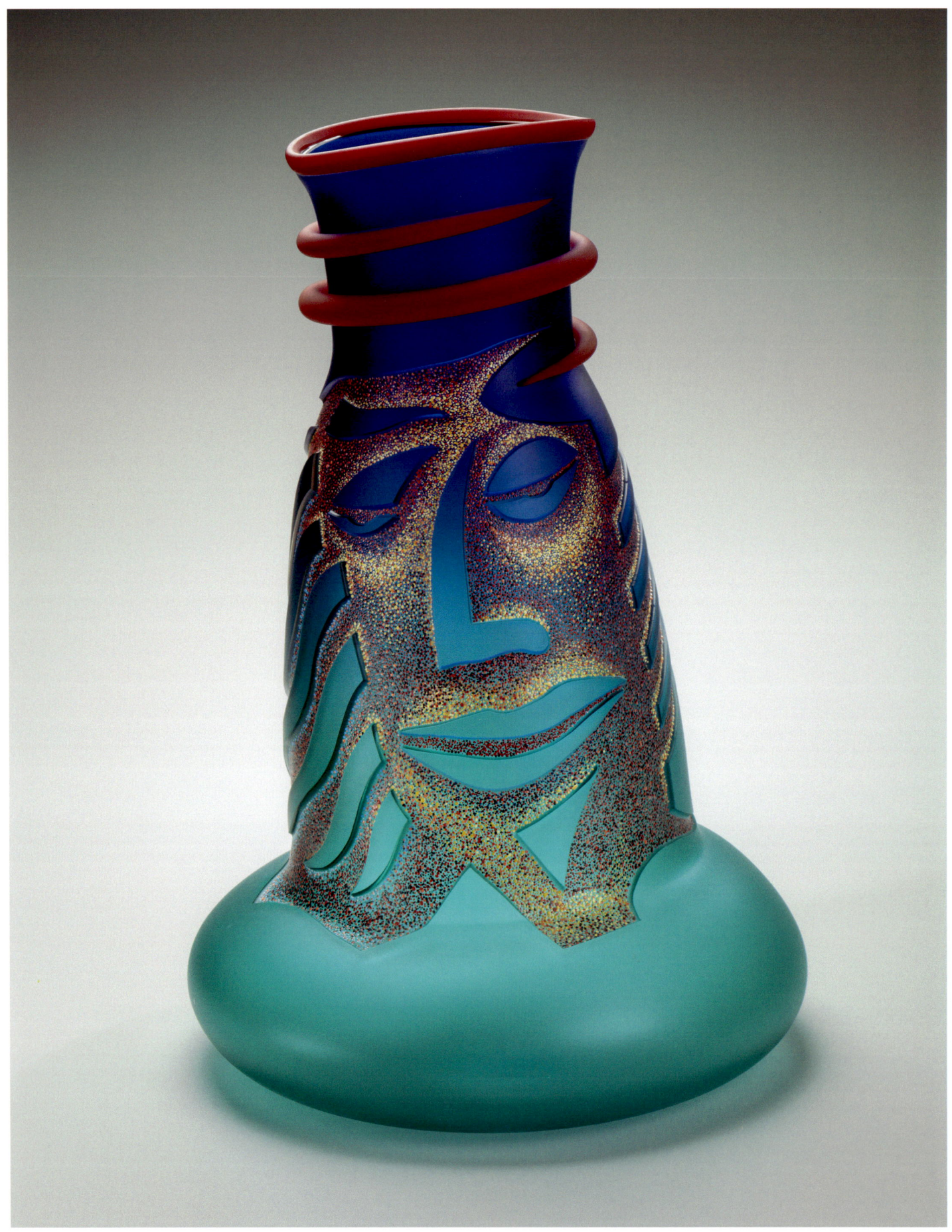

15

Dan Dailey
born 1947, United States

Banana Woman, 1990, from the *Face Vase* series, 1988–97.
Blown glass and applied vitreous enamel, 22¼ × Diam. 14½ in. (56.52 × 36.83 cm)

Fritz Dreisbach

born 1941, United States

Mongo Bowl, 1981, from the ongoing
Mongo series.
Blown glass, 6⅞ × 9¼ × 8¾ in.
(17.46 × 23.5 × 22.23 cm)

Stephen Dee Edwards

born 1954, United States

Head, 1991.
Blown, cast, cut, and fused glass,
17⅜ × 7½ × 6½ in. (44.13 × 19.05 ×
16.51 cm)

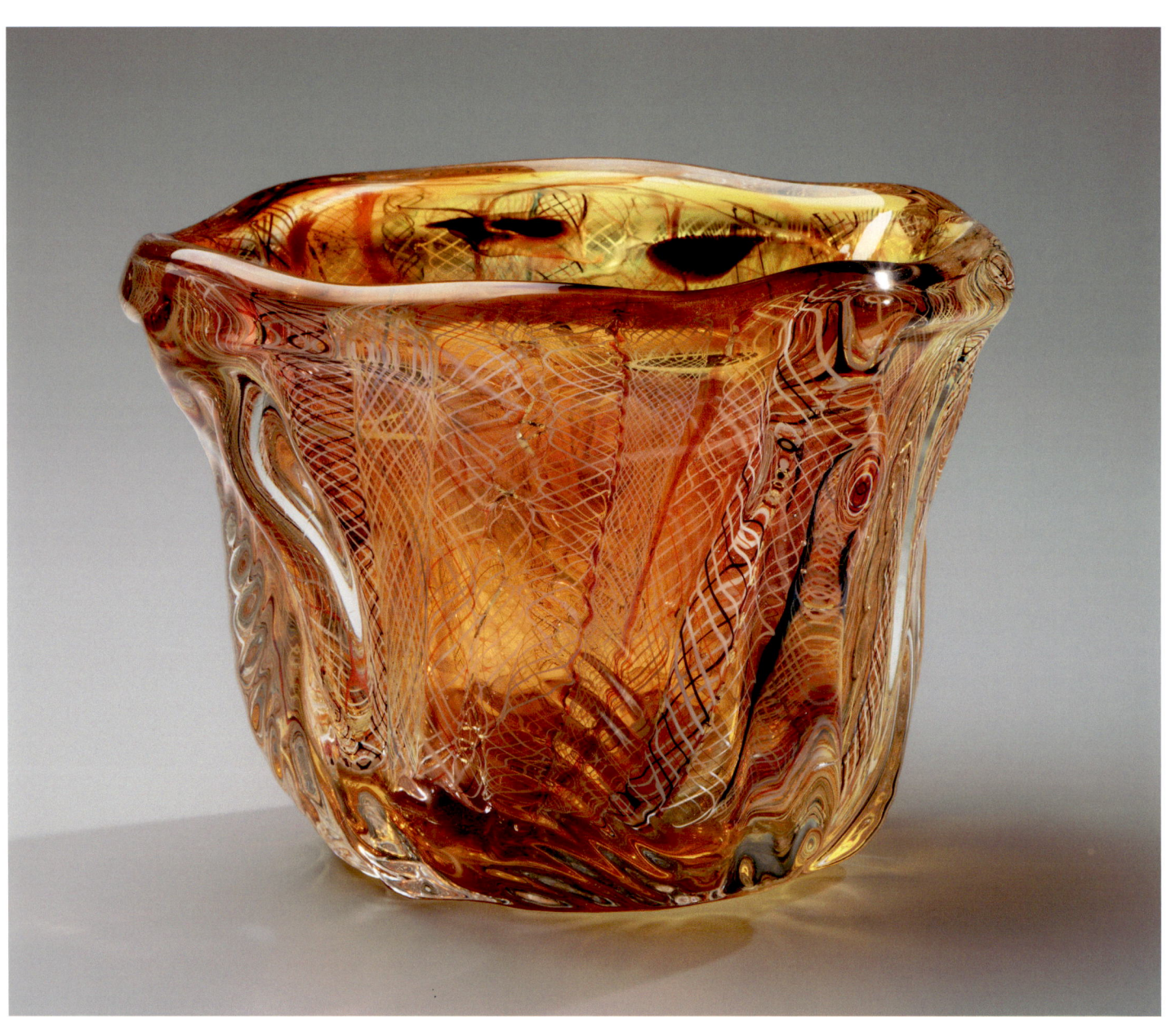

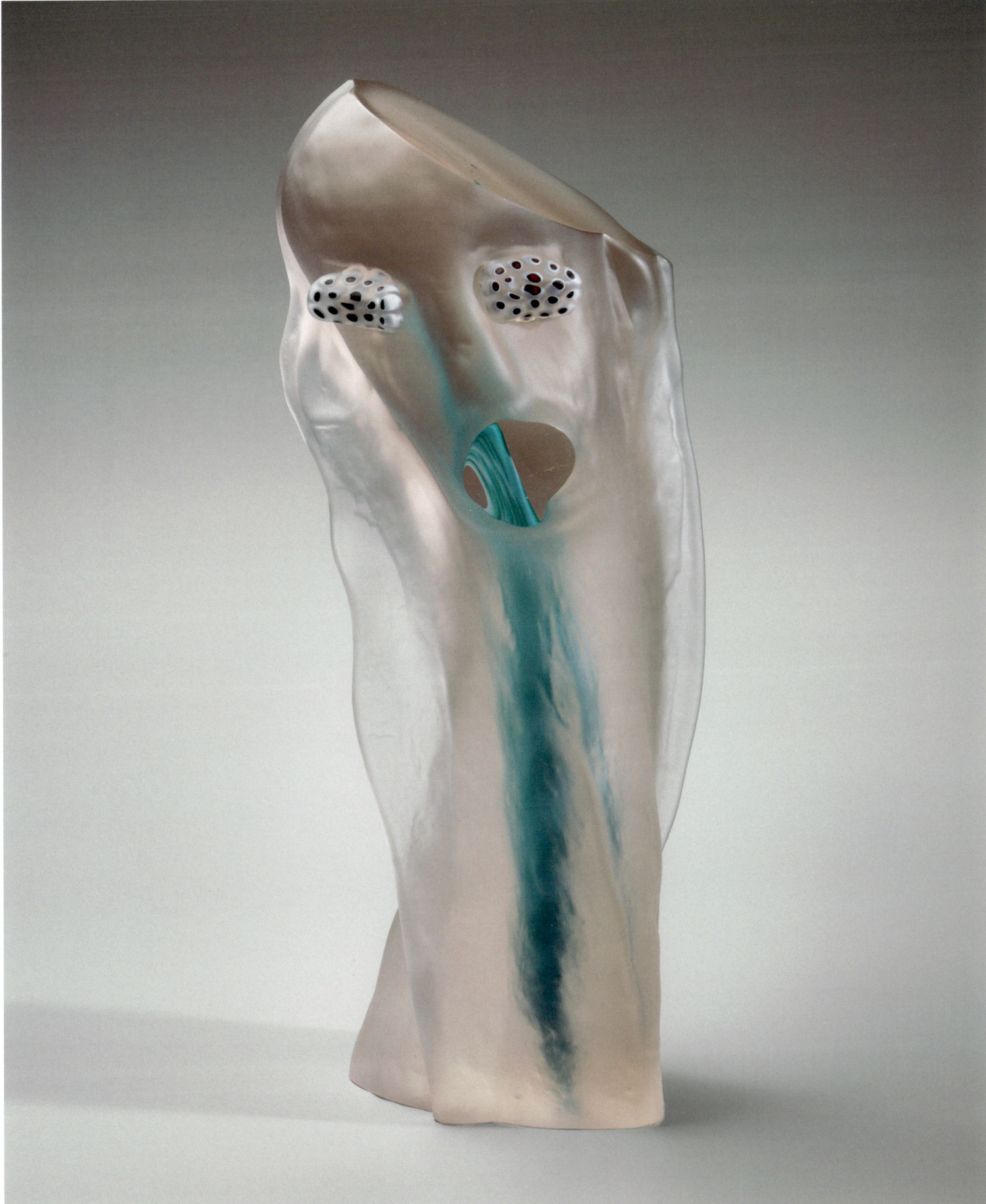

18

Kyohei Fujita

1921–2004, Japan

Kaguya-hime 141-114, ca. 1988.
Mold-blown glass with enamel,
silver, and gold and platinum foil,
6¼ × 4⅞ × 4⅞ in. (15.88 × 12.38 ×
12.38 cm)

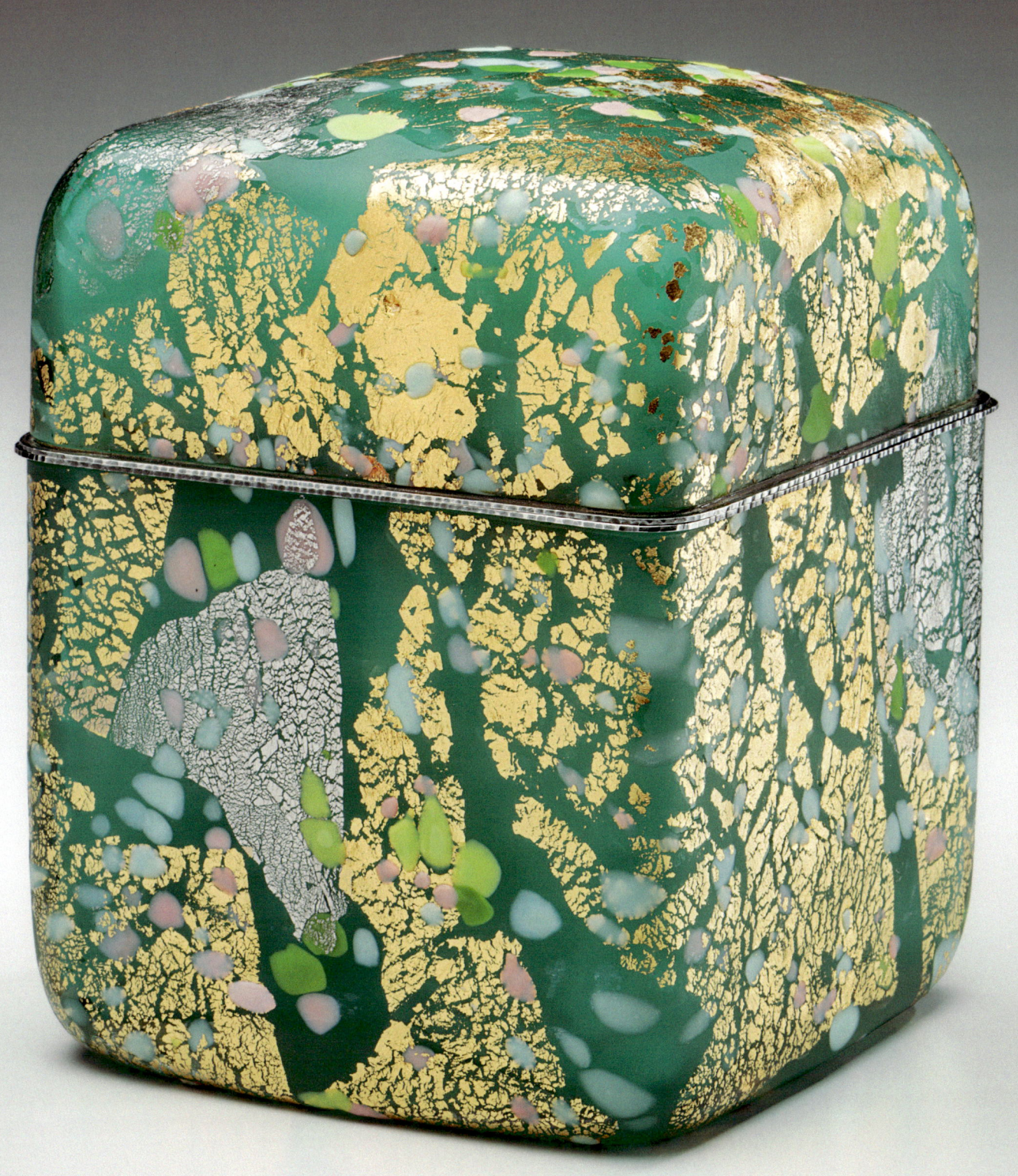

19

Michael Glancy

1950–2020, United States

Crystal Sentinel, 1982.
Blown, engraved, and electroplated
glass with copper, and industrial
plate glass, cylinder: 9⅝ × Diam.
2⅜ in. (24.45 × 6.03 cm), base: 12 ×
12 × ¼ in. (30.48 × 30.48 × 0.64 cm)

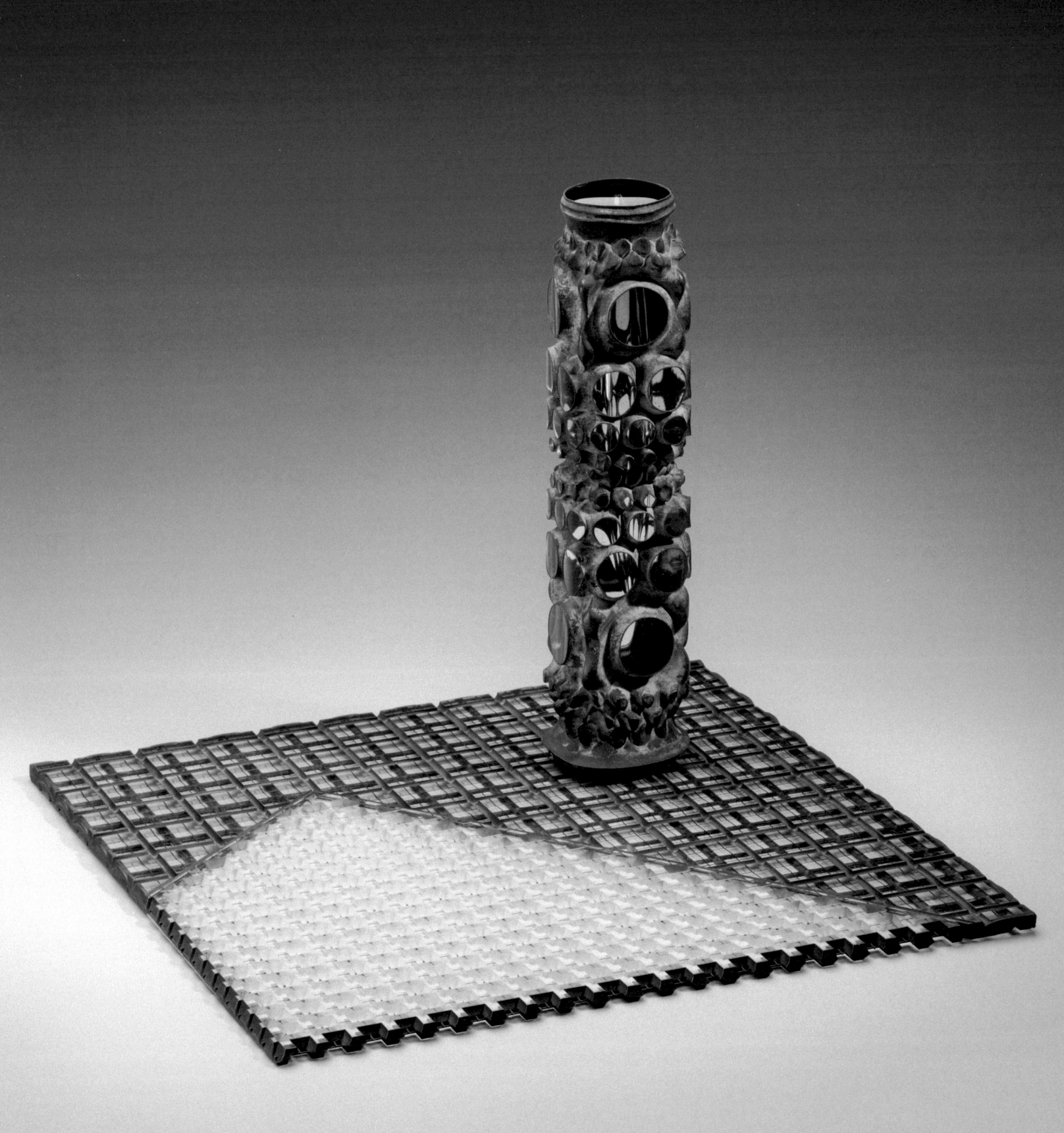

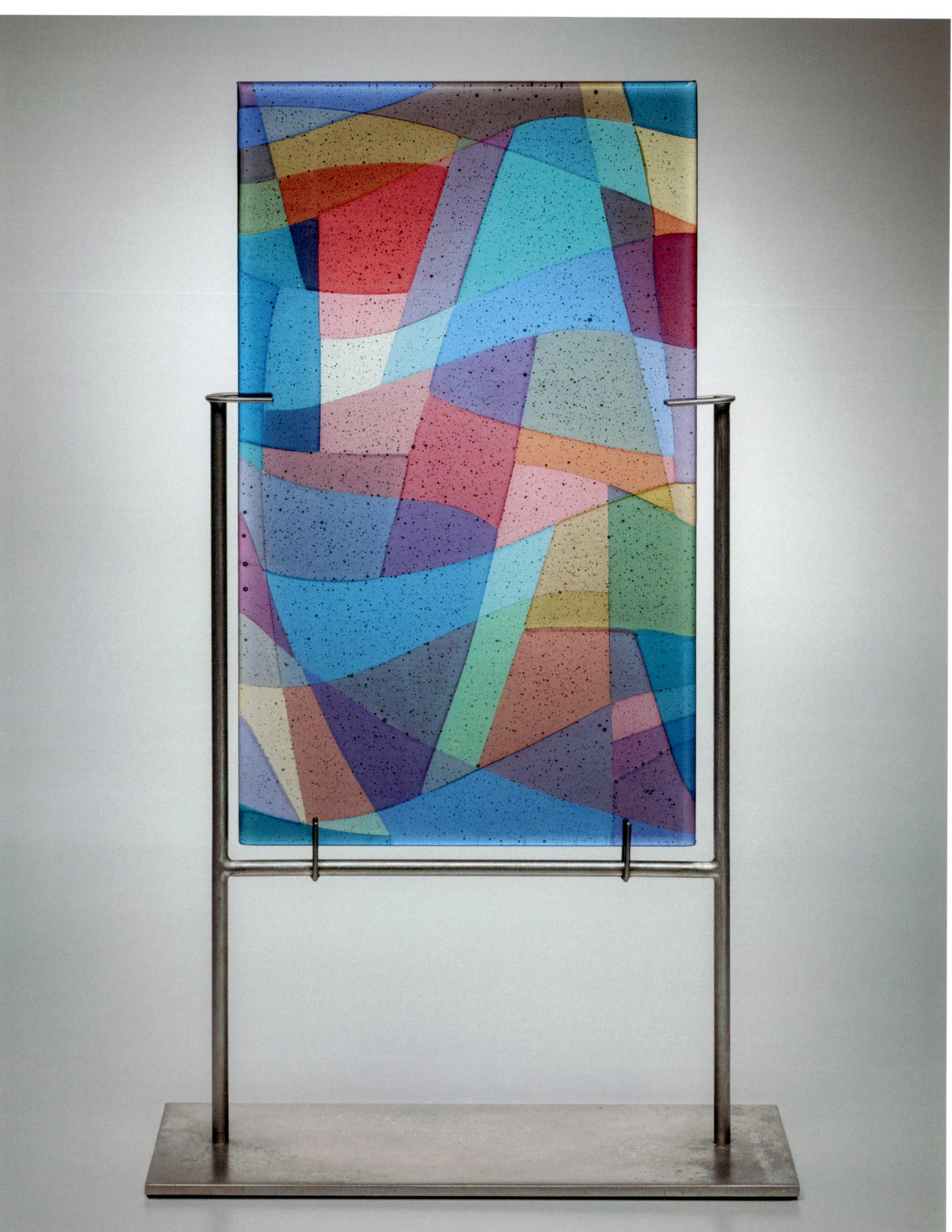

20

Dorothy Hafner

born 1952, United States

Blue Cascade, 2007.
Multi-layer fused glass and metal,
24½ × 14¼ × 6 in. (62.23 × 36.2 ×
15.24 cm)

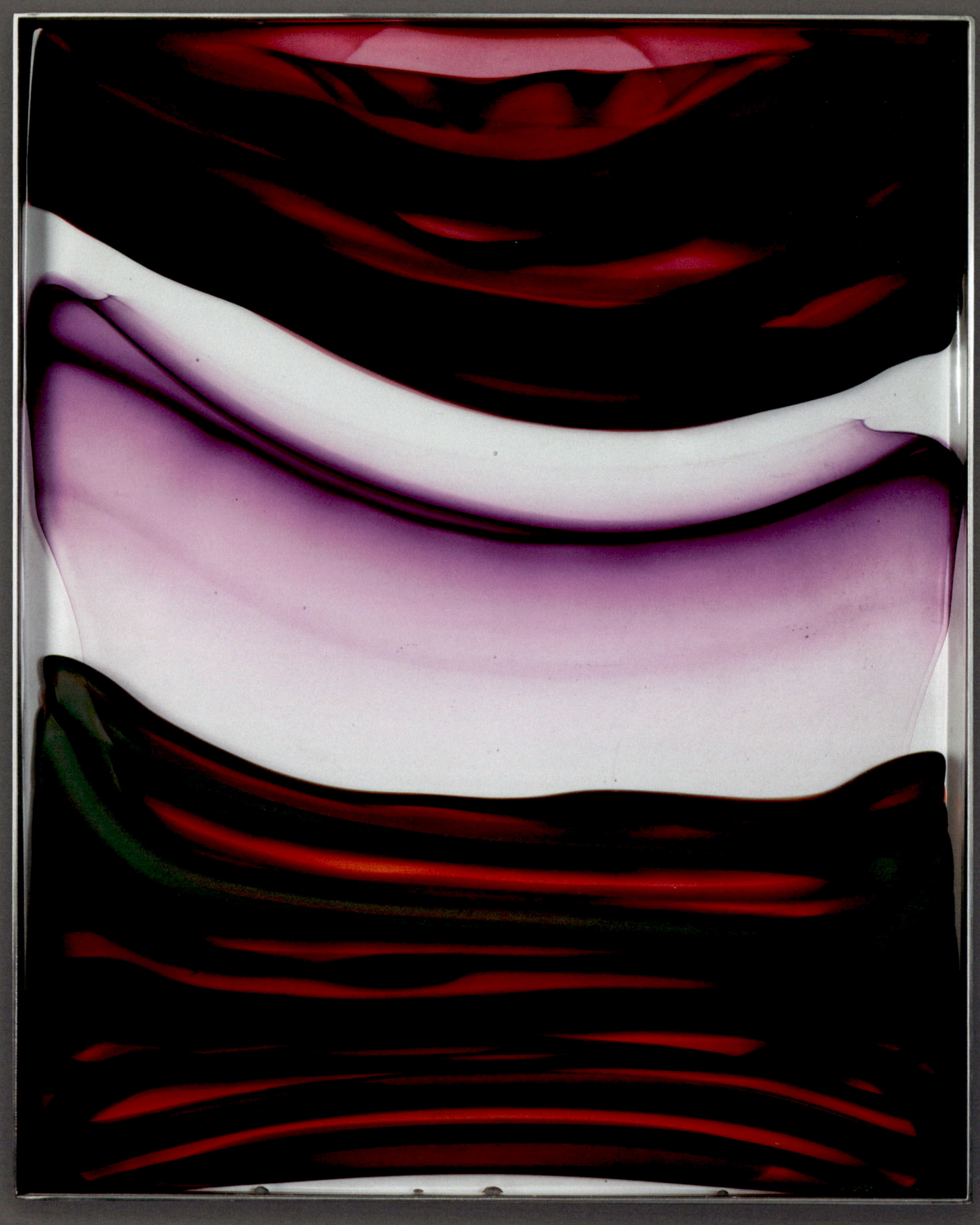

21

Jamie Harris

born 1975, United States

Modulated Infusion Wall Panel, 2008, from the ongoing *Infusions* series.
Blown glass, cast glass, and metal, 24 × 19⅜ × 1⅜ in. (60.96 × 49.21 × 3.49 cm)

22

Chris Hawthorne

born 1953, United States

James Nowak

born 1956, United States

Vessel, 1990, from the *Aquarium* series.
Blown glass, 18¼ × 23½ × 12½ in. (46.36 × 59.69 × 31.75 cm)

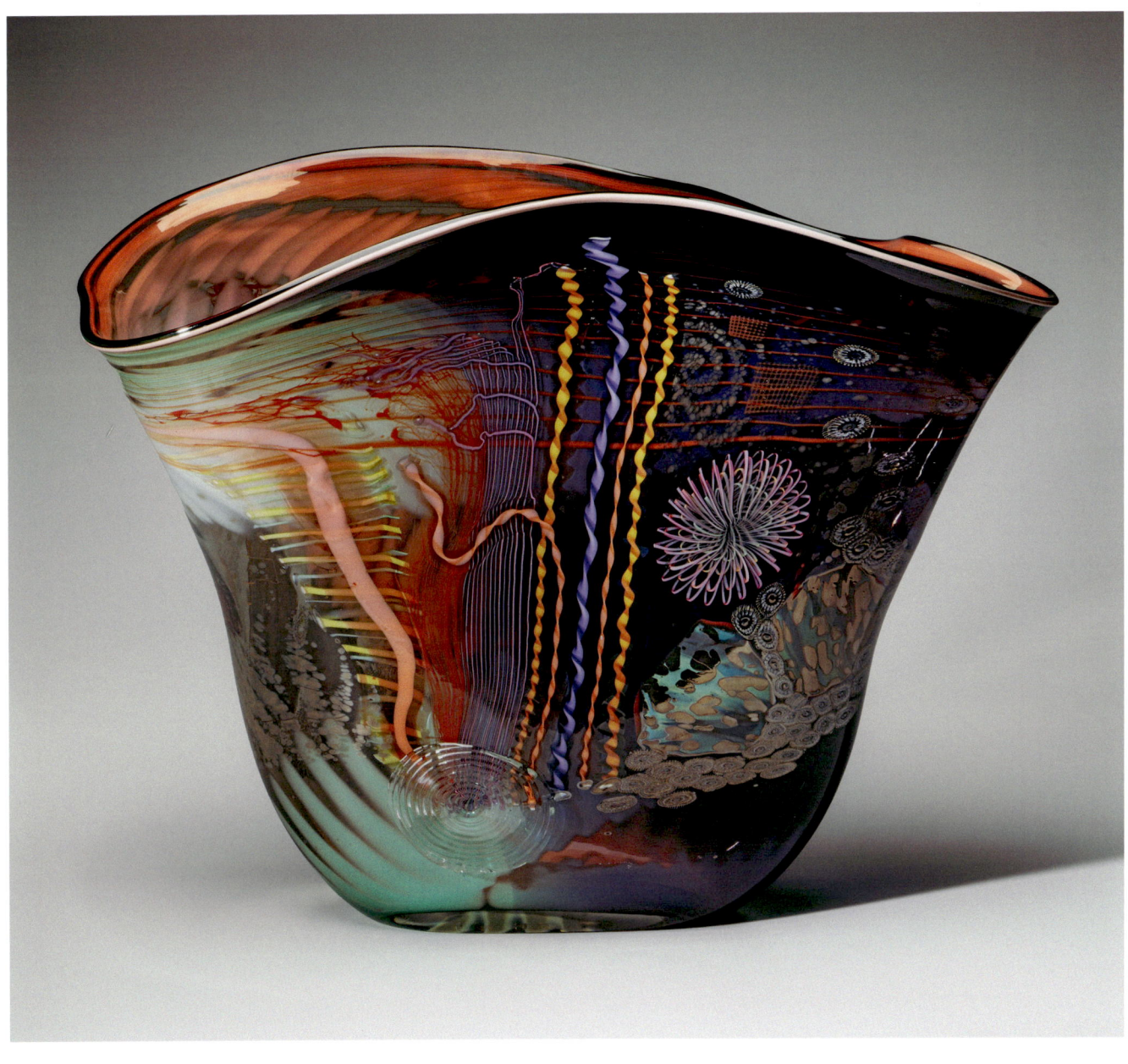

Kimiake Higuchi

born 1948, Japan

Cyclamen V-3, 1995.
Pâte de verre, 15¾ × 14⅛ × 6 in.
(40.01 × 35.88 × 15.24 cm)

Kimiake Higuchi achieved the delicate florals and opaque colors in her *Cyclamen V-3* vase through the centuries-old glassmaking process of *pâte de verre*. First employed in ancient Greece, this technique became popular among late nineteenth-century French glassmakers working in the Art Nouveau style. Higuchi and her husband and collaborator, Shin-ichi, are masters of *pâte de verre*, which they began experimenting with in the 1980s. While both artistically trained in Italy, they are entirely self-taught when it comes to glass. Through careful study, they came to the slow and deliberate process they now use to create their pieces. Of this process, Higuchi says, "You can't break through your limitations by sitting comfortably in your environment. You have to use your head, your limbs and sharpen your five senses."[1]

Today, Higuchi calls Nikko, Japan, home. She and Shin-ichi exemplify a wave of international studio glassmakers who began spreading the movement globally in the 1980s. Their home studio is surrounded by a garden they designed, from which the artist draws her greatest inspiration. There, she grows, tends, and observes her plants, sometimes harvesting them at their peak to serve as imprints for her molds. Her process involves the careful selection of color, grinding pigments herself, and making her own plaster molds. Pouring the ground glass into a mold, it is then fused in a kiln. She then grinds and polishes the work to achieve a lifelike surface. "I always challenge myself to express more and more through my nature pieces," she says, "I hope to move people."[2] LM

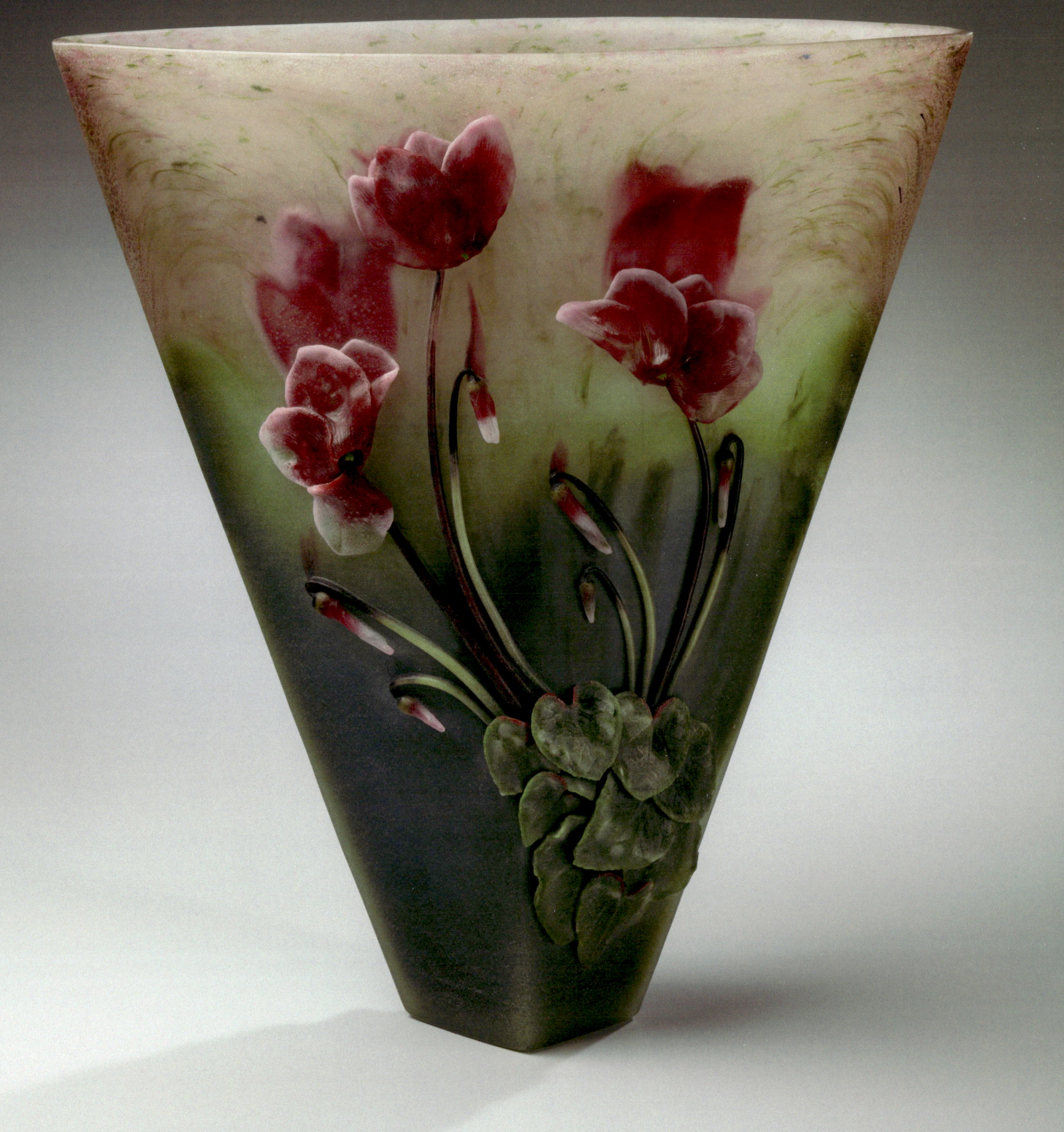

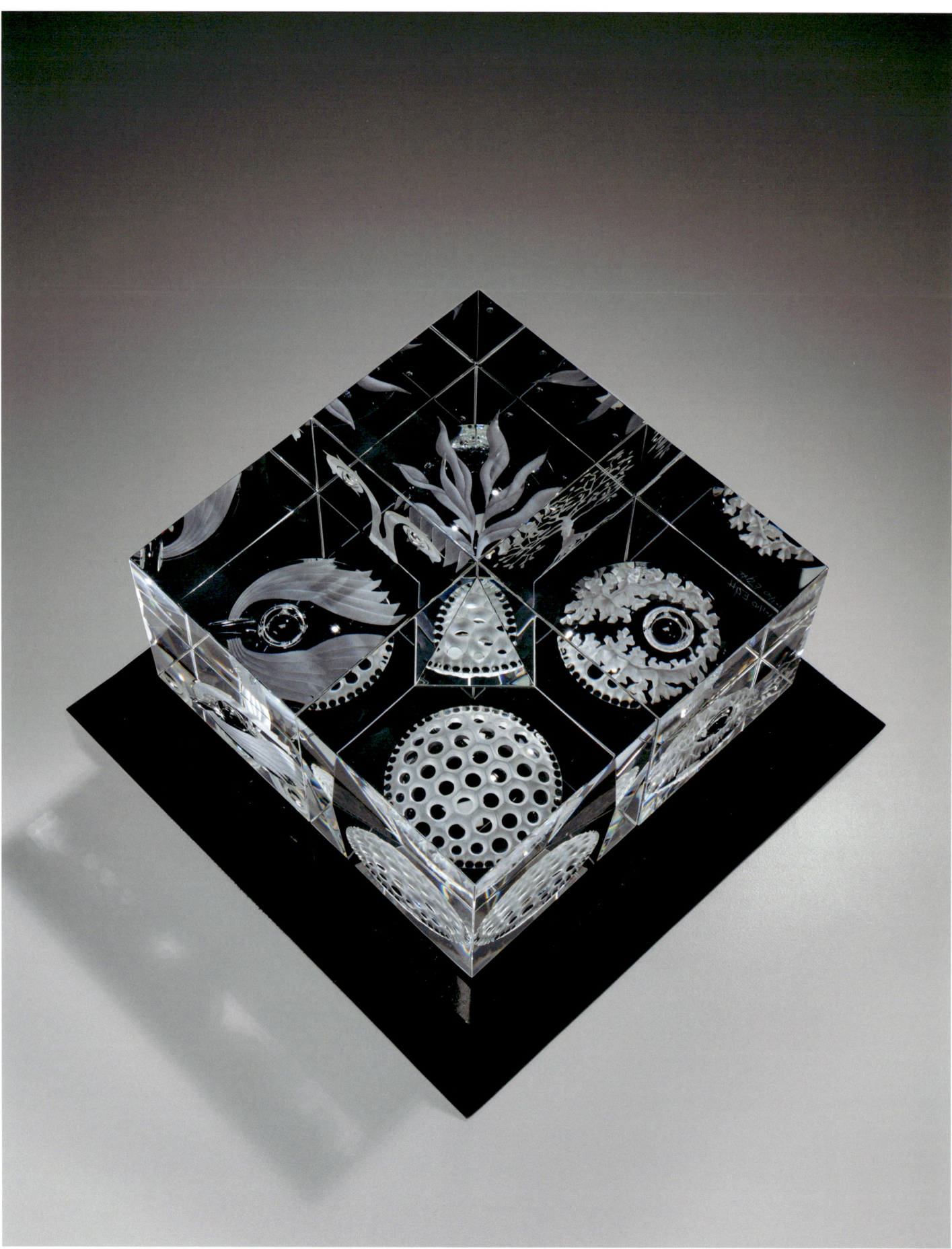

24

Eric Hilton

born 1937, United Kingdom,
for Steuben Glass Works,
United States

Infinite Journey, 20th–21st century.
Cast and sandblasted glass, and
granite, 5 × 9⅜ × 9⅜ in. (12.7 ×
23.81 × 23.81 cm)

"Art, for me, is the vehicle that
synthesizes order into the awe
of existence. It is the vehicle
for dance, music, poetry,
literature, and the visual arts. It
represents the soul of human
consciousness."
—Eric Hilton

25

Pavel Hlava

1924–2003, Czech Republic

Nature and Autumn, 1992.
Blown, cut, polished, and laminated
glass, 13¼ × 15¾ × 4¼ in. (33.66 ×
40.01 × 10.8 cm)

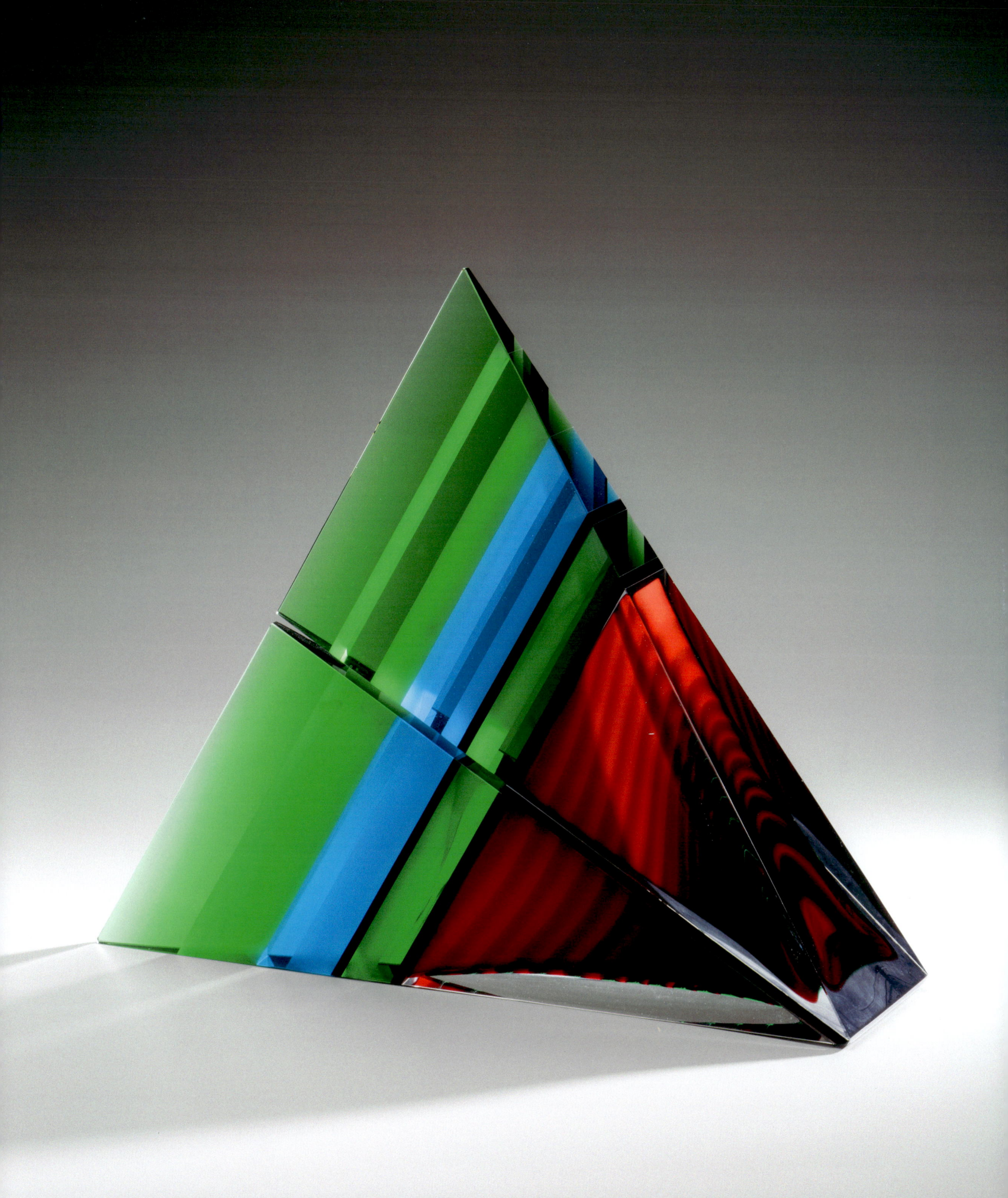

26

Sidney Hutter

born 1954, United States

Turned Jerry Vision Vase #126, 2001, from the ongoing *Solid Vase Form* series.
Cut, ground, and laminated plate glass, 16½ × 9½ × 8⅜ in. (41.91 × 24.13 × 21.27 cm)

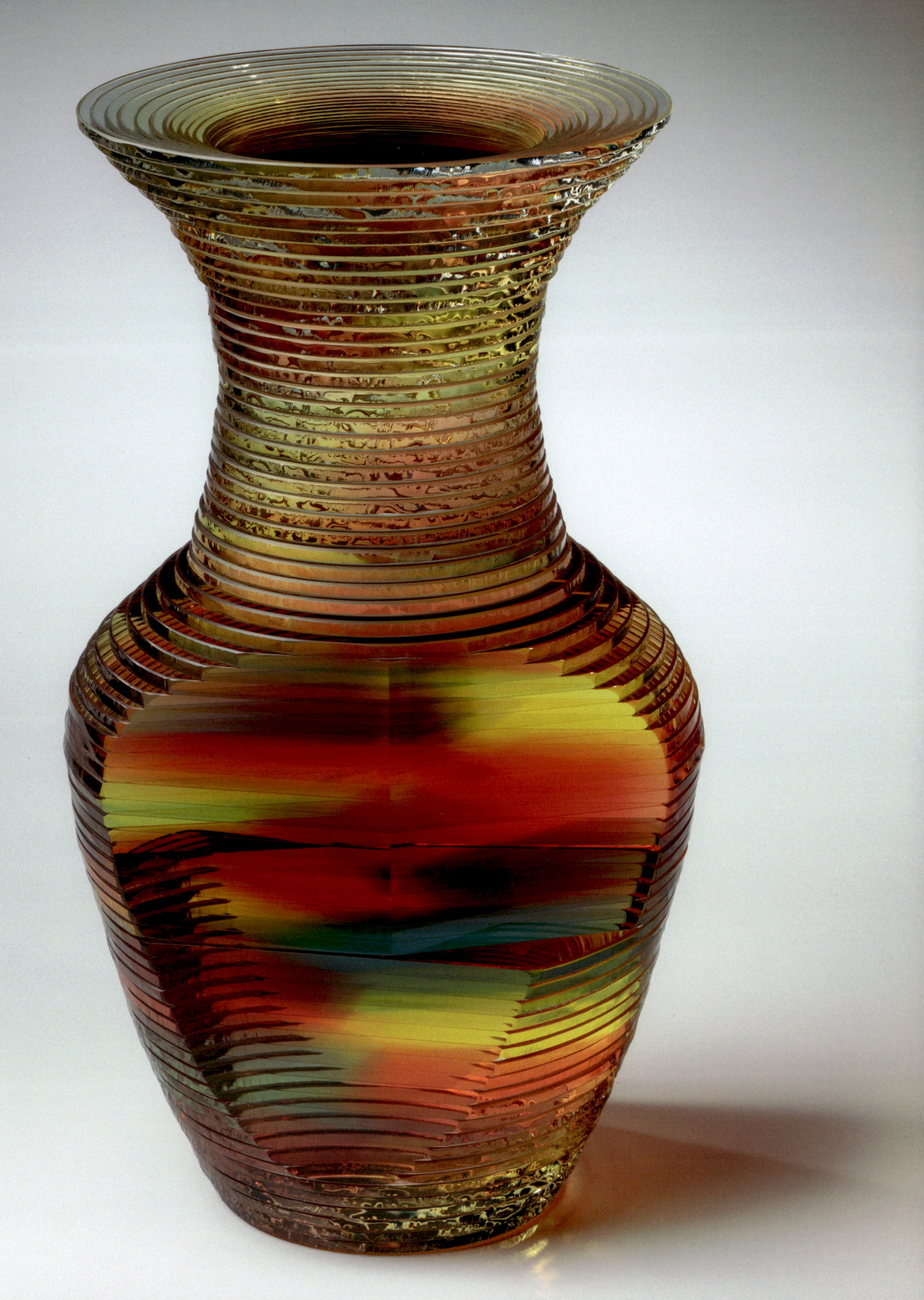

27

Margie Jervis

born 1956, United States

Susie Krasnican

born 1954, United States

Black and white pitcher with glasses,
1983, from the *Profiles and
Silhouettes* series.
Fused glass with enamel, 13½ ×
18⅞ × 7 in. (34.29 × 47.94 × 17.78 cm)

28

Jon Kuhn

born 1949, United States

Symbiosis II, 1991.
Ground and polished cut optical lead
glass, 12½ × 11 × 11 in. (31.75 ×
27.94 × 27.94 cm)

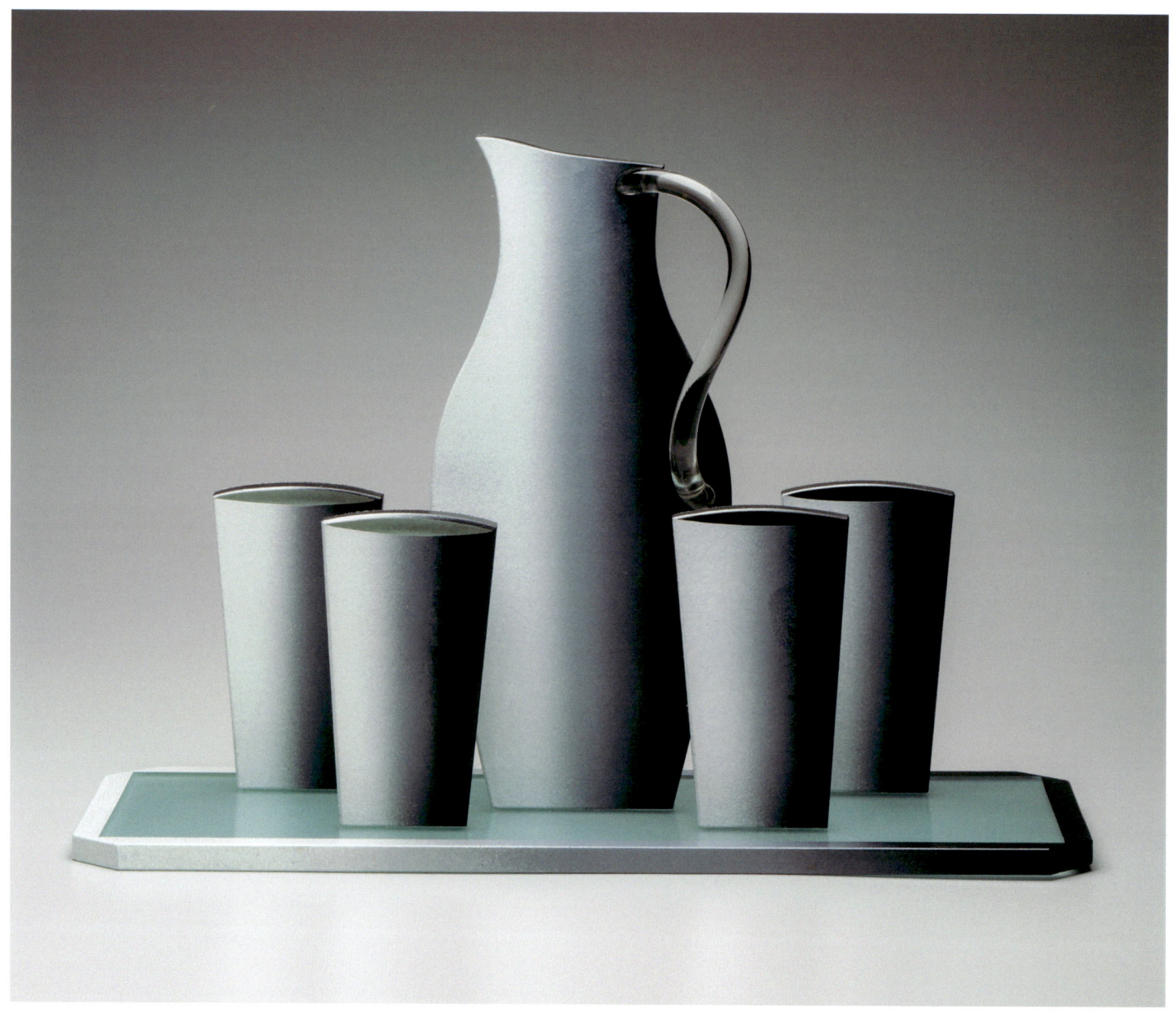

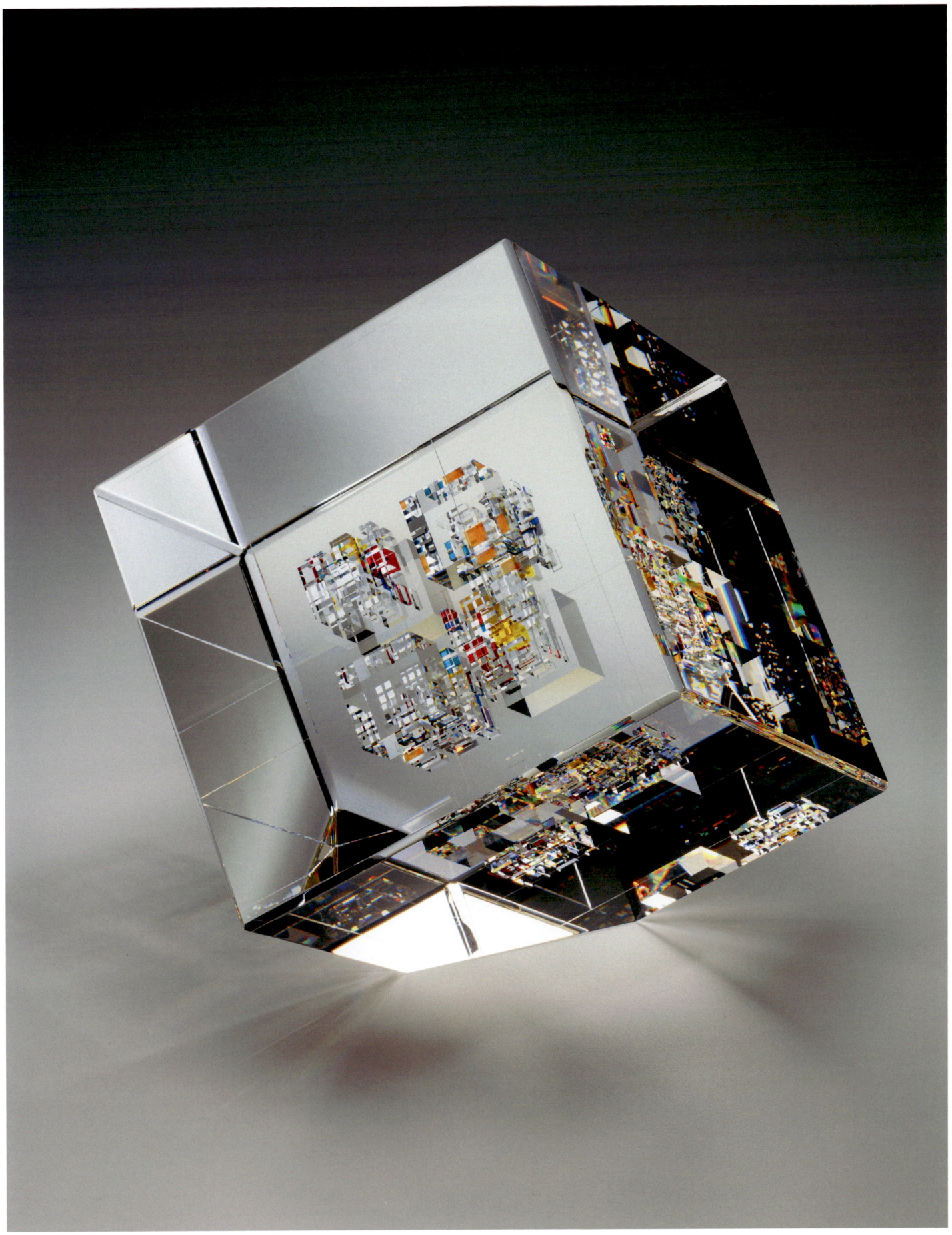

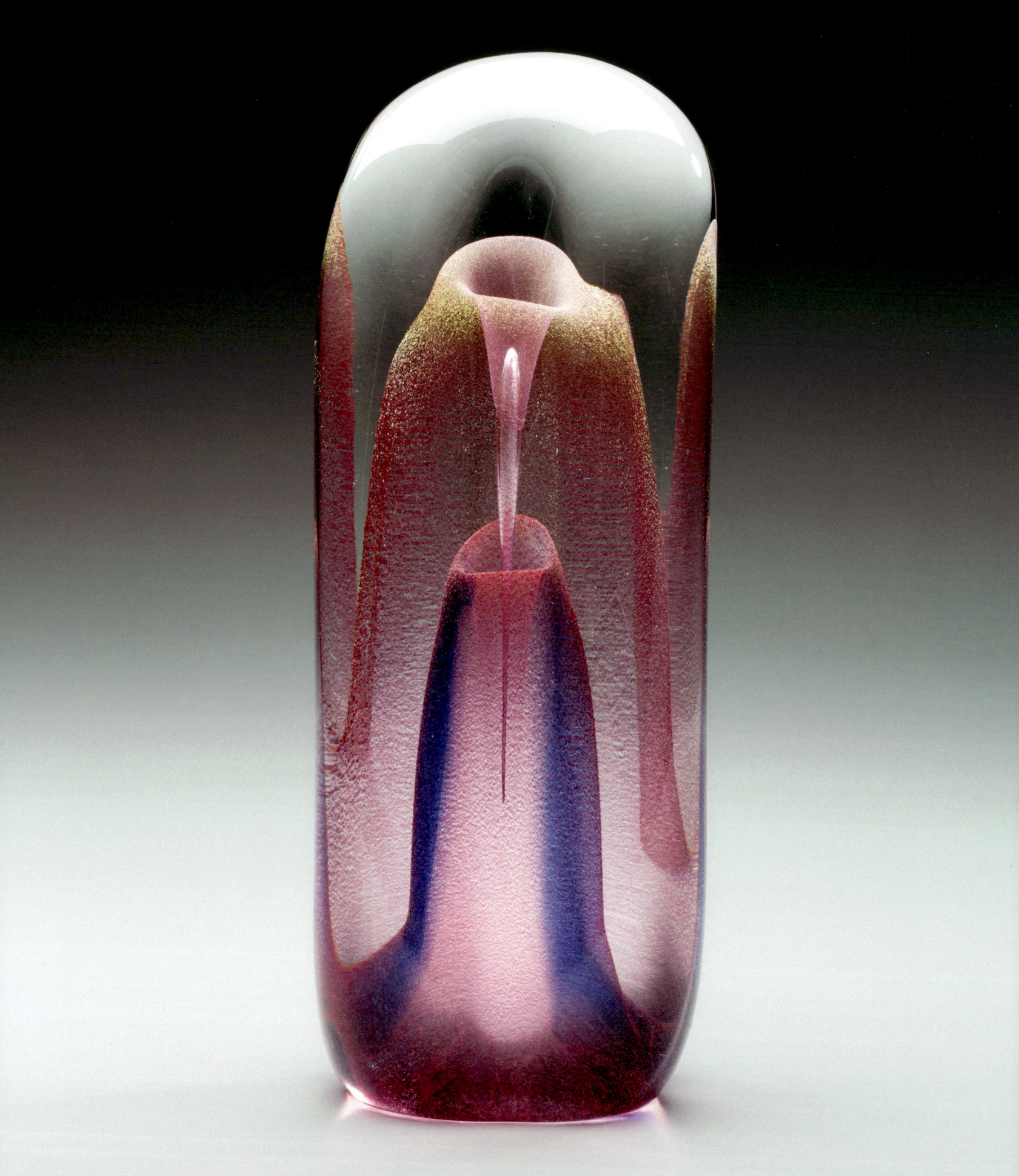

Dominick Labino

1910–1987, United States

Sculpture, 1981, from the *Emergence* series, 1971–84.
Blown, cut, and polished glass, 7⅛ × Diam. 2½ in. (18.1 × 6.35 cm)

"Art is art and technology is technology. But technology comes before art: it's the scientist that leads the way and art is always behind. . . . You can do more things with glass than any other medium. There are absolutely no limits as to what you can do in the way of color with glass."
—Dominick Labino

Karen LaMonte

born 1967, United States

Child's Dress, 2004.
Cast glass, 13¼ × 13 × 10 in. (33.66 × 33.02 × 25.4 cm)

For Karen LaMonte, the body—or the lack thereof—speaks volumes. Her ethereal draped figures are absent of a body, but heavy with corporeal form. While her work bears connotations of the expressive language of drapery in art history, she notes, "Artworks have infinite interpretations that change with time."[1]

LaMonte employs lost-wax casting, a process in which a glass mold is made through a series of negative molds, which are cast and then melted away. This highly technical, highly physical process is crucial to the expressive nature of her sculptures, allowing her to achieve dramatic movement in a variety of materials, which also include bronze and iron.

LaMonte's *Child's Dress* expresses optimism. At once playful and ghostly, the dress brings instant associations with the innocence and care of childhood. Etched details of embroidered steamships at sea on the dress's yoke similarly reference the beginning of a journey.[2] Details, according to LaMonte, are crucial—they provide a bridge from the viewer to the sculpture, and thus create a connection to the artist.[3] LM

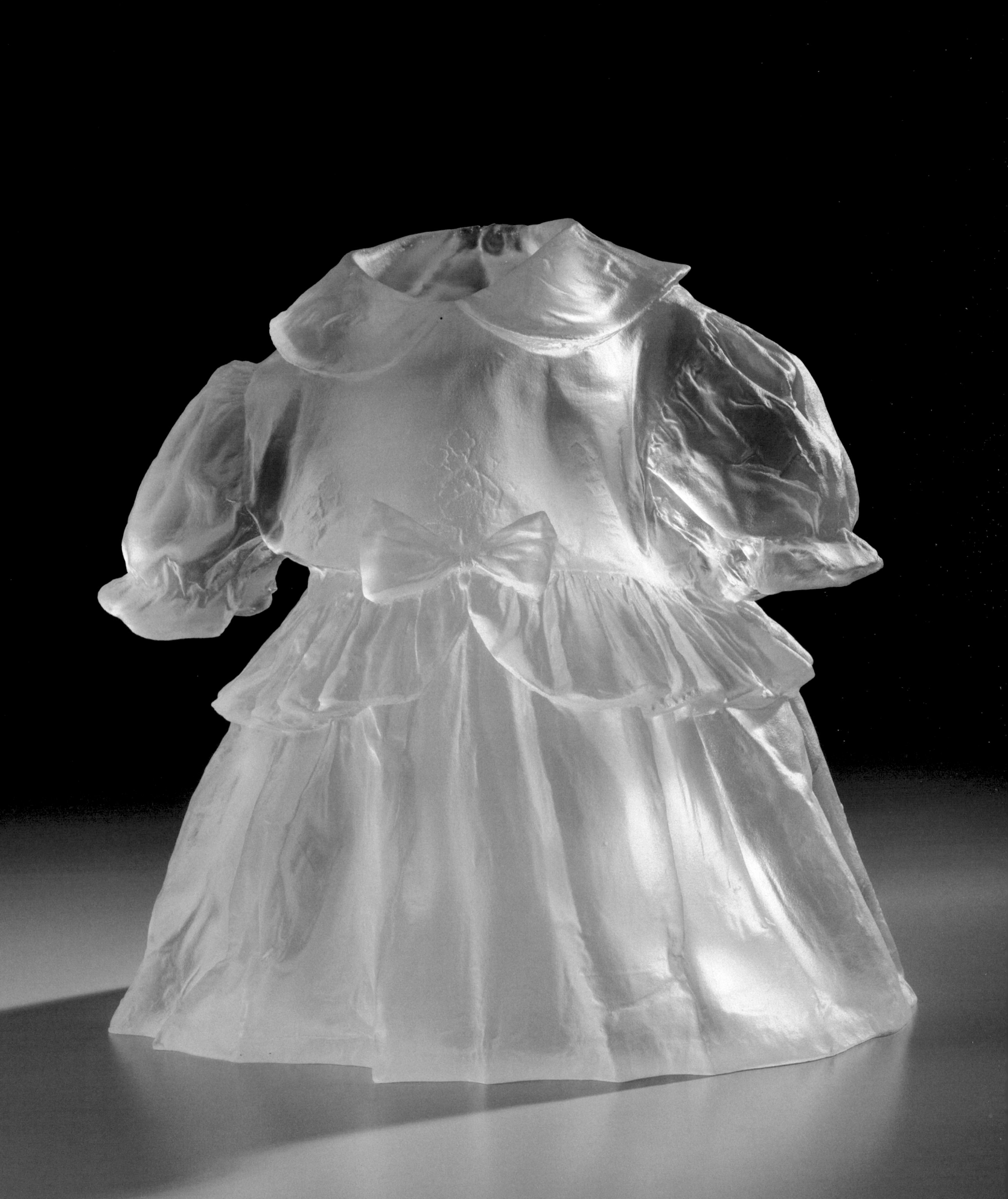

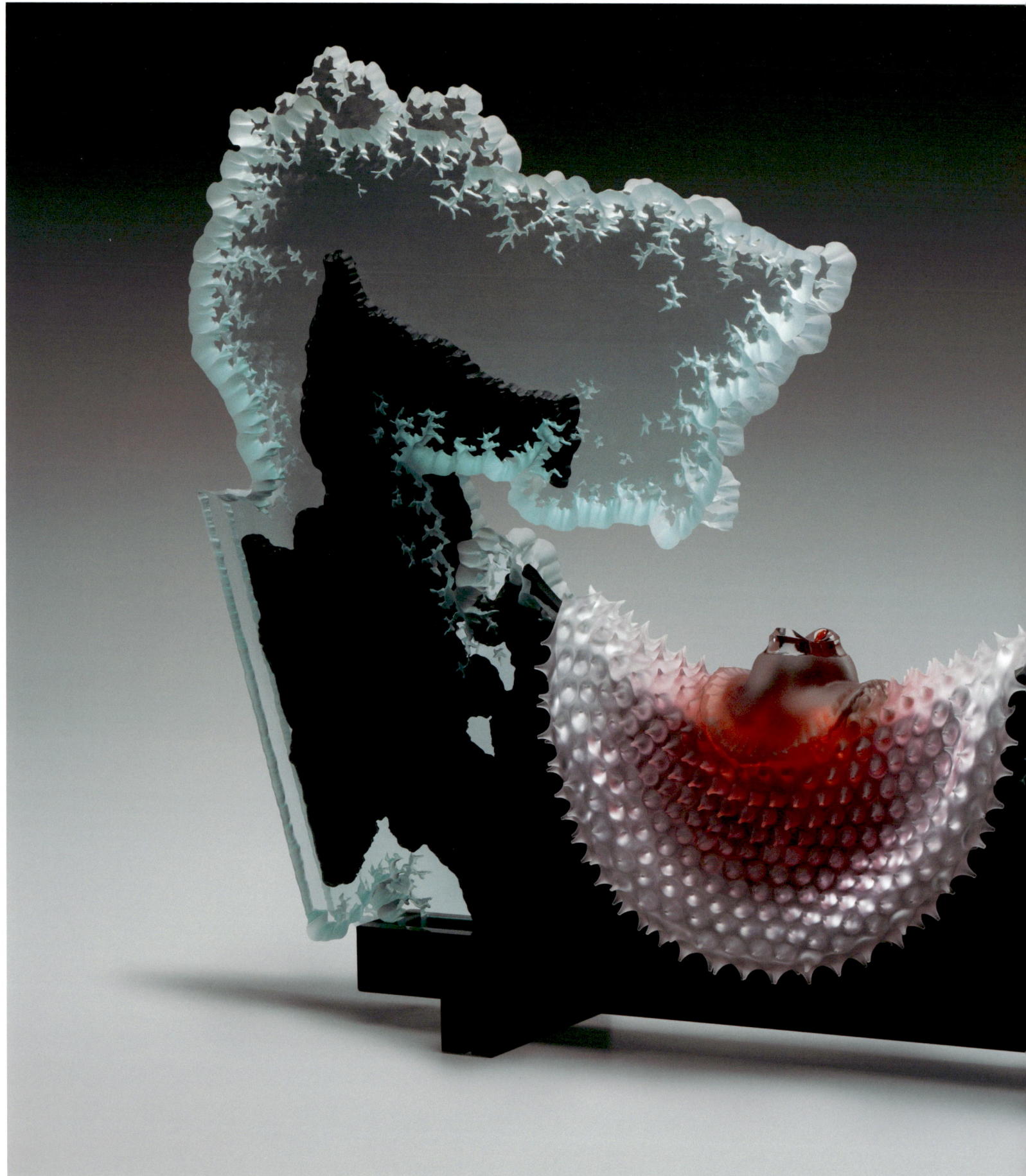

K. William LeQuier

born 1953, United States

Sentinel #17, 1986, from the *Sentinel* series.
Blown and plate glass, 18¾ × 24 × 4¾ in. (47.63 × 60.96 × 12.07 cm)

"My work is inspired by the drama of everyday events in the natural world where weather and time are catalysts for change."
—K. William LeQuier

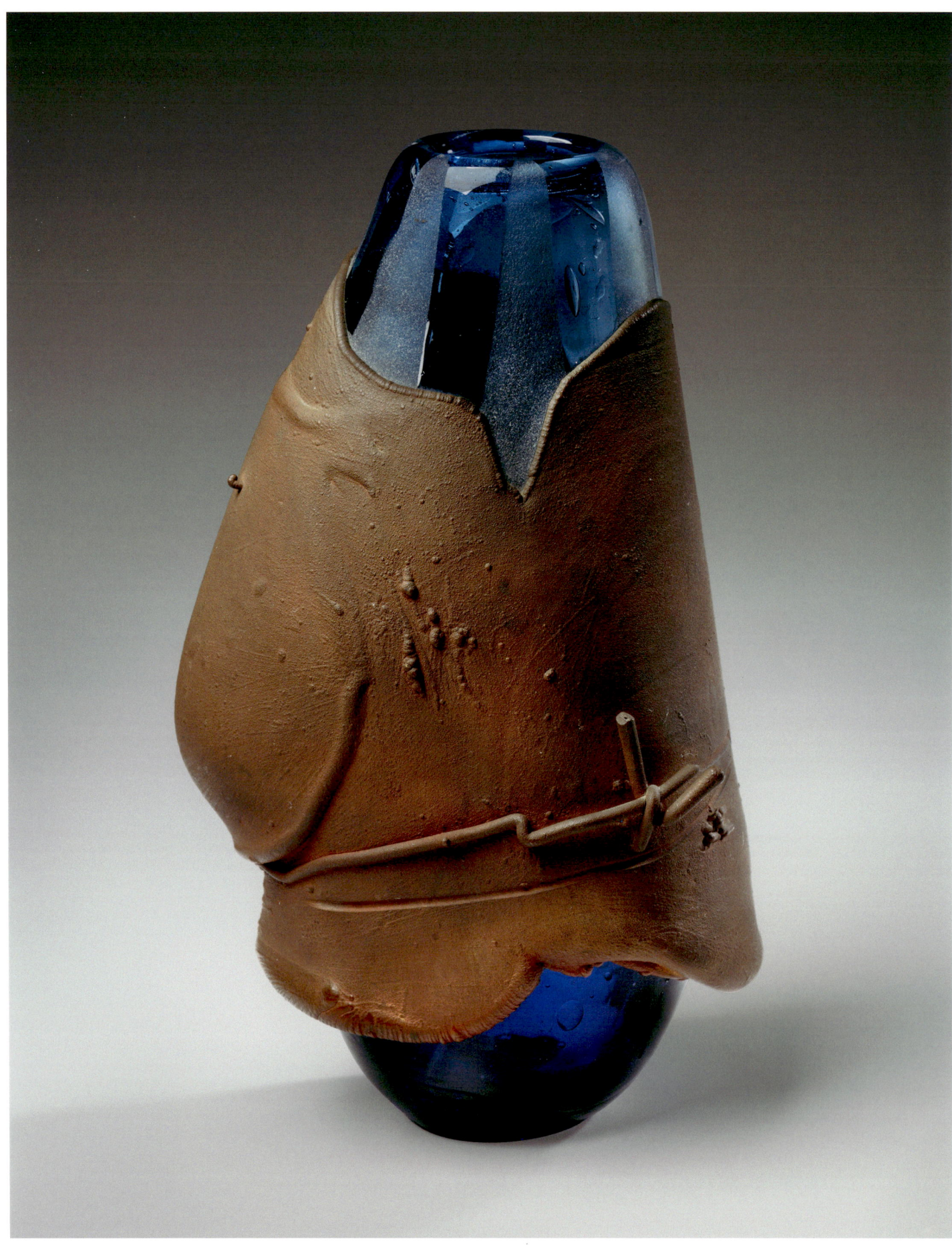

32

Marvin Lipofsky

1938–2016, United States

Vase, 1966.
Blown glass and copper, 12¾ × 7 ×
5 in. (32.39 × 17.78 × 12.7 cm)

33

Harvey K. Littleton

1922–2013, United States

Crested Form, 1976.
Blown and cut glass, 16½ × 10½ ×
5½ in. (41.91 × 26.67 × 13.97 cm)

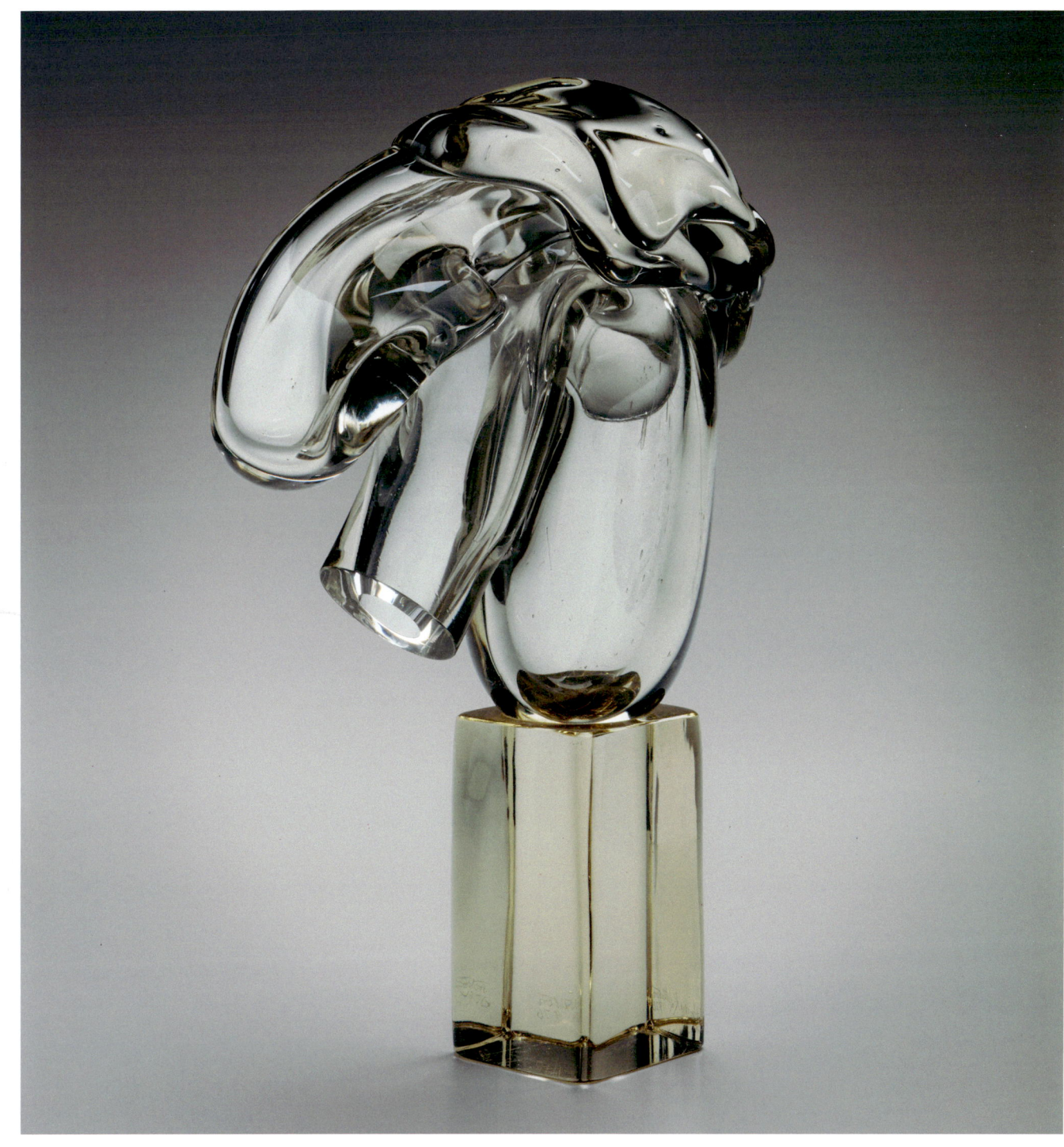

Harvey K. Littleton

1922–2013, United States

Ruby Blue Linked Forms, 1989.
Blown, cut, and polished cased
glass, overall: 13⅜ × 17½ × 12 in.
(33.97 × 44.45 × 30.48 cm)

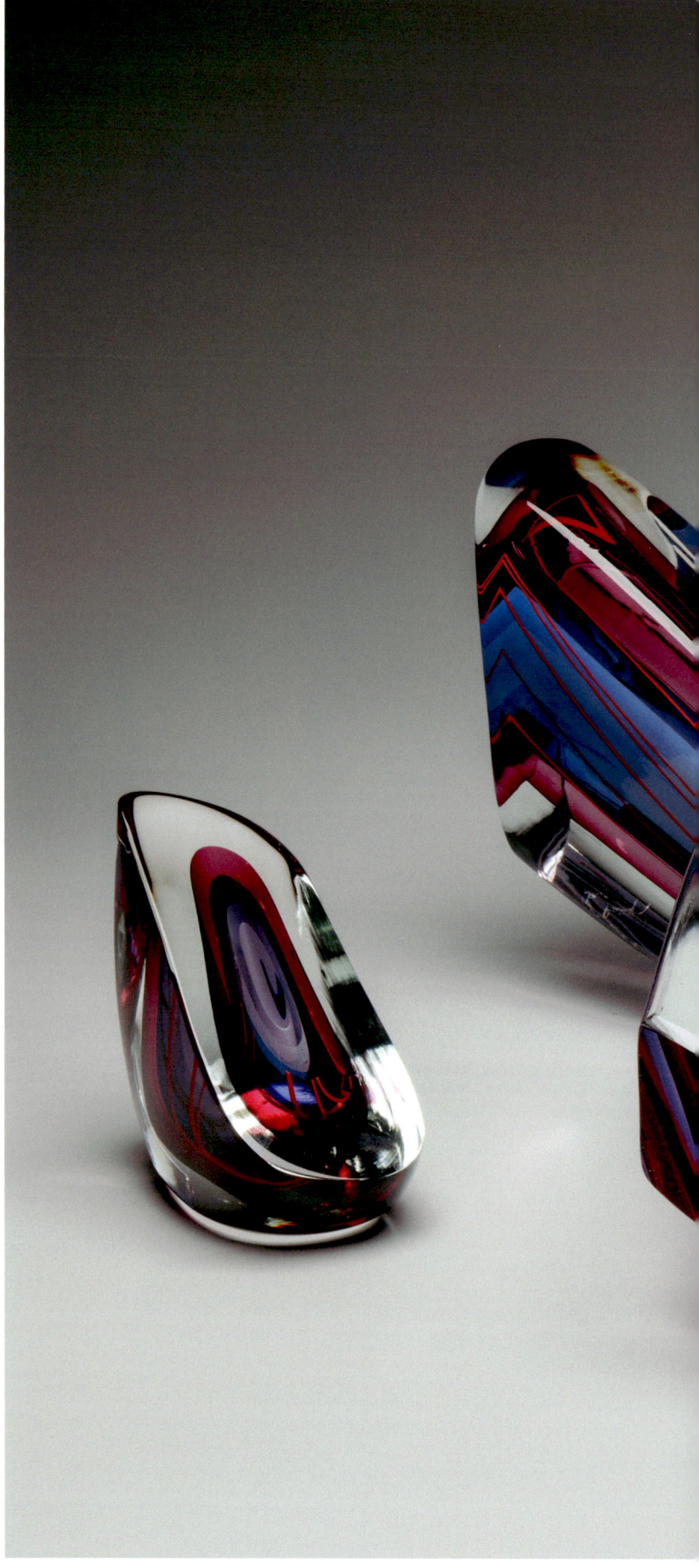

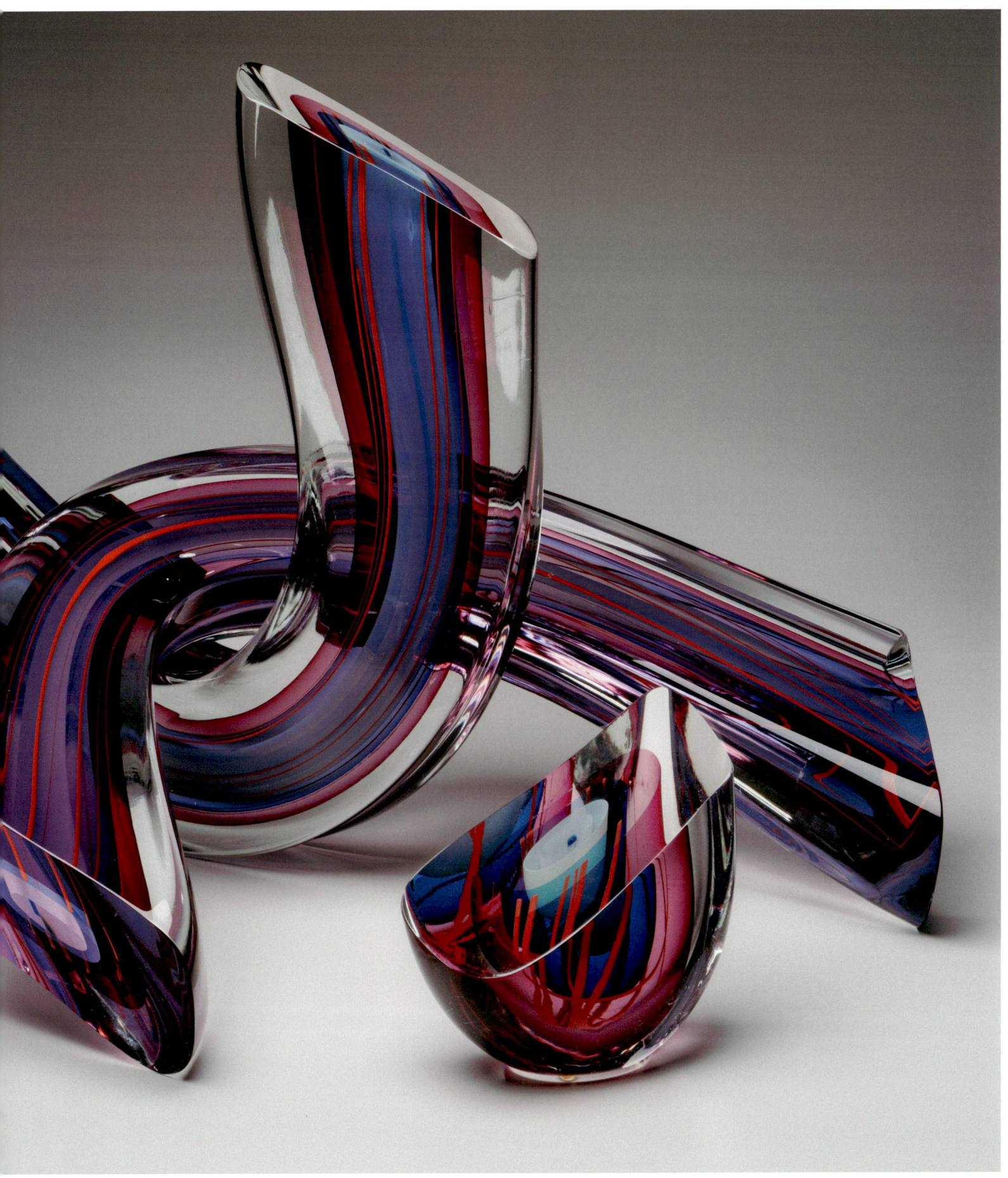

Kristina Logan

born 1964, United States

Red Teapot #5, 2001.
Pâte de verre, flameworked glass,
and sterling silver, 7 × 6¾ × 4 in.
(17.78 × 17.15 × 10.16 cm)

Dante Marioni

born 1964, United States

Vessel, 1986.
Blown glass, 30 × 8 × 6¼ in. (76.2 ×
20.32 × 15.88 cm)

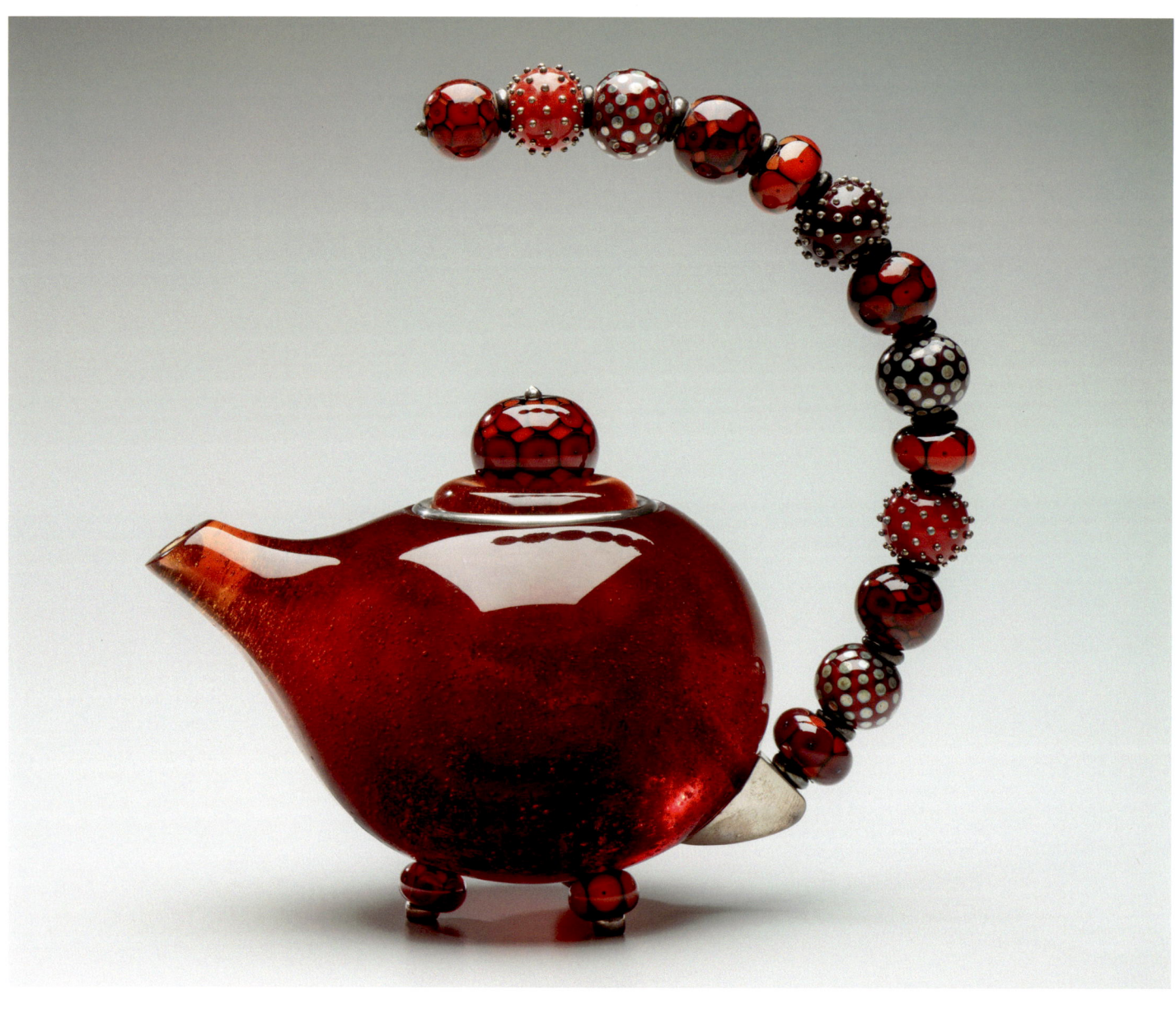

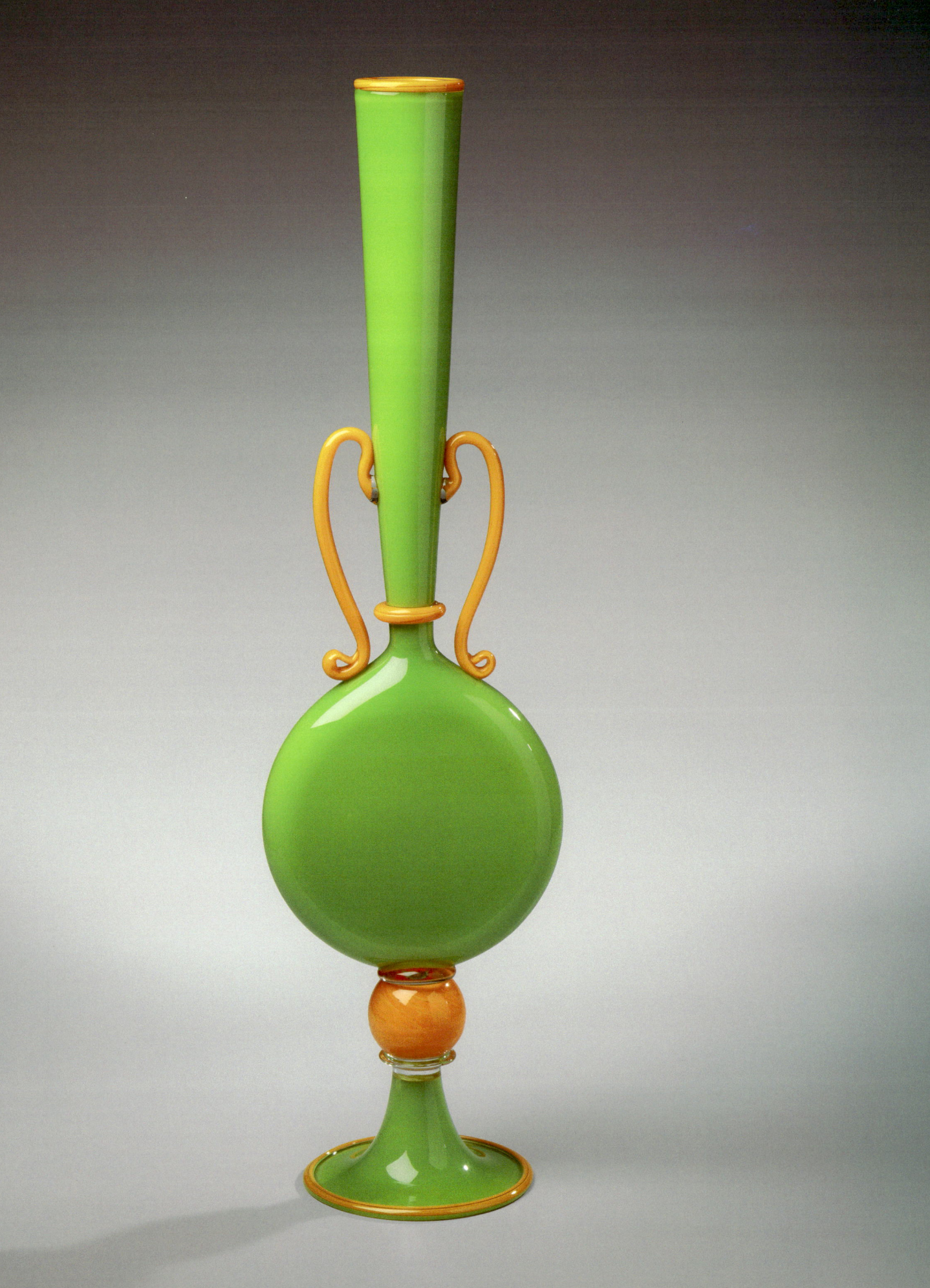

Richard Marquis

born 1945, United States

Crazy Quilt Teapot, 1979, from the
Crazy Quilt series.
Fused and blown *murrine* and
aventurine glass, 4¾ × 5¾ × 4⅞ in.
(12.07 × 14.61 × 12.38 cm)

Richard Marquis

born 1945, United States

Marquiscarpa #29, 1991, from the
Marquiscarpa series, 1991–2011.
Fused, slumped, blown, and
wheel-carved *murrine*, 6½ × 8½ ×
3⅛ in. (16.51 × 21.59 × 7.94 cm)

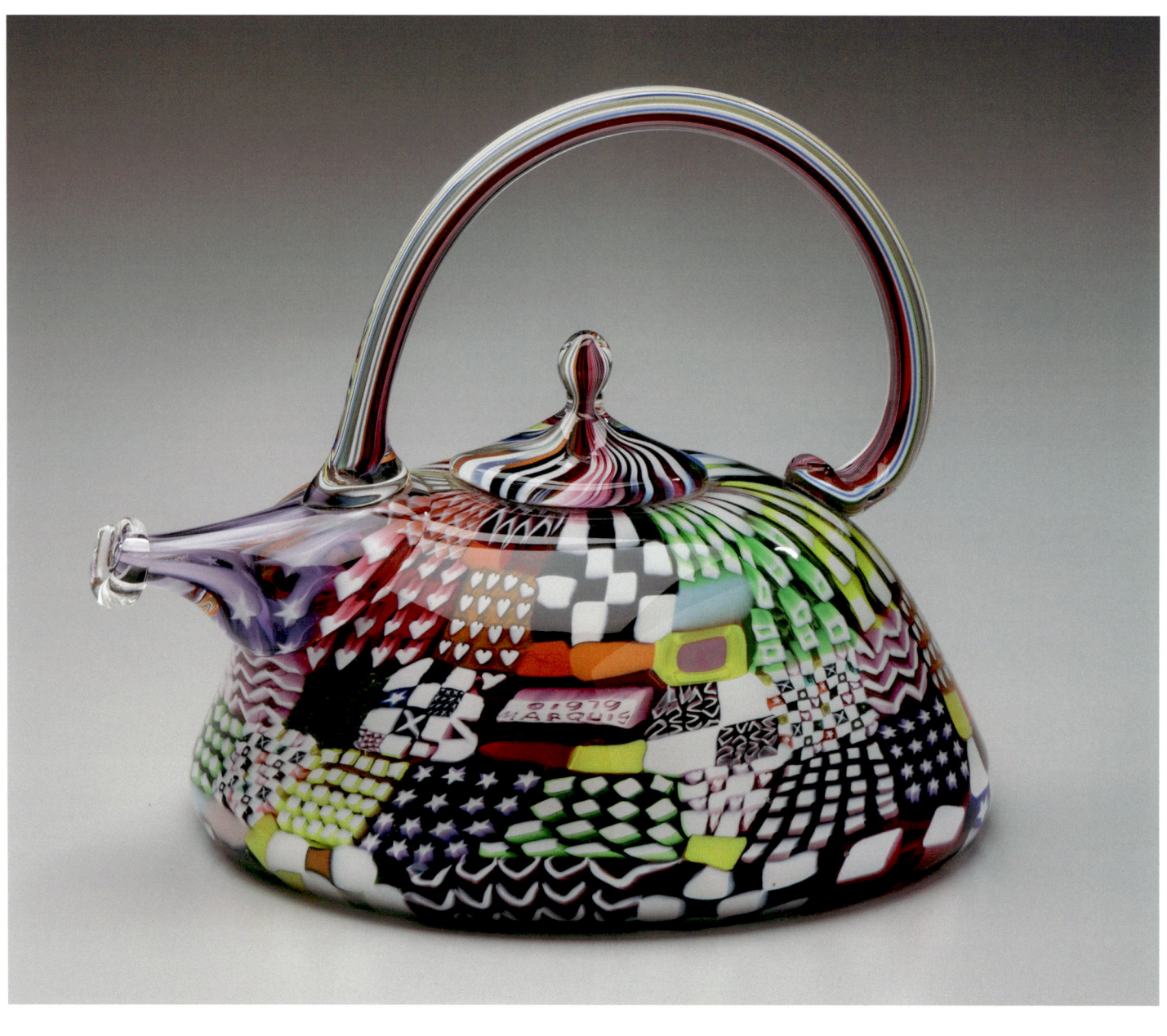

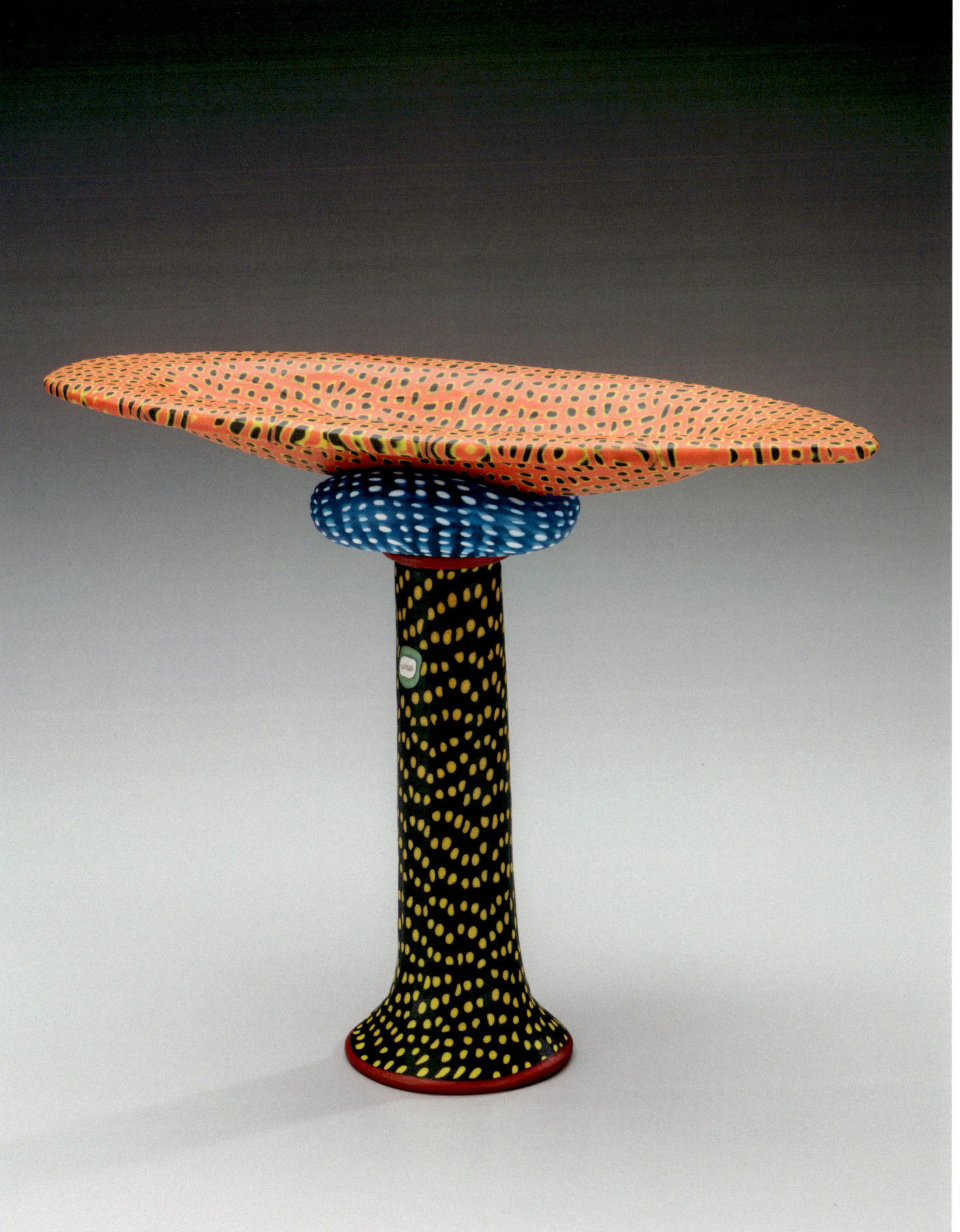

Charles Miner

born 1947, United States

Roswell Frogs, 2006.
Cast lead glass (crystal), 10¼ × 21 ×
20½ in. (26.04 × 53.34 × 52.07 cm)

Klaus Moje

1936–2016, Germany, worked in
Australia

Untitled #10, 1997.
Fused, slumped, and ground glass,
Diam. 20⅞ × 2¾ in. (53.02 × 6.99 cm)

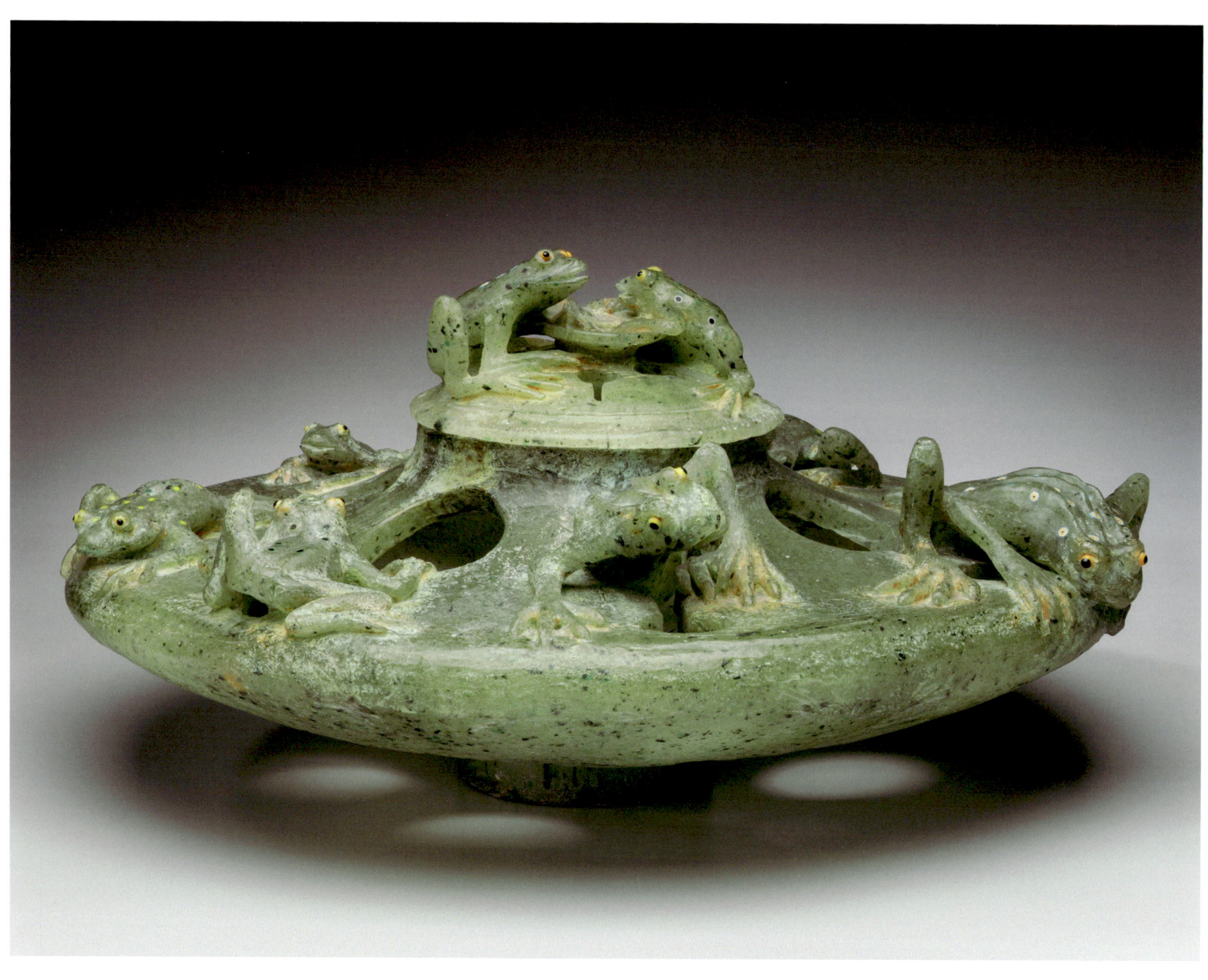

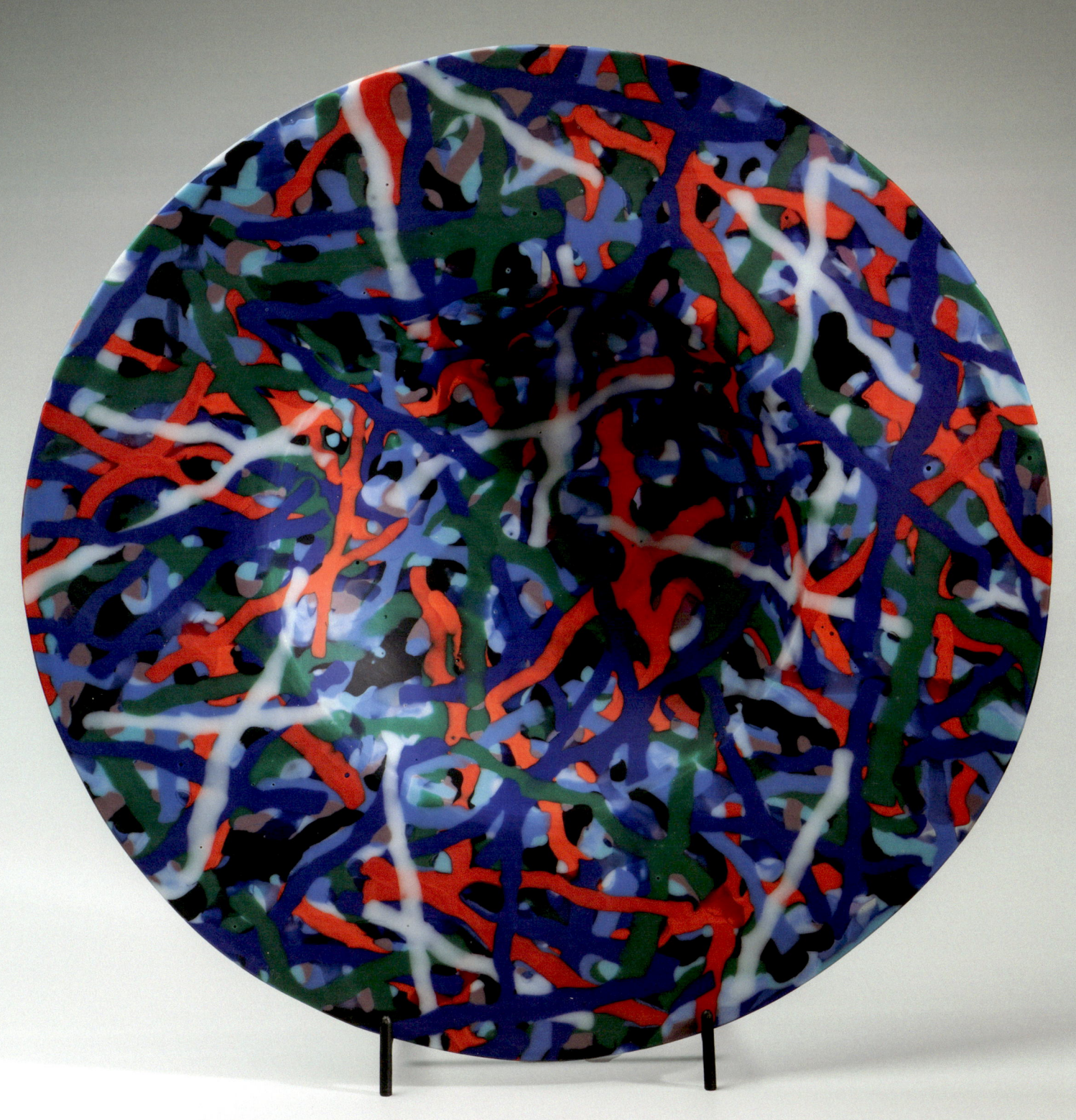

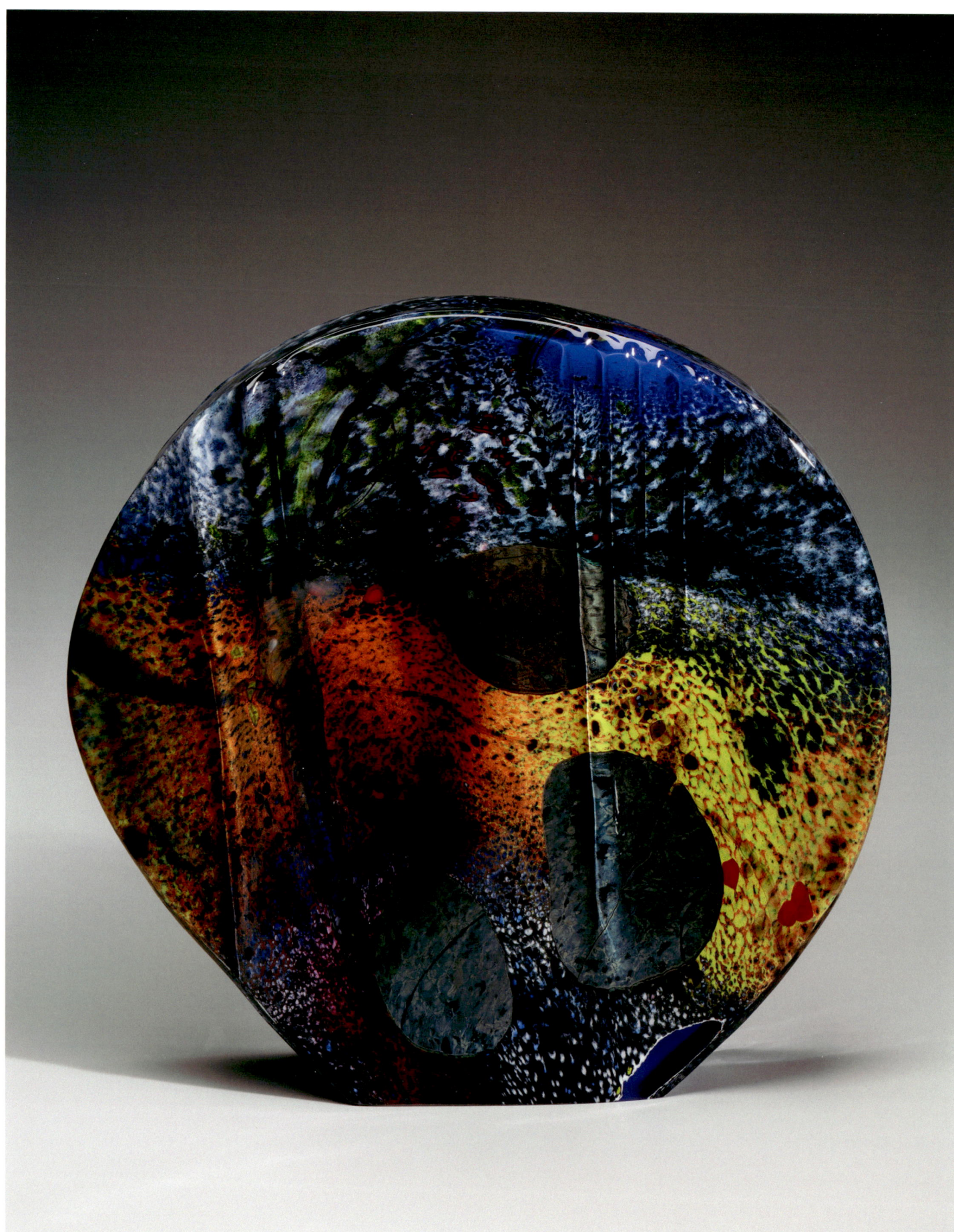

41

William Morris

born 1957, United States

Standing Stone, 1984.
Mold-blown glass, 18 × 18¼ × 6 in.
(45.72 × 46.36 × 15.24 cm)

42

Jay Musler

born 1949, United States

Cityscape, 1995.
Blown, acid-etched, and painted
glass, 8⅛ × Diam. 18 in. (20.64 ×
45.72 cm)

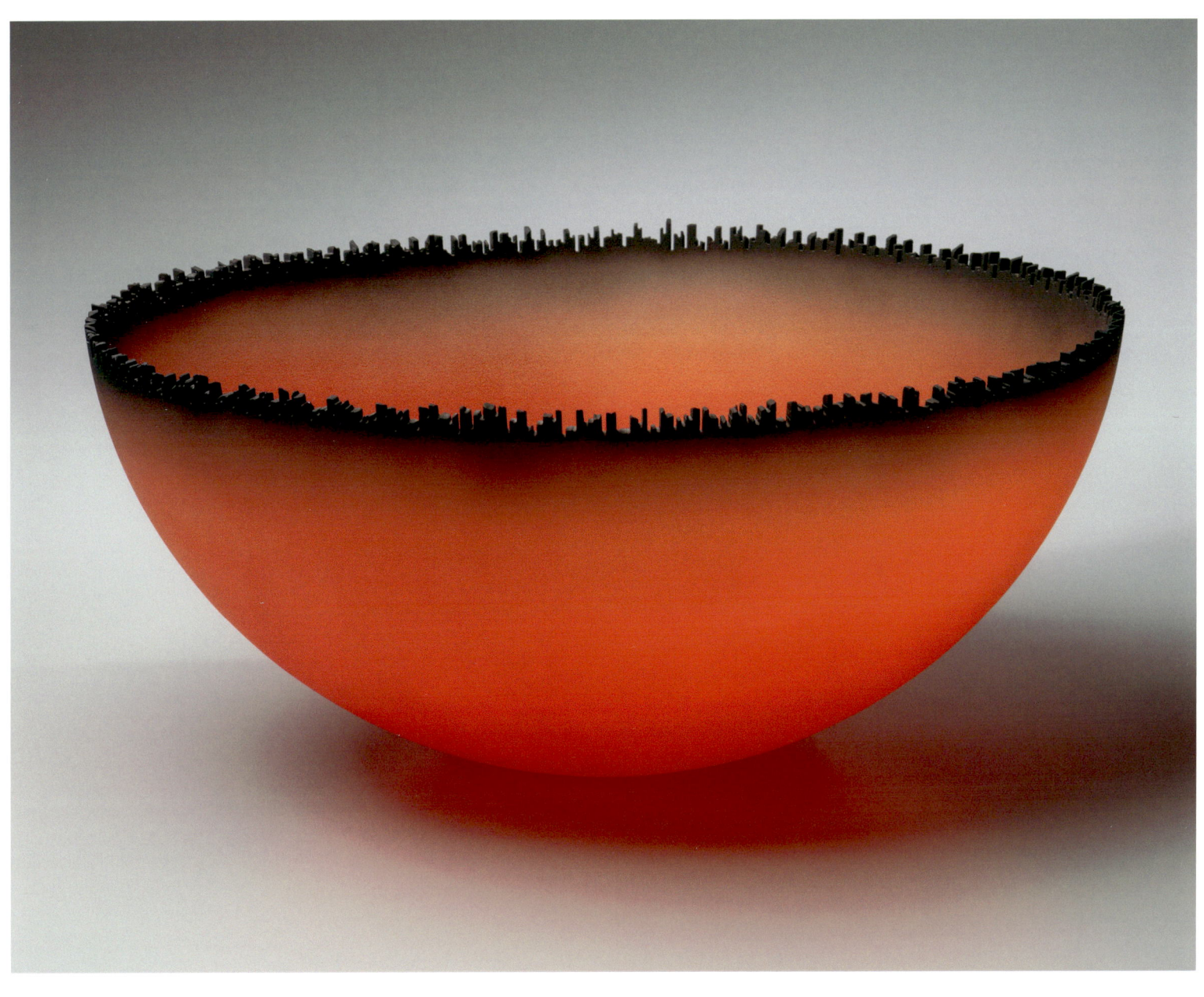

43

Tom Patti

born 1943, United States

Solar Gray Soltex Riser, 1979, from
the *Solar Riser* series, 1977–81.
Blown, fused, and laminated glass,
5¼ × 4 × 3¾ in. (13.34 × 10.16 ×
9.53 cm)

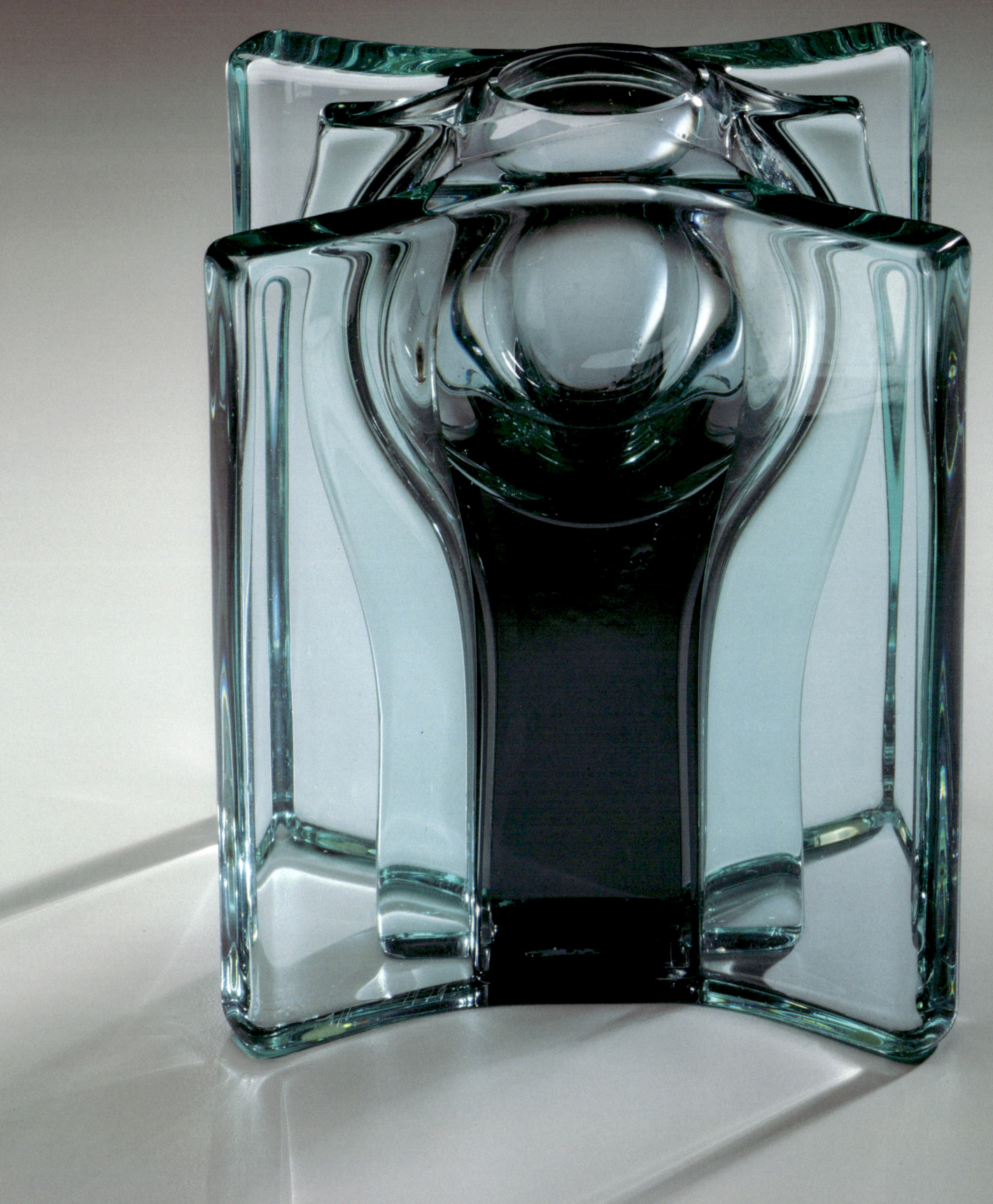

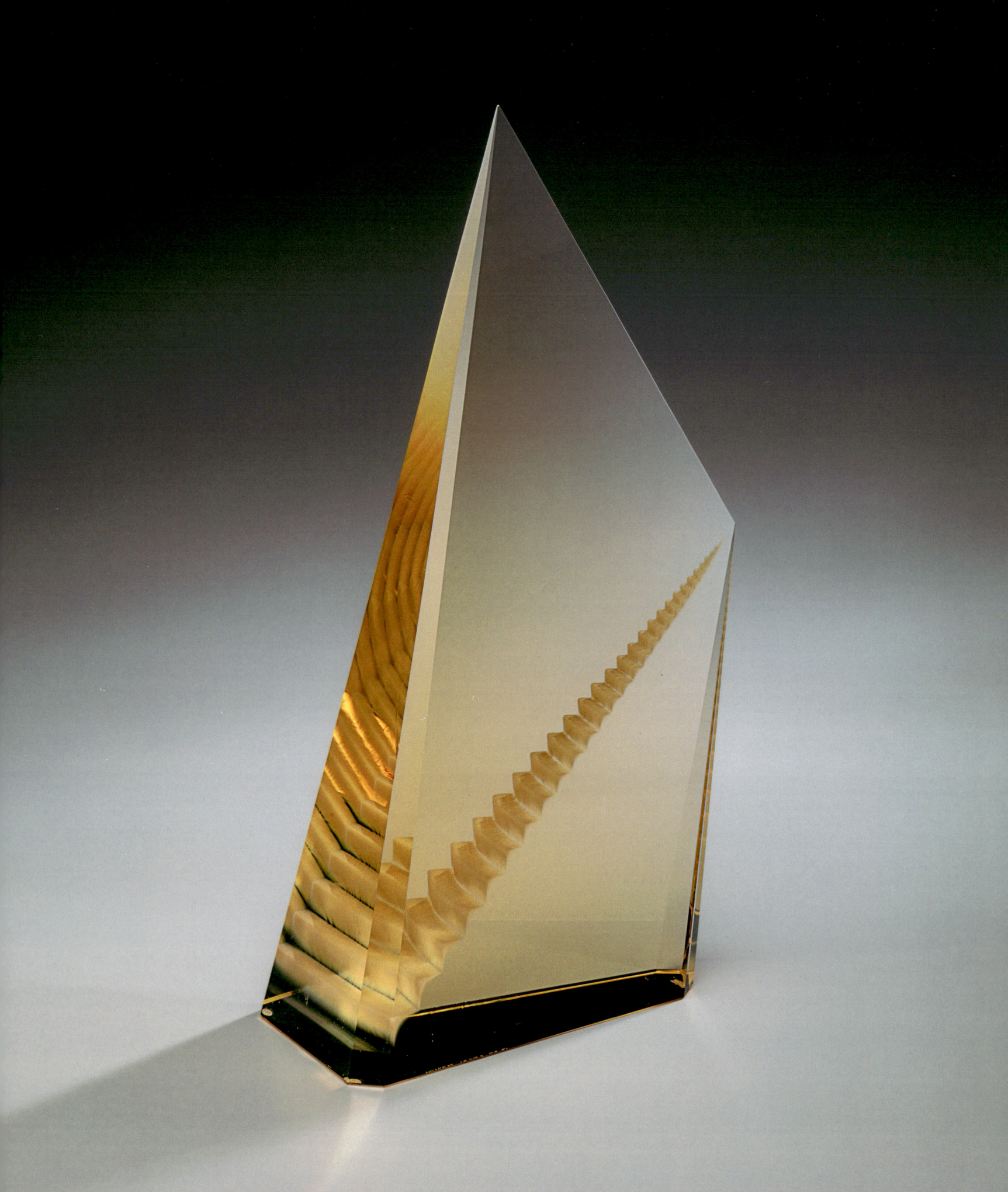

44

Mark Peiser

born 1938, United States

Ascension, 1985.
Uranium and cast glass, 13⅝ × 6¼ ×
3½ in. (34.61 × 15.88 × 8.89 cm)

46

Ann Robinson

born 1944, New Zealand

Neodymium Generation Bowl, 1995. Cast lead glass (crystal), 8 × Diam. 15¼ in. (20.32 × 38.74 cm)

Ann Robinson's mastery of lost-wax casting has grown from constant and meticulous experimentation. She began her artistic practice with bronze casting and, later, glassblowing, before turning to casting in glass. At the time, she was the first artist to revive the ancient technique in her native New Zealand. Lost-wax casting, the process in which Robinson carves a wax model, builds a mold around it, and melts it away to create a cavity for the glass, has allowed her to work towards her ever-changing formal objectives. She has perfected each technical aspect of her process, exploring new ways of approaching her glass recipes, molding, and annealing processes to achieve her signature large, heavy forms and unique surface textures. "To me," she says, "working on a piece is an act of love; the more effort that you put in, the more that comes shining back out. I respect technique and enjoy the rich interplay between process and idea."[1]

Robinson's *Generation Bowl* is one of a series of bowl forms in her repertoire. Featuring an overlapping v-shape around the perimeter, thick walls, and an opaque, acid-washed body, it represents the bold, spare, and luminous forms that are her signature. The bowl, she says, is timeless, bearing meaning that spans the ages and functions as "the receiver, the holder, the protector, the offerer, and the transmitter."[2] The history of vessel making, Robinson feels, connects her with generations of craftspeople. It "goes hand-in-hand with human history, and I am proud to be a part of that lineage, especially when I consider that the arm of the craftsperson reaching out from the past is probably that of a woman."[3] LM

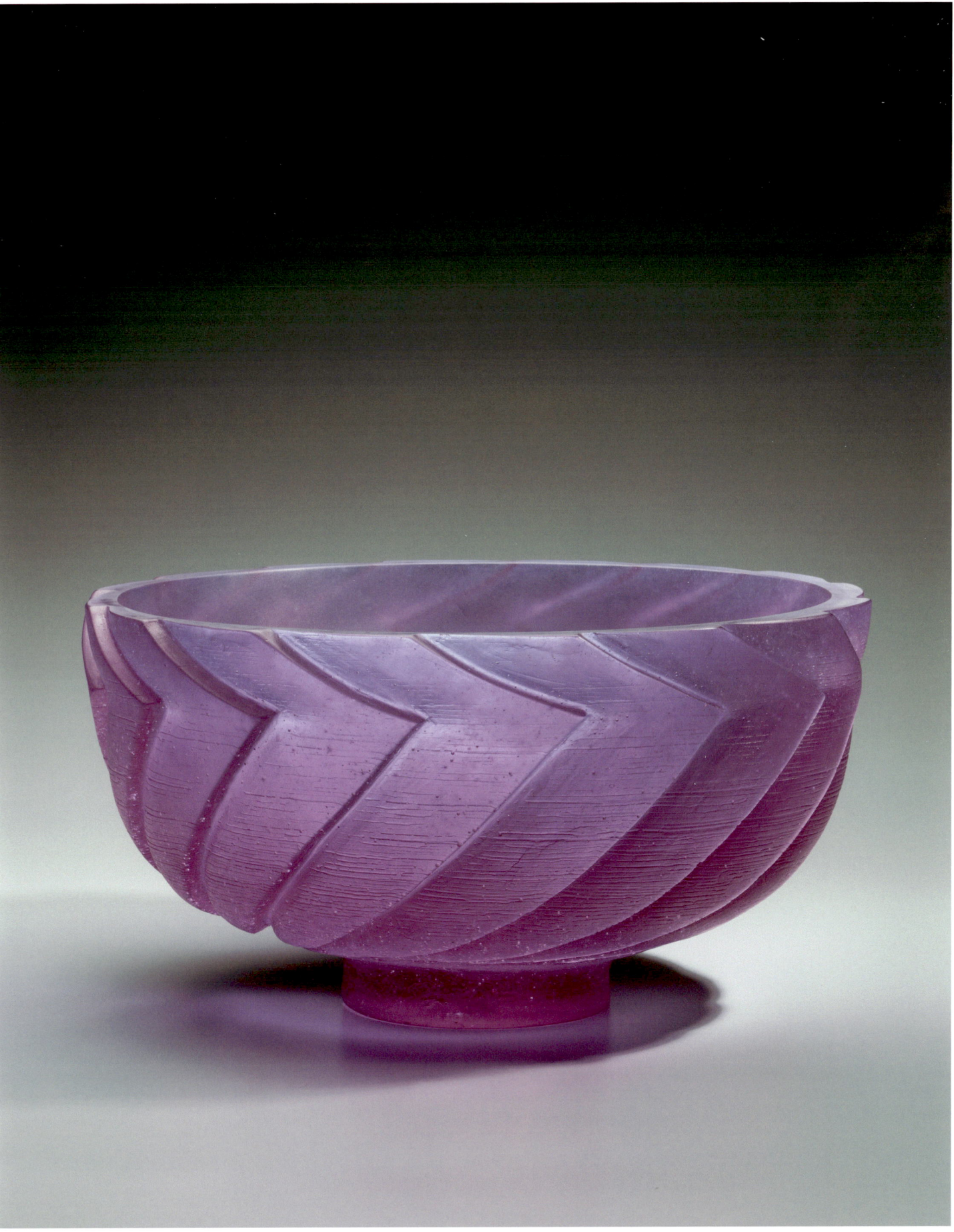

47

Erica Rosenfeld

born 1975, United States

Fulton Street, 1:30 am, 2007–09. Hotworked, carved, and sewn *murrine* on mesh, 17½ × 30½ × 1 in. (44.45 × 77.47 × 2.54 cm)

Erica Rosenfeld is a multi-media artist and teacher known for her sculptures, jewelry, installations, and performance art. Working across glass, paint, and found objects, her art is responsive to the times, including themes of memory, fear, growth, and nostalgia.[1]

Fulton Street, 1:30 am is the artist's exploration of a tumultuous moment in her life. In the midst of a heated discussion, her mild-mannered then-husband threw the box of tiles he was carrying into the street. "I was beyond surprised and at that moment I realized how unhappy we were in our marriage—this realization changed the course of our life together which made the piece I was making an artifact of that time in my life. My ex felt terrible and started scrambling to gather all of the glass in the middle of the street before any cars passed. We worked together to pick up as many pieces as we could. . . . I left the next morning and we decided to get divorced the following day. I continued to work on the tapestry and finished it four months later."[2]

Rosenfeld constructed her tapestry using hundreds of thin glass slices, called *murrine*, to evoke the soft folds of a length of fabric. While not her original intention, the armorlike effect of the work the artist now associates with the armor she needed at a time of great loss in her life. She painstakingly sewed each individual *murrina* to a mesh substrate. This process of repetitively affixing multiples derives from her interest in beadwork, a craft Rosenfeld has been practicing since the age of seven. The structure for the softly undulating peaks and valleys of the piece was achieved through unconventional means: the work is padded using discarded socks. LM

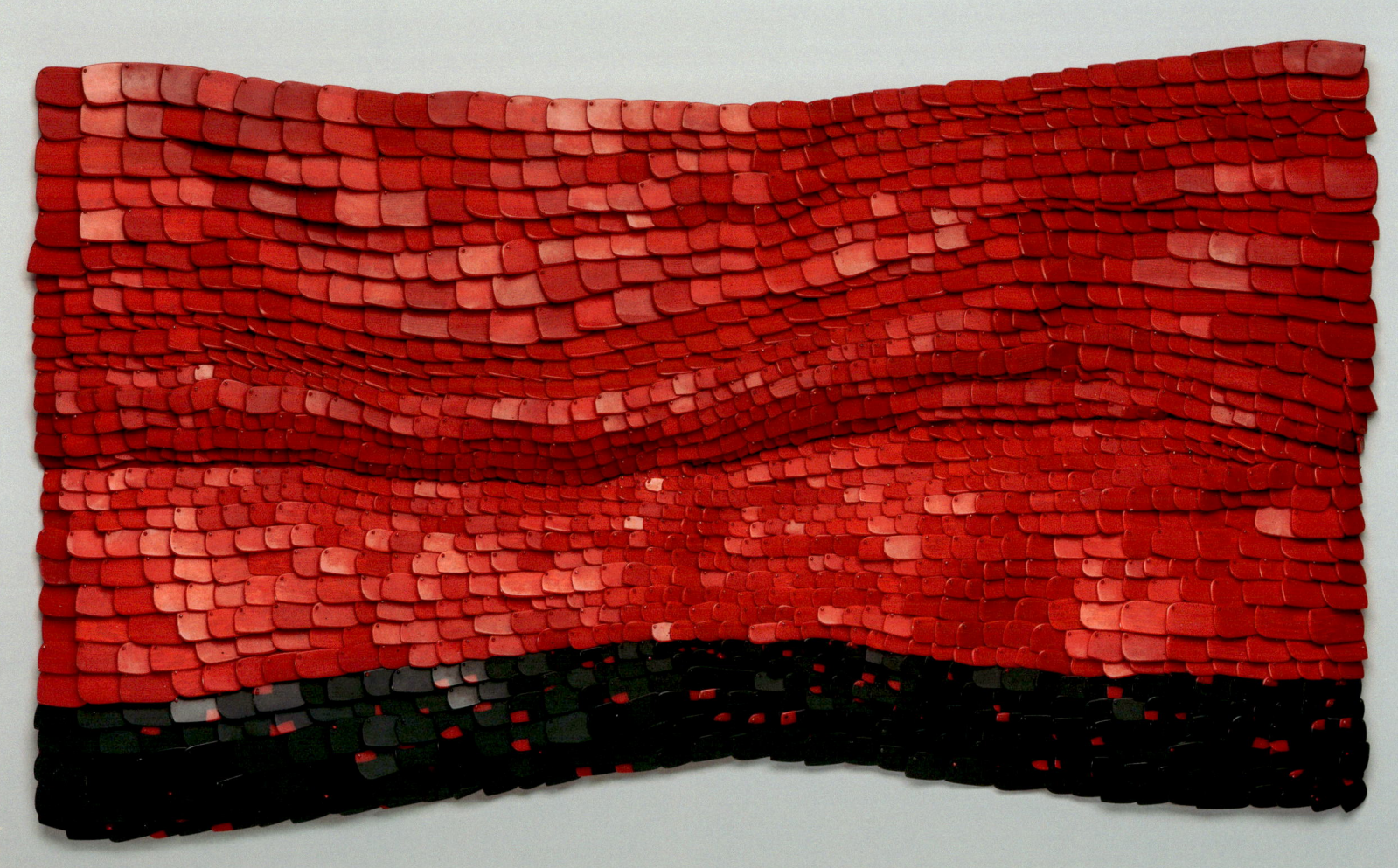

48

Ginny Ruffner

1952–2025, United States

Elements of a Still Life II, 1996, from the *Conceptual Narrative* series. Flameworked and painted glass, 17¾ × 20 × 12 in. (45.09 × 50.8 × 30.48 cm)

Ginny Ruffner has been creating art in diverse media for over five decades. It is fitting that Marcel Duchamp, an artist known for pushing boundaries in the traditional art world with wit, irreverence, and humor, first inspired her to combine her drawing and painting skills with the medium of glass.[1] Soon after this realization, Ruffner embarked on learning glassmaking, apprenticing with an artist in Atlanta who specialized in flameworking with borosilicate glass.[2] She spent five years mastering the techniques before relocating to Seattle to teach flameworking at Pilchuck Glass School. Working in a field largely dominated by men, Ruffner's mastery of traditional glassmaking techniques allowed her to develop her own vision and style that influenced many other artists in the art of flameworking, including Kari Russell-Pool (pl. 49).[3]

Ruffner's sculptures delight the viewer with their humor and joyful use of color that obliquely address complicated subjects such as feminism, beauty, and the history of art. In *Elements of a Still Life II*, 1996, a fused line of colorful figures, including fruit and tropical fish, form a three-dimensional frame around the essential elements of a picnic. Her long-running *Conceptual Narrative* series invokes the traditional art historical canon with a feminist lens. In the past, women artists were limited to painting still life subjects, while their male counterparts were allowed to paint nudes. But Ruffner says, "... Still lifes are sexy too.... I think that the fruit is female, growing and changing, beautiful and nutritious, functional. So, I paint them to provoke conversation about all that."[4] SNC

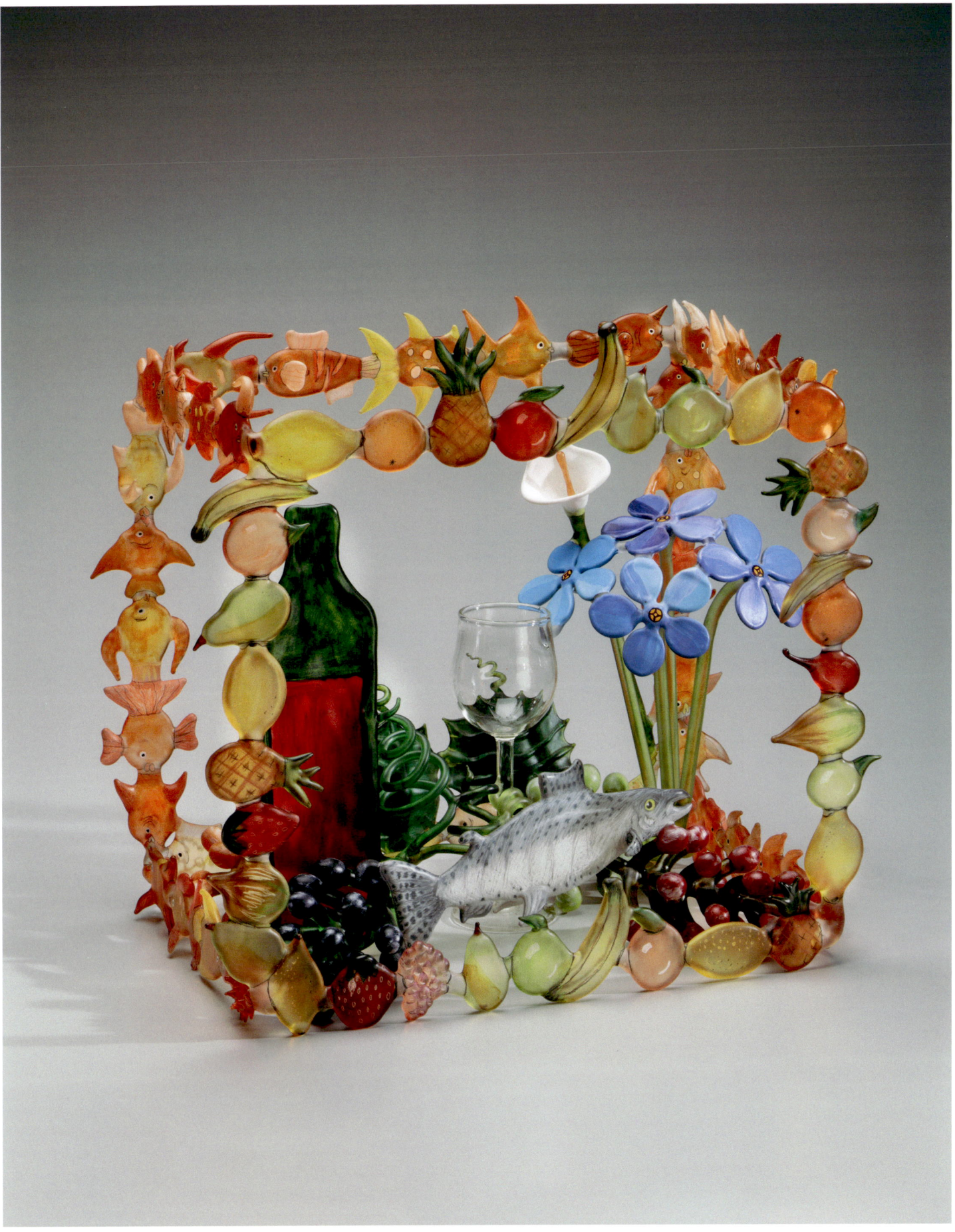

49

Kari Russell-Pool

born 1967, United States

Marc Petrovic

(*assistant*), born 1967, United States

3 Birds, Flowers, 2001, from the
Banded Vessels series, 2001–
ongoing.
Blown and flameworked glass, 19 ×
Diam. 9½ in. (48.26 × 24.13 cm)
2022.6.139

Kari Russell-Pool creates her delicate vessels through flamework, the process of manipulating colored glass canes over an open flame. Born in Salem, Massachusetts, she first began experimenting with glass during art school. At the suggestion of a teacher, she took a course at the Pilchuck Glass School in Washington with famed flamework artist Ginny Ruffner.[1] Russell-Pool was immediately drawn to the method because it allowed her to work with form and color simultaneously. Over the course of her career, she has explored themes including politics, parenthood, nature, and identity, and her work often references traditional vessels and glassmaking techniques.

In *3 Birds, Flowers*, a latticed band of twisting flowers, grapes, and plump birds separates two sides of a sinuous, broad-shouldered vase. Juxtaposing the textures of a luscious overgrowth with the smooth, opaline surface of the vase, Russell-Pool evokes a feeling of precarious abundance. Her husband, the glass artist Marc Petrovic, collaborated with Russell-Pool on the fabrication. Petrovic blew the birds, based off of titmice, and the vessel to Russell-Pool's specifications.[2] The thickest point of the vessel's wall was then scored and broken apart so that the flameworked flora and fauna created by Russell-Pool could be inserted within. Russell-Pool's inspiration for her *Banded Vessels* series, which brings to mind gardens blooming from within vases, came from a dream she had when she was expecting her second daughter. LM

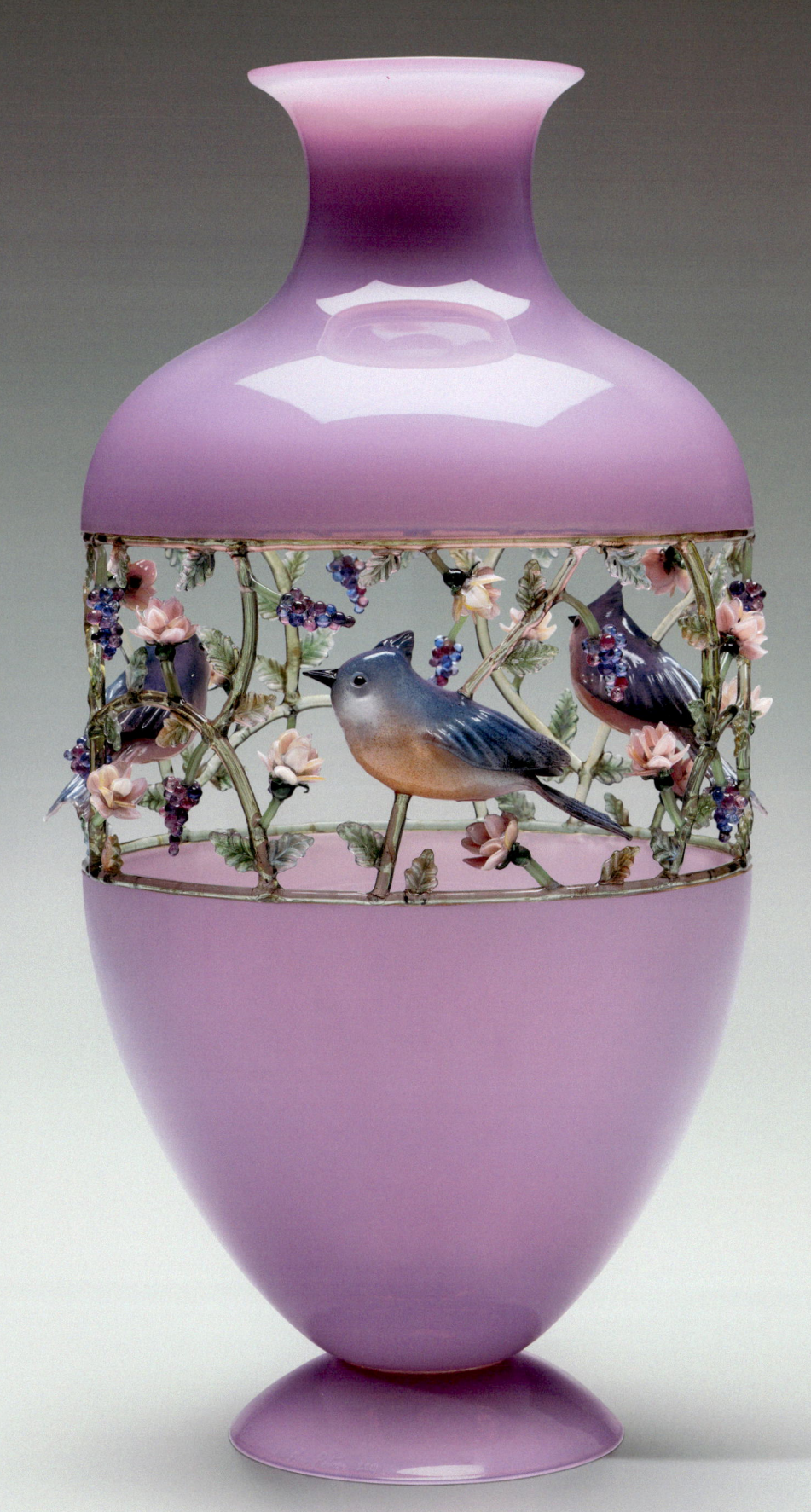

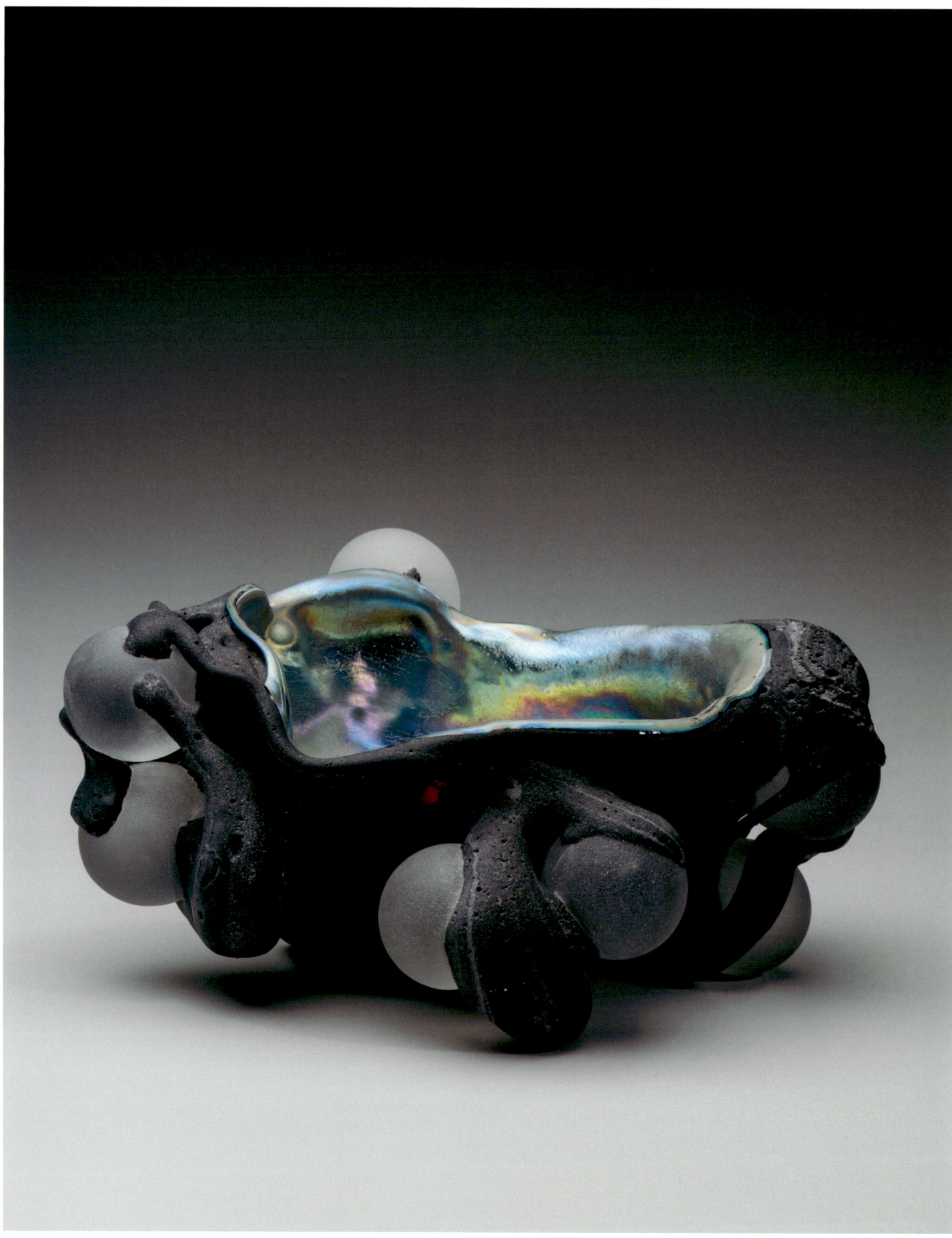

50

Josh Simpson

born 1949, United States

Iridescent Tektite, 1981, from the ongoing *Tektite* series.
Tektite meteorite formula glass, iridescent silver glass, and crystal spheres, 4 × 8 × 7 in. (10.16 × 20.32 × 17.78 cm)

51

Preston Singletary

born 1963, United States (Tlingit)

Oystercatcher, 2006.
Blown and sand-carved glass, and
steel, 16⅛ × 12 × 15 in. (40.96 ×
30.48 × 38.1 cm)

Preston Singletary is internationally renowned for his glass sculptures
that interpret Tlingit stories and retell family histories using the formline
design of Indigenous Northwest Coast artists.[1]

Singletary began blowing glass in his hometown of Seattle, Washington, in 1982, twenty years after Harvey Littleton led the Toledo Glass
workshops that ignited the Studio Glass movement in the United States.
Singletary honed his skills working in production glass for many years
before working in the Seattle studio of Benjamin Moore, where he had the
opportunity to assist artists including Dante Marioni, Richard Royal, Dan
Dailey, and Lino Tagliapietra. There, he was exposed to the larger international world of glass and began to develop his own independent work. He
cites all of those leaders in the glass field, and the Pilchuck Glass School,
as influential to his work, but Singletary also became an influential artist in
his own right as part of the first generation of Native glassblowers that
shaped new directions and spurred creativity in Indigenous glass over the
past fifty years. Many types of art continue to inspire Singletary's cre-
ations, including the sculptures of Isamu Noguchi, Henry Moore, Constan-
tin Brâncuși, and Jean Arp, but Tlingit culture and style remain the ultimate
inspiration.[2] However, his work is groundbreaking for the ways in which it
diverges from conventional design strictures of Northwest Coast art,
reimagining them in entirely new ways.

Tlingit shamans living on the Pacific Northwest coast identified with
the oystercatcher, a shorebird notable for its long, vivid, red-orange bill.
The oystercatcher inhabits the liminal space between water and land,
living in the sky but diving beneath the water for food, while shamans
inhabited the realm between the human and spirit worlds. As such, the
oystercatcher was frequently used as the main form of shamans' rattles.

Although Singletary has replicated oystercatcher rattles, in this work
the bird stands firmly on his feet rather than tucked in for flight. The
opaque brown glass Singletary chose is subtly mottled, evoking the
surface of wood, the time-honored material of Northwest Coast rattles.
Sandblasted designs in glass recreate Tlingit relief carving, representing
frogs on the belly and tail of the bird. Perched on his back is another
crouching frog in black glass. SNC

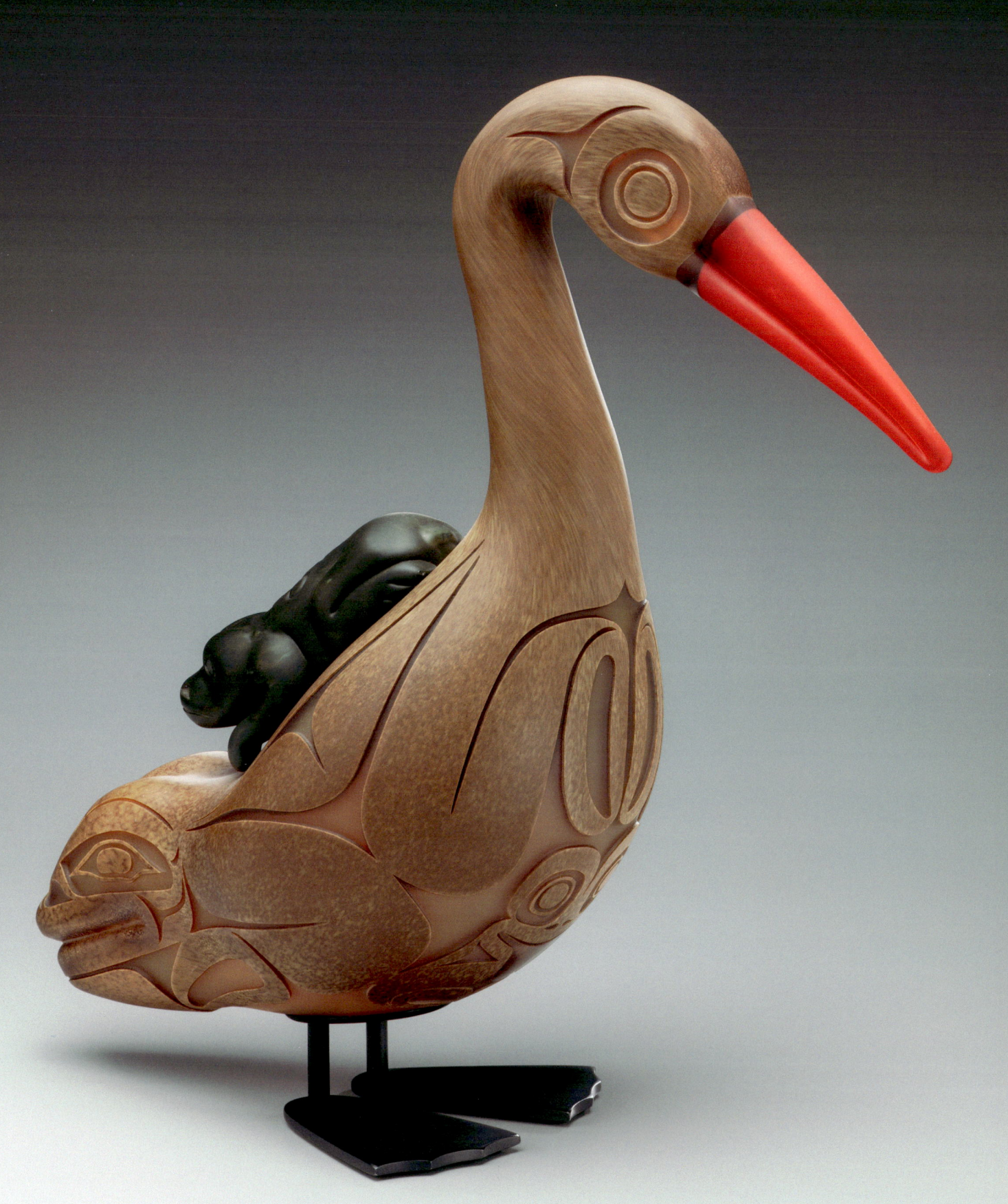

52

Paul Stankard

born 1943, United States

Honeybee Swarm with Flowers and Fruit, 2012.
Flameworked glass, 5½ × Diam. 5½ in. (13.97 × 13.97 cm)

Miniature worlds reveal themselves in Paul Stankard's intricate paperweights. Handheld studies of clustered flora, fauna, root systems, and insects, his work invites viewers to lose themselves within each finely rendered detail. *Honeybee Swarm with Flowers and Fruit* is one of Stankard's largest paperweights, with the inclusion of hovering bees and gestural botanical bouquets. Suspended in crystal, the work feels like a snapshot of a spontaneous moment, capturing each feature in varying states of movement, bud, and bloom.

Each of Stankard's artworks reflects the artist's deep appreciation for nature and a lifetime of skilled experimentation with glass. Stankard first trained at Salem Community College, in Carneys Point, New Jersey, in the scientific glassblowing program. He began his career fabricating scientific instruments, but soon left to pursue work on his globe sculptures. He has since come to be known as a founder and pioneer of the Studio Glass movement. He achieves the movement and complexity of each artwork through flamework, building each layer up before encasing them in crystal. Stankard has experimented with the elements he includes over time, expanding beyond botanicals to include tiny words and small beings. The themes of his work, however, remain focused on the beauty of the natural world. He cites the poetry of Walt Whitman as an inspiration for his keen observation of the environment, as well as his nostalgia for his experiences in nature as a child. LM

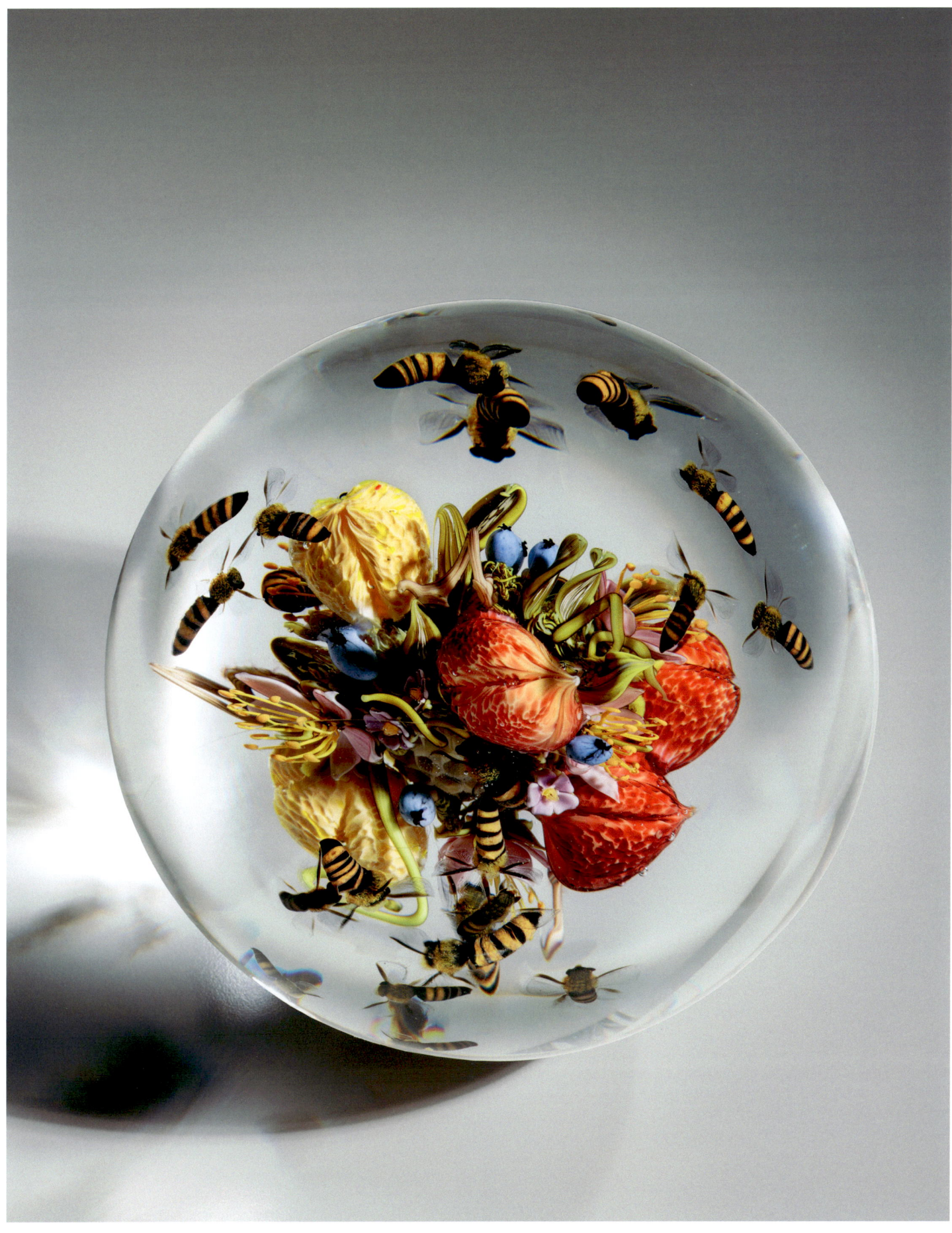

53

Lino Tagliapietra

born 1934, Italy

Notte del Redentore, 1988.
Blown glass, 13 × 9½ × 9¼ in.
(33.02 × 24.13 × 23.5 cm)

54

Lino Tagliapietra

born 1934, Italy

Spirale, 1996.
Blown glass, 25¼ × Diam. 4 in.
(64.14 × 10.16 cm)

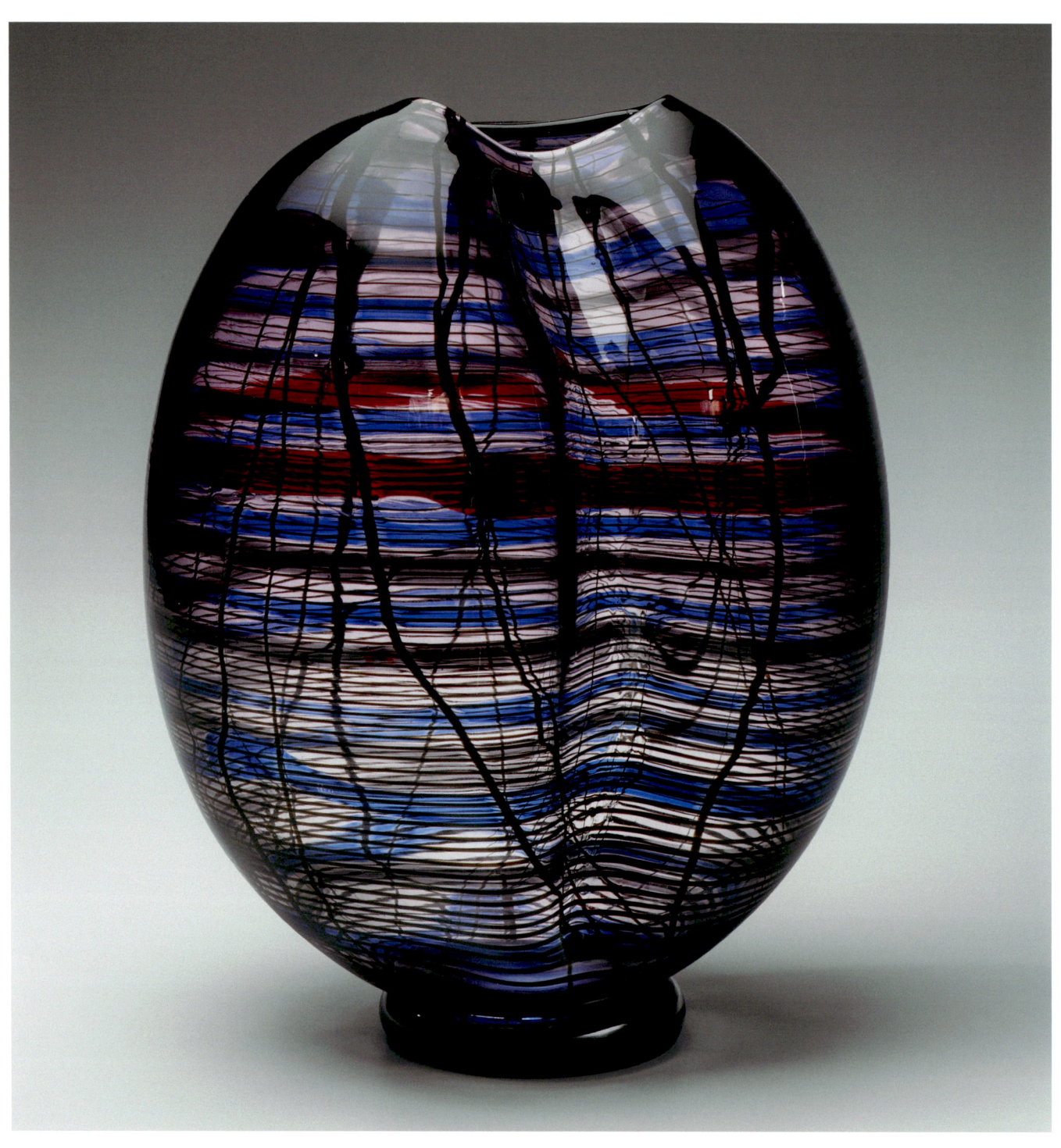

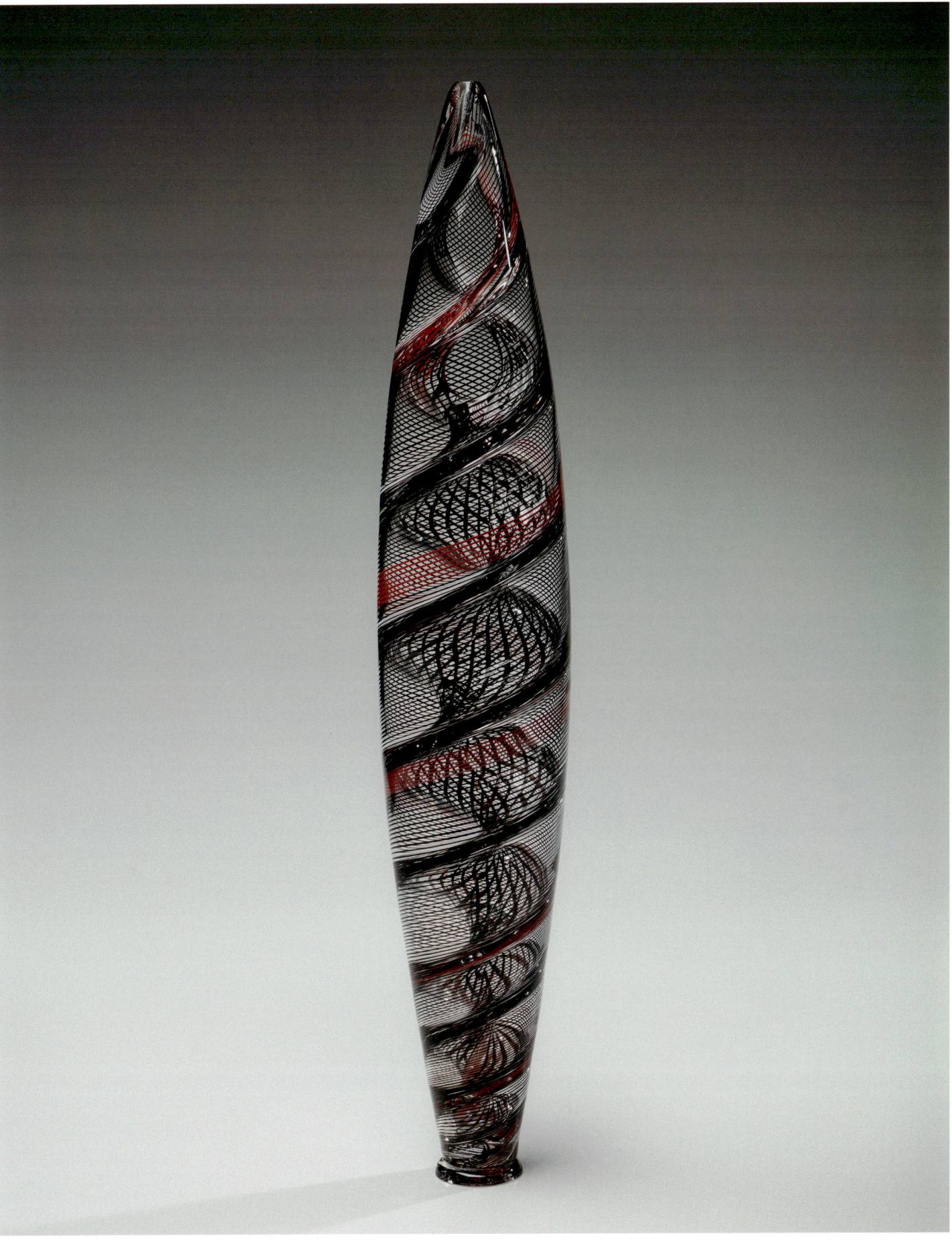

55

Lino Tagliapietra

born 1934, Italy

Odissea, 1998.
Fused hand-pulled cane, *murrine,*
and metal, 70¼ × 24 × 12 in. (178.44 ×
60.96 × 30.48 cm)

Lino Tagliapietra is acknowledged the world over as a master glass artist and teacher who has transformed the world of contemporary glass with his expertise, skill, and limitless creative vision. Reaching the age of 90 at the writing of this book, he has worked with glass consistently for nearly 8 decades since beginning his apprenticeship in glassmaking at the age of 11 in his home of Murano, Italy. He became a *maestro vetraio* (master glassmaker) at the age of 21 and worked in the factory glass system in Murano for decades before eventually breaking out as an independent glass artist. In 1979, Tagliapietra famously visited Seattle at the invitation of Dale Chihuly to introduce students at the Pilchuck Glass School to the traditions of Venetian glassblowing, an exchange that would forever transform the development of the American and International Studio Glass movements and also the *maestro*'s own work.

In the fall of 1998, Tagliapietra stepped outside of his expertise in blown glass to embark on an entirely new series of work using kilnformed glass at the Bullseye Glass Co. in Portland, Oregon, ultimately creating a series of more than twenty works called *La Carta dei Sogni* (Dream Sketchbook). The large-scale abstract panels, which he thinks of as paintings, represent a carefully arranged assemblage of cut cane lengths interspersed with *murrine*.[1] Tagliapietra describes the dynamics between space and color in a composition: "The division of space, the broken wall, the broken paper, the division where it is possible to be shocked. This is what I'm always looking at and looking for. I translate energy into one kind of space, one color."[2]

In *Odissea* (Odyssey), the colors and patterns of the cane vibrate with energy from the strong vertical bifurcation between the red and yellow sides of the panel. Nancy Callan has fond memories of making this piece at Bullseye with Lino's team, including David Walters, John Kiley, and Paul Cunningham. Callan had only begun working with Lino in 1996 and recalls how much she learned about cane pulling on this project. "I remember him pulling the yellow cane and how surprised I was to see what he did with it. . . . We had so much cane for him to work with, he had a huge palette of different colors to create the fused compositions."[3]

Lino and Lina Tagliapietra must have had a fondness for this work, as they lived with *Odissea* in their Seattle home.[4] Dale Chihuly reportedly saw the piece soon after it was created and declared it "a masterpiece."[5] SNC

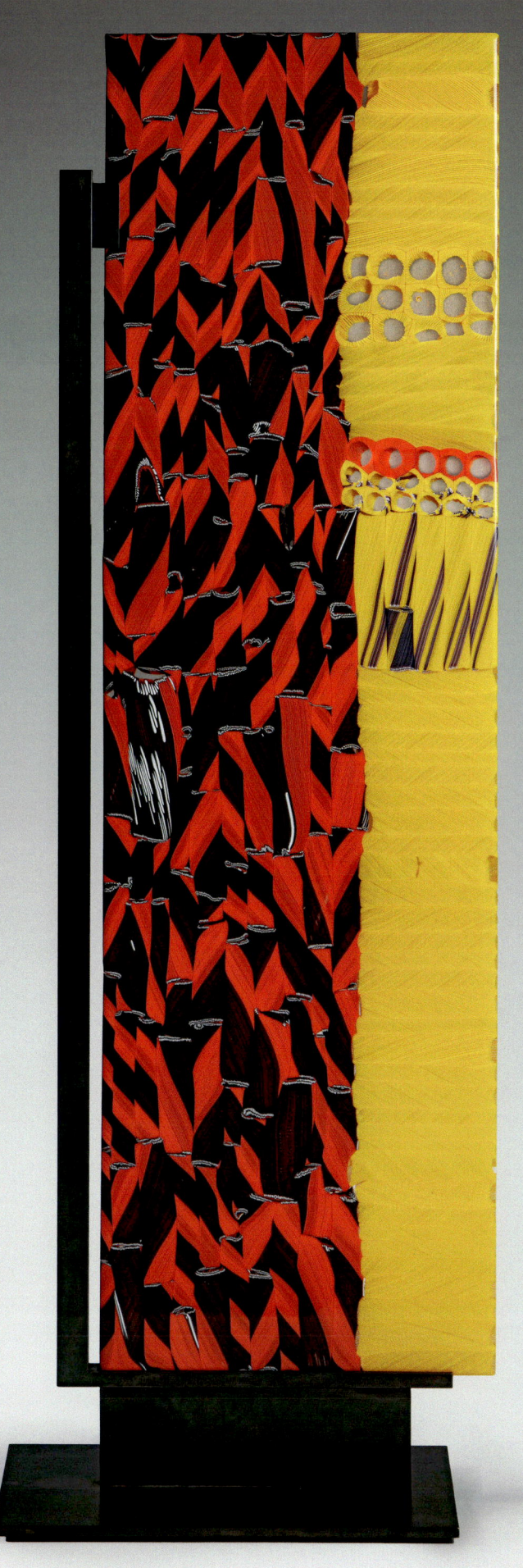

56

Lino Tagliapietra
born 1934, Italy

Endeavor, ca. 2000.
Blown and carved glass, and metal,
13 × 71⅜ × 4¾ in. (33.02 × 181.29 ×
12.07 cm)

57

Lino Tagliapietra
born 1934, Italy

Vienna, 2009.
Blown glass, 40⅝ × 19 × 8½ in.
(103.19 × 48.26 × 21.59 cm)

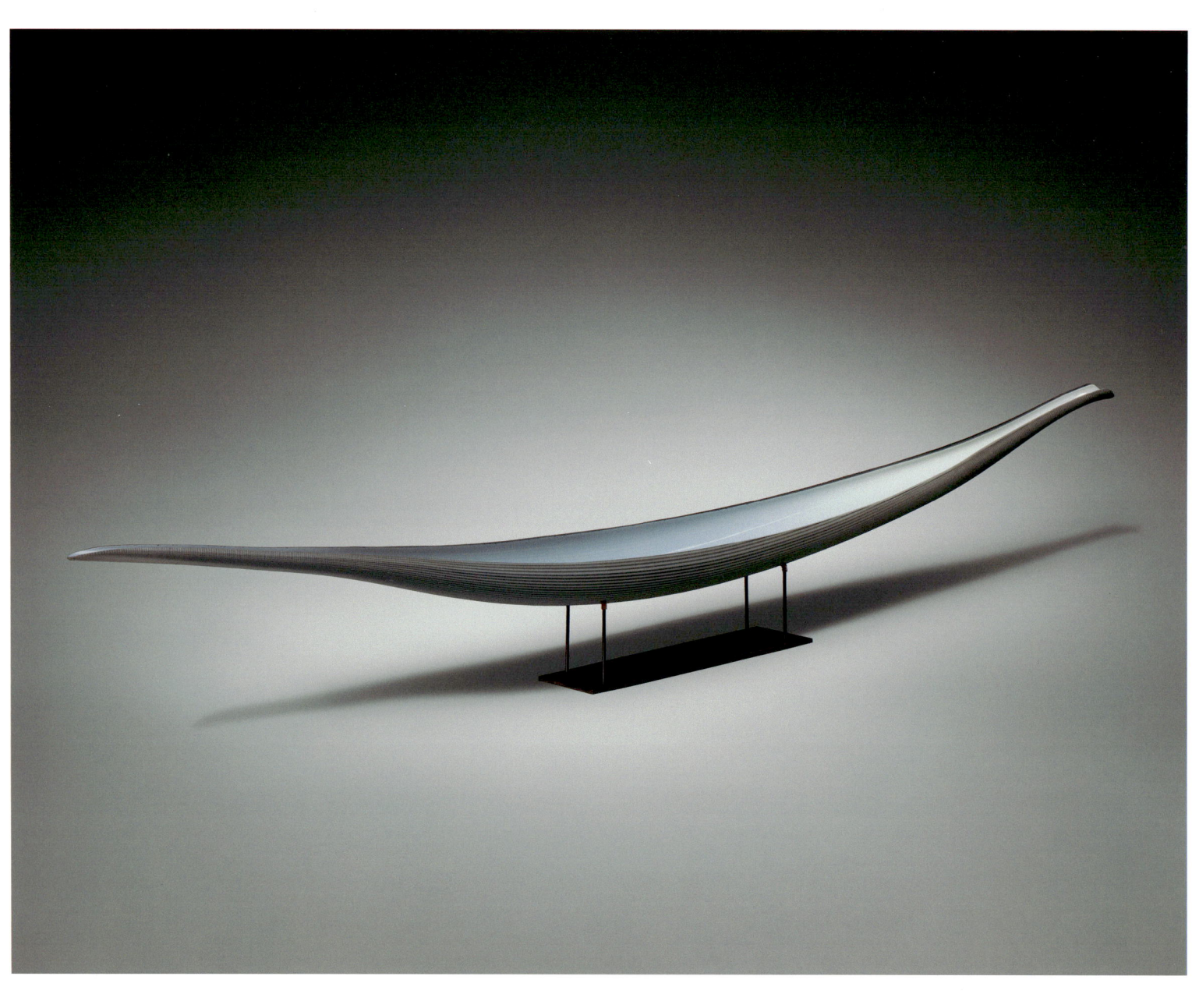

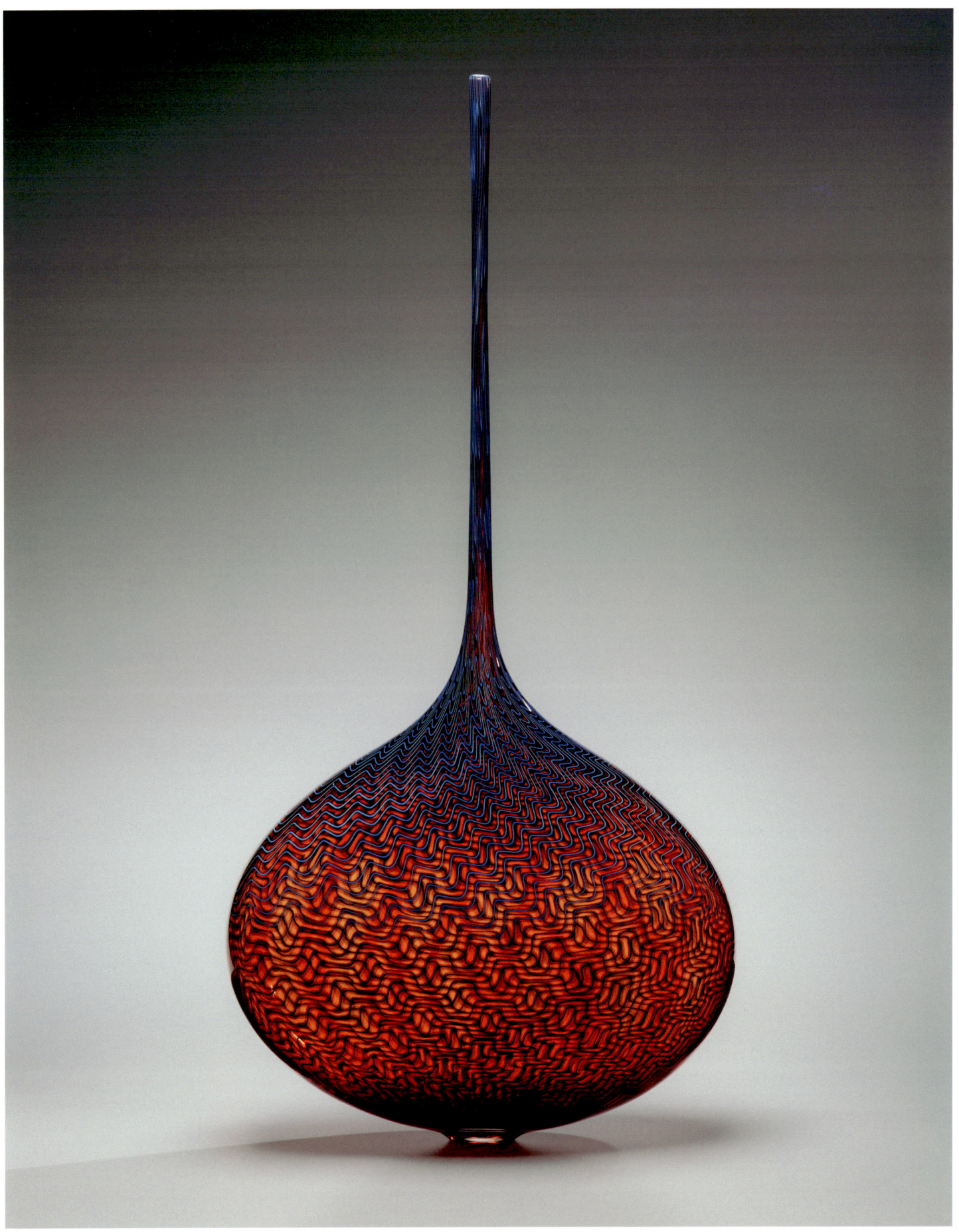

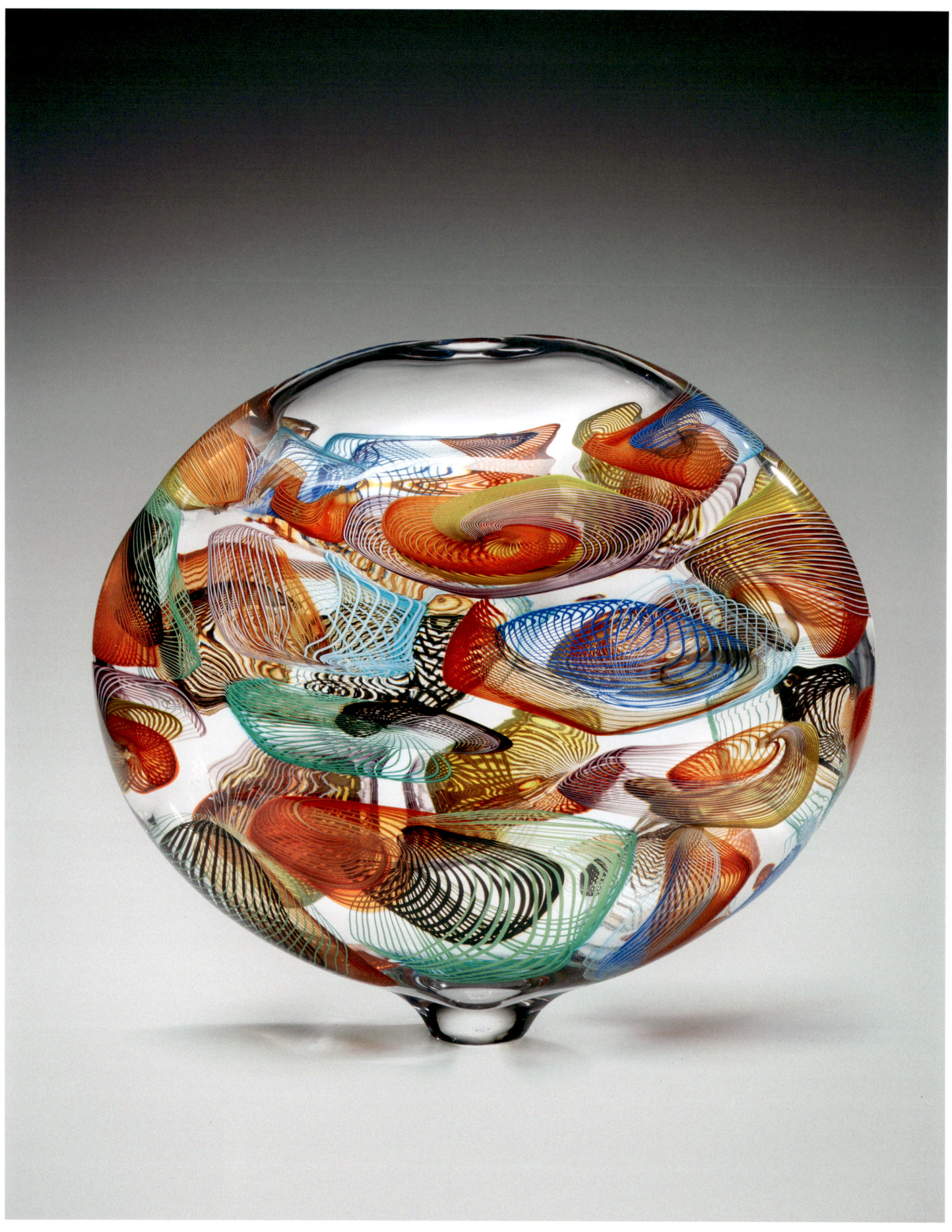

58
Lino Tagliapietra

born 1934, Italy

Kira, 2010.
Blown glass, 15½ × 16½ × 6½ in.
(39.37 × 41.91 × 16.51 cm)

59
Lino Tagliapietra

born 1934, Italy

Saturno, 2010.
Blown glass and metal, 69 × 17¾ ×
17¾ in. (175.26 × 45.09 × 45.09 cm)

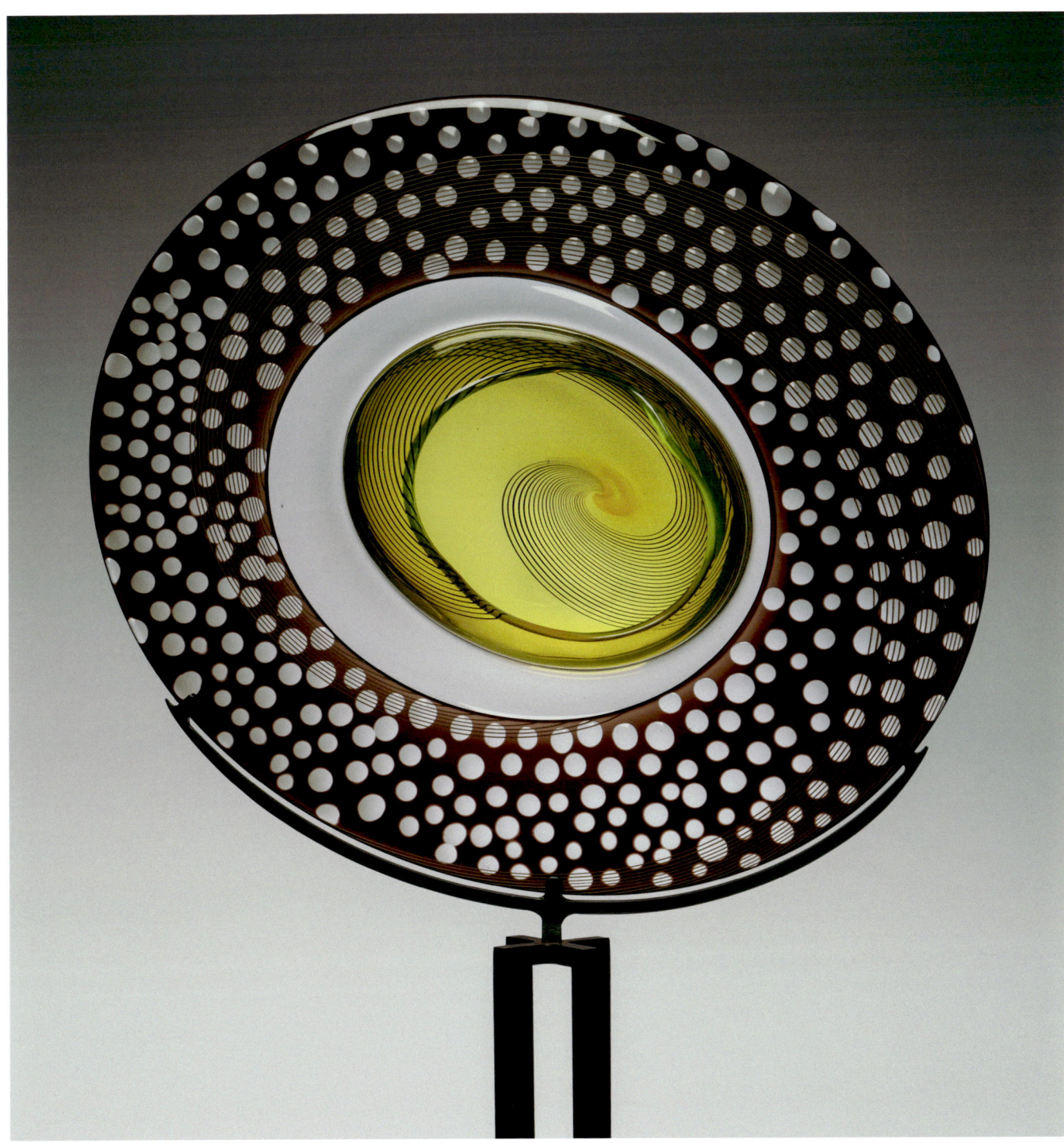

Lino Tagliapietra

born 1934, Italy

Florencia, 2019.
Blown glass, 25 × 10 × 8 in. (63.5 × 25.4 × 20.32 cm)

Lino Tagliapietra

born 1934, Italy

Dinosaur, 2019.
Blown glass, 55 × 9 × 9 in. (139.7 × 22.86 × 22.86 cm)

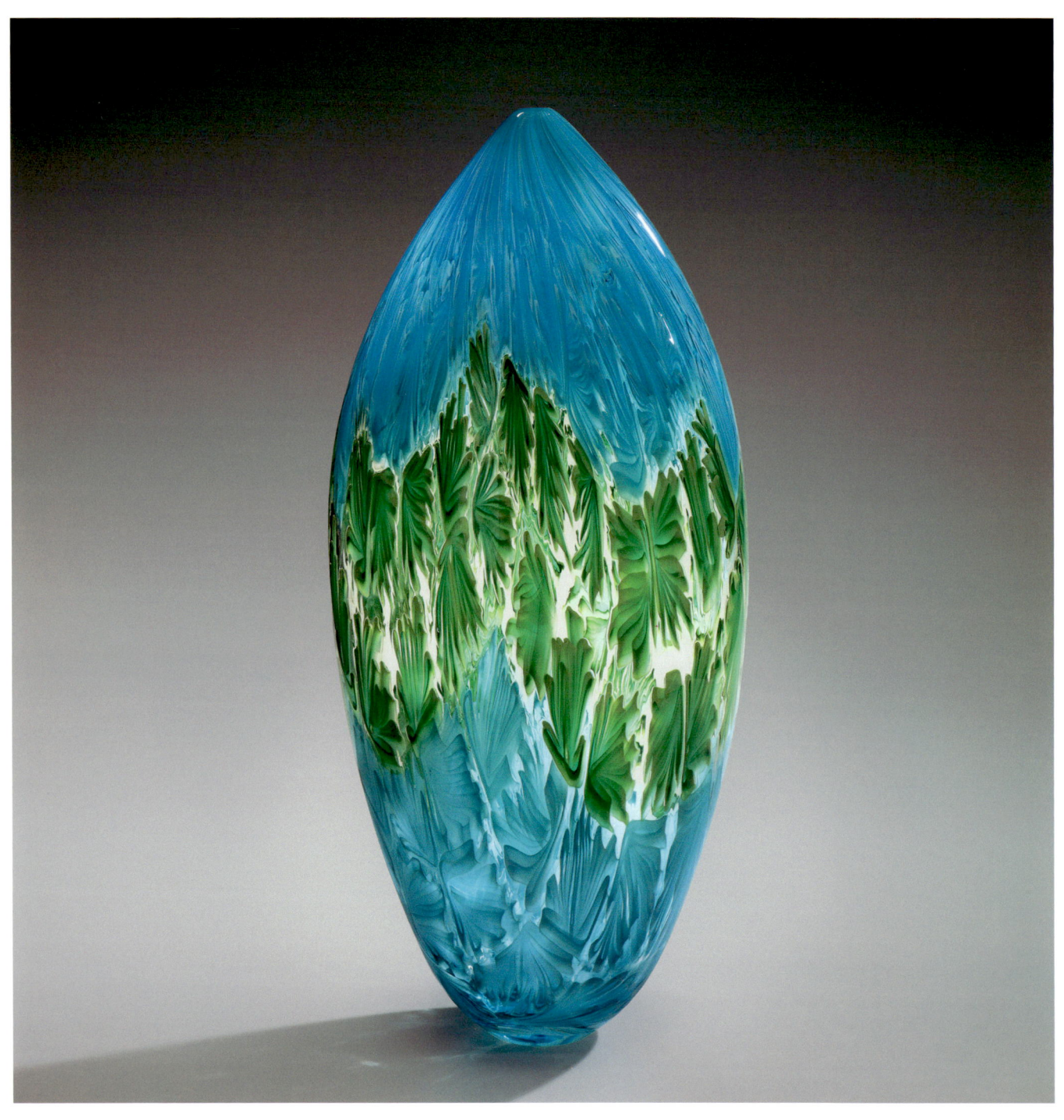

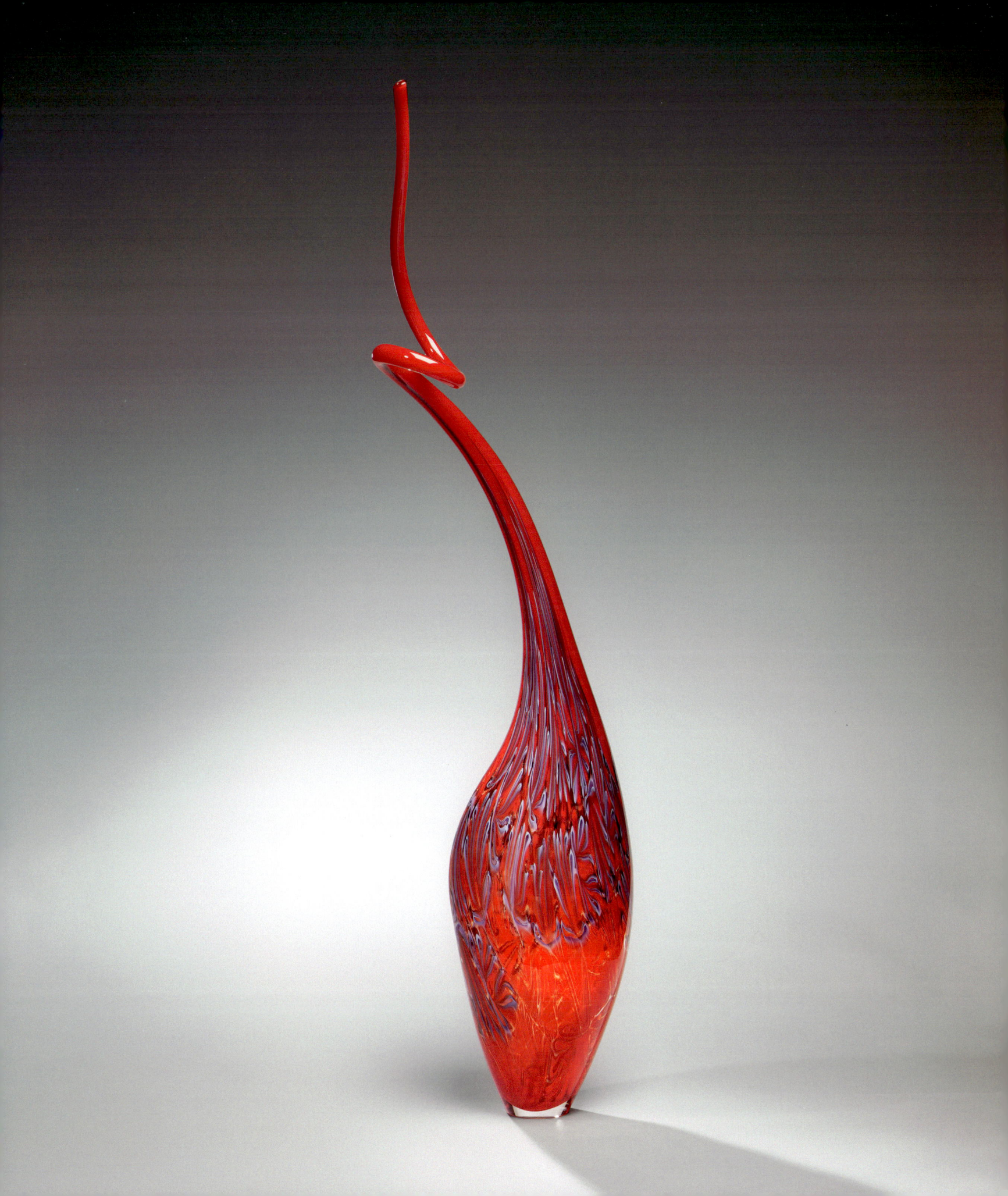

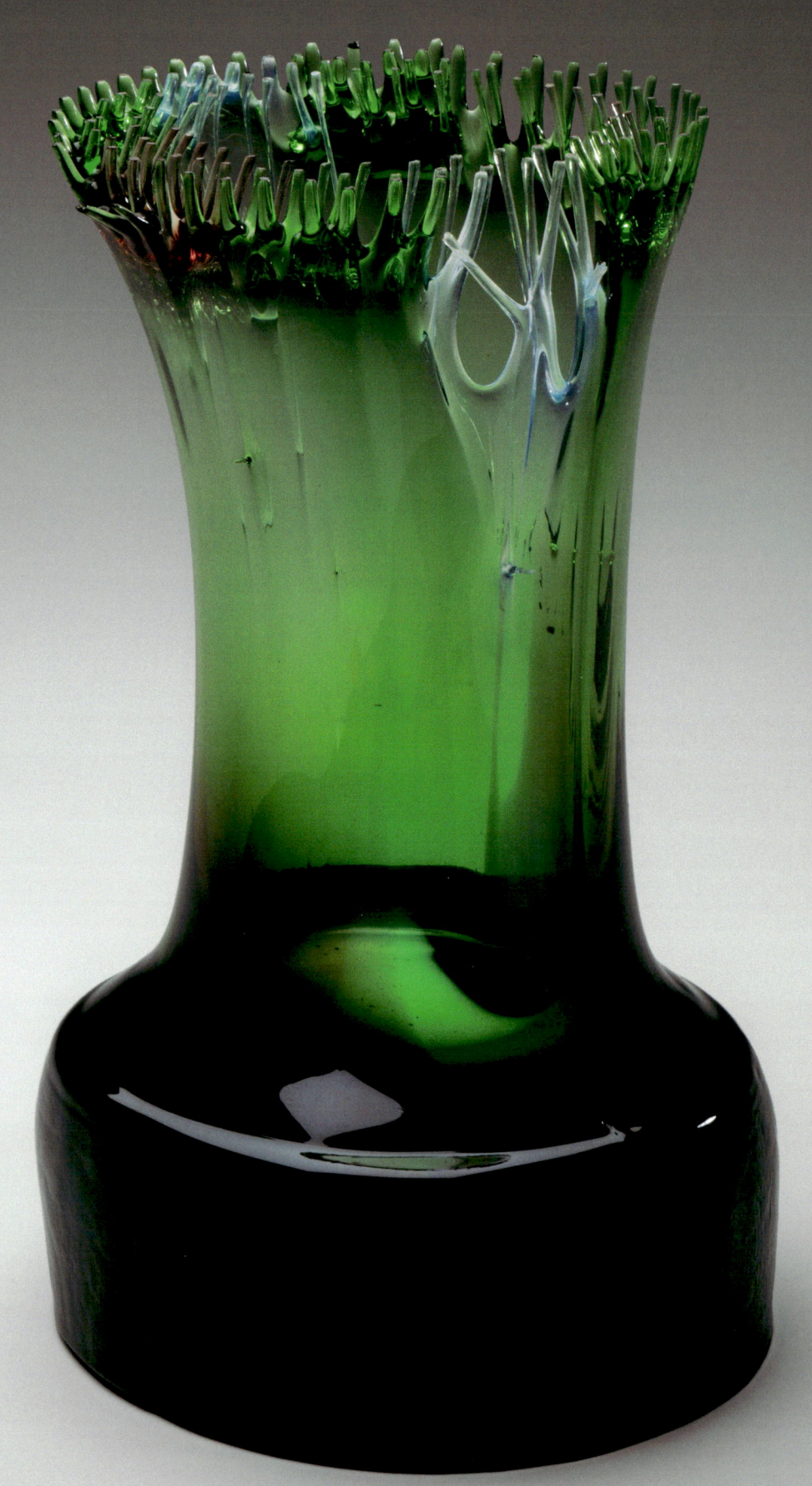

62

Dalibor Tichý

1950–1985, Czech Republic

Emerald Ring, 1982.
Cast and hotworked glass, 9¾ ×
5½ × 6 in. (24.77 × 13.97 × 15.24 cm)

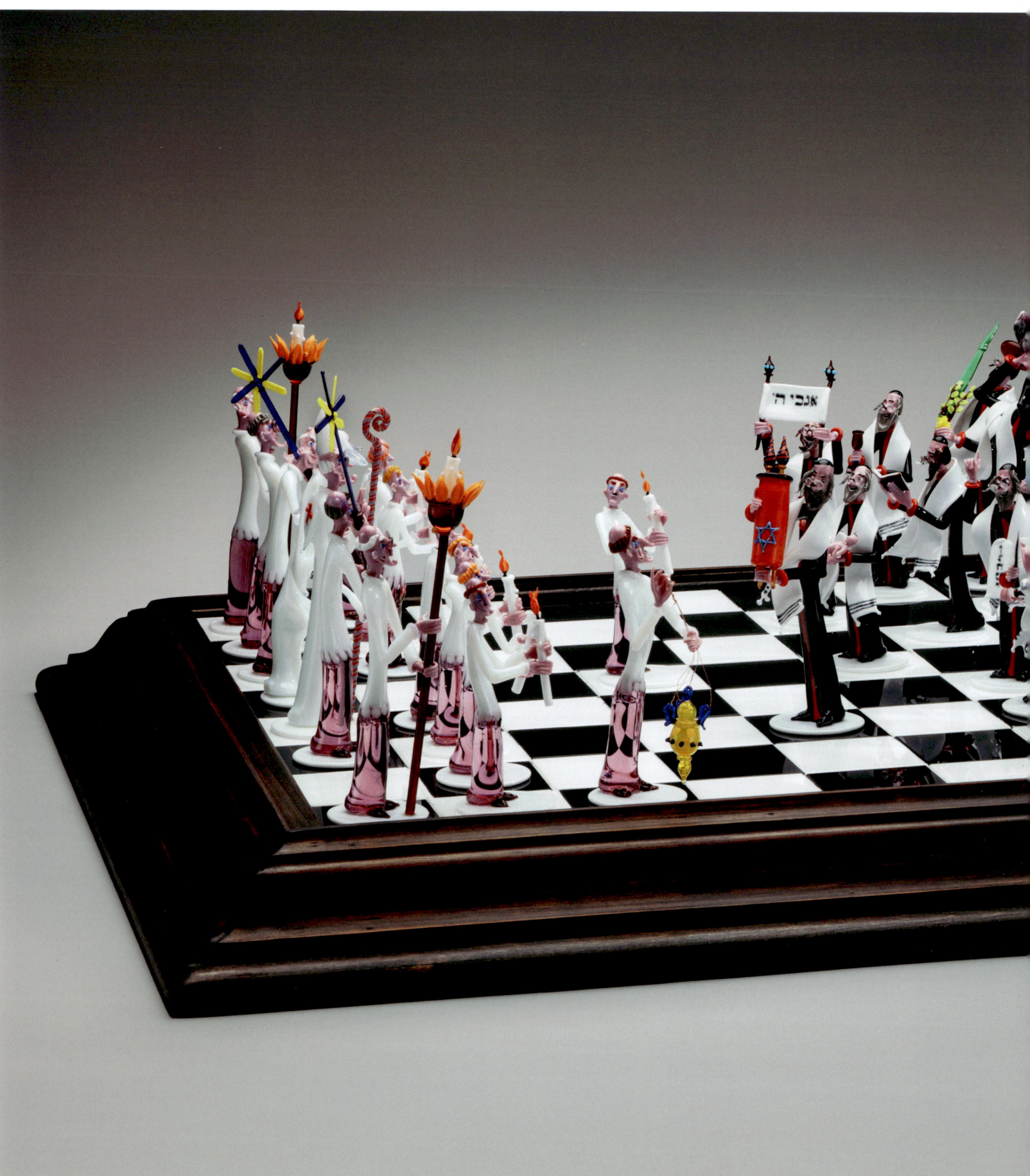

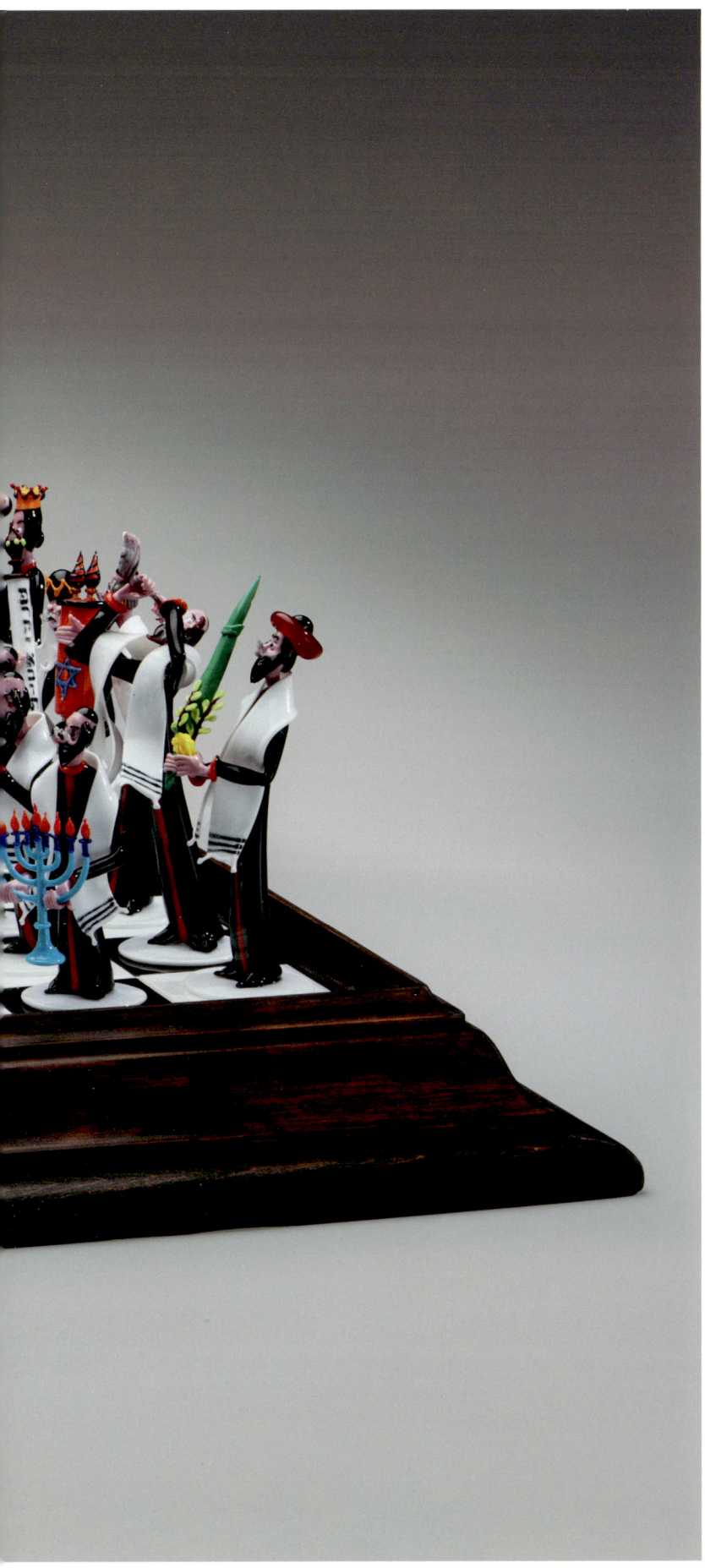

63

Gianni Toso

born 1942, Italy, works in the United States

Chasidim-Franciscan Chess Set, 1983. Flameworked glass and wood, 10½ × 26½ × 26½ in. (26.67 × 67.31 × 67.31 cm)

64

Karla Trinkley

born 1956, United States

Widow's Walk, 20th–21st century.
Cast glass, 7 × 8½ × 8½ in. (17.78 ×
21.59 × 21.59 cm)

65

Bertil Vallien

born 1938, Sweden

Dorian Bay, 1985.
Sandcast glass, 5¼ × 16¾ × 4½ in.
(13.34 × 42.55 × 11.43 cm)

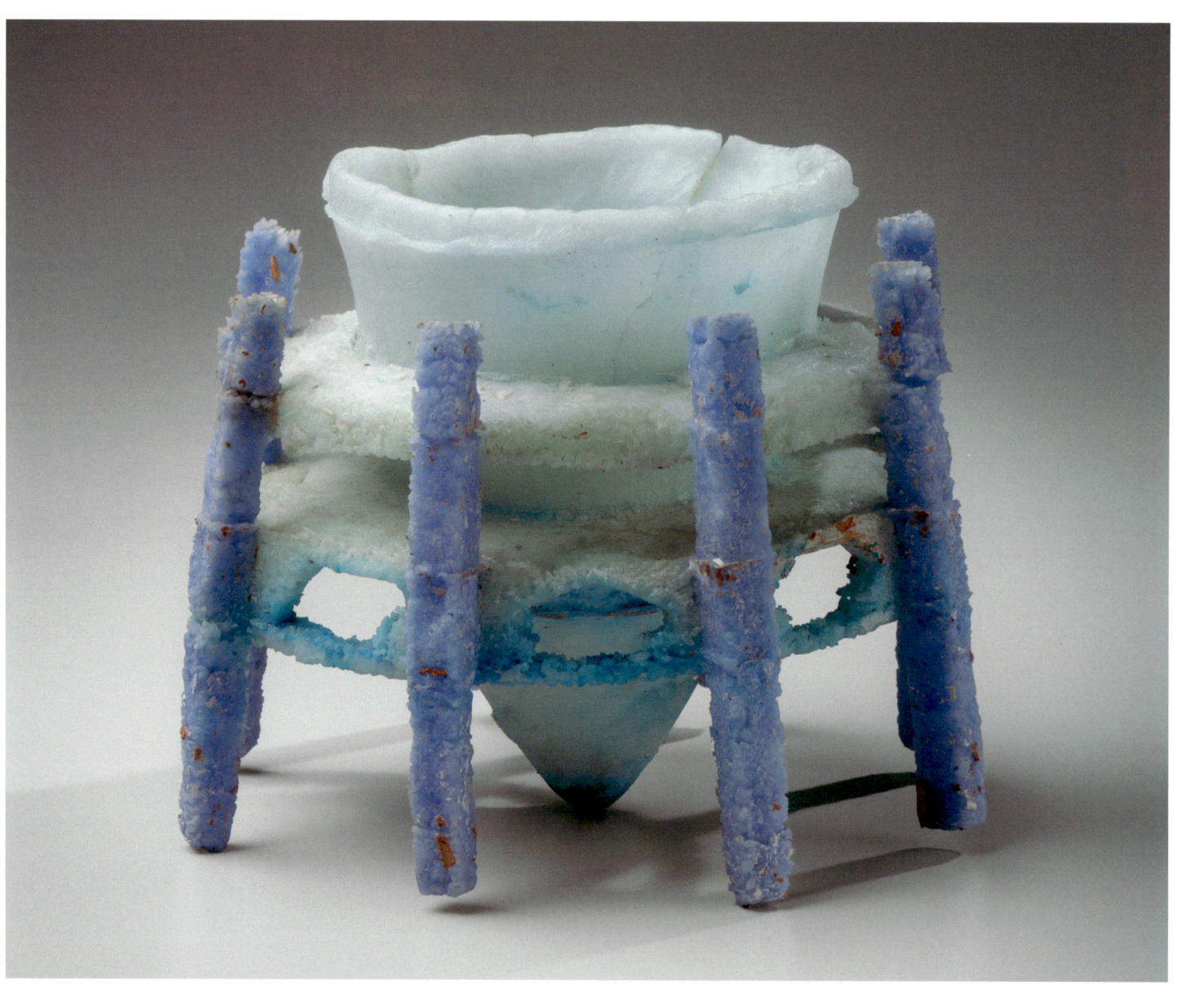

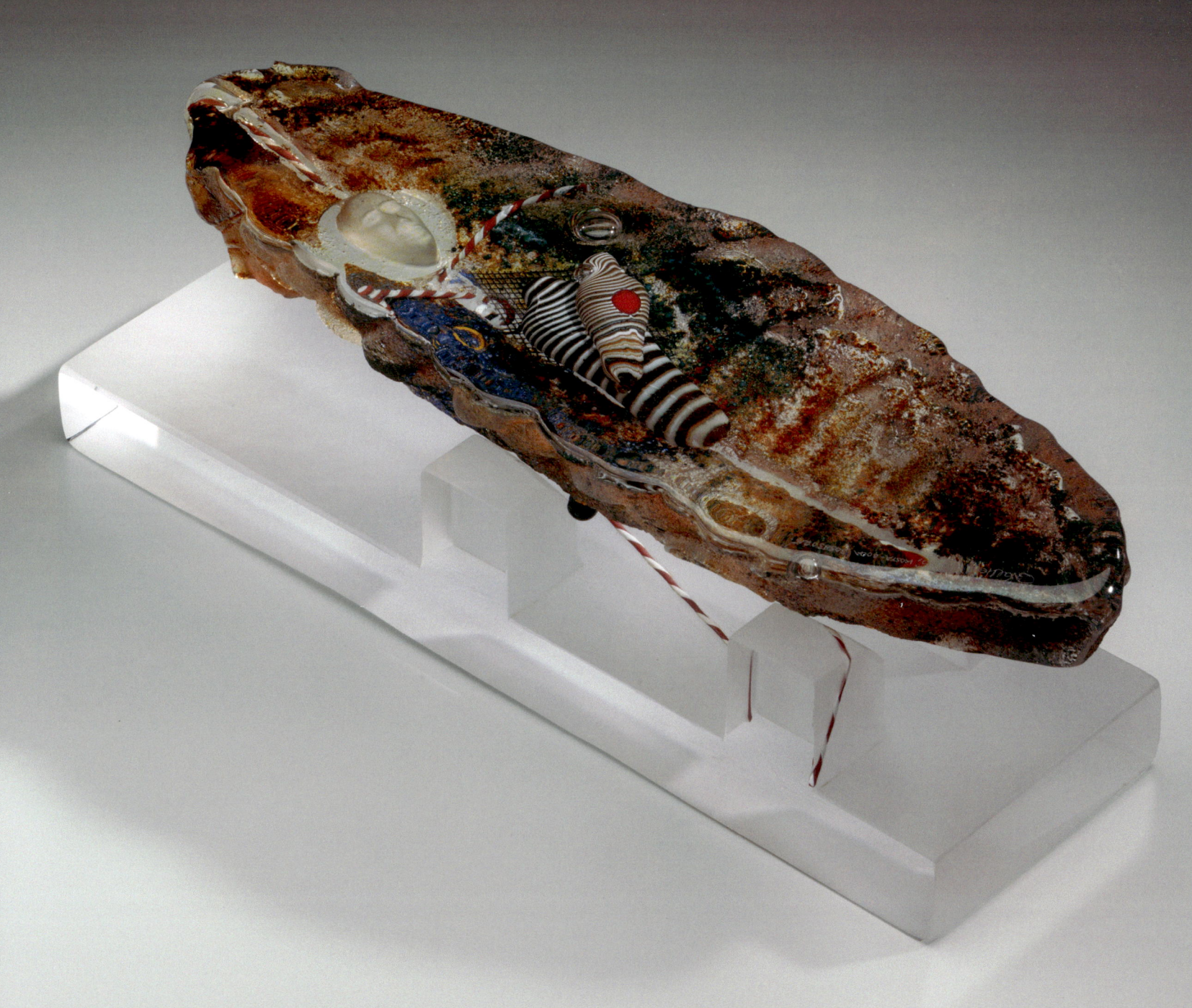

66

František Vízner

1936–2011, Czech Republic

Red bowl with peak, 2006.
Cut glass, shaped on the grindstone,
3½ × Diam. 10⅝ in. (8.89 × 26.99 cm)

67

James Watkins

born 1955, United States

Bottle with Window and Frame, 1991.
Pâte de verre, 18⅜ × 10¾ × 5 in.
(46.67 × 27.31 × 12.7 cm)

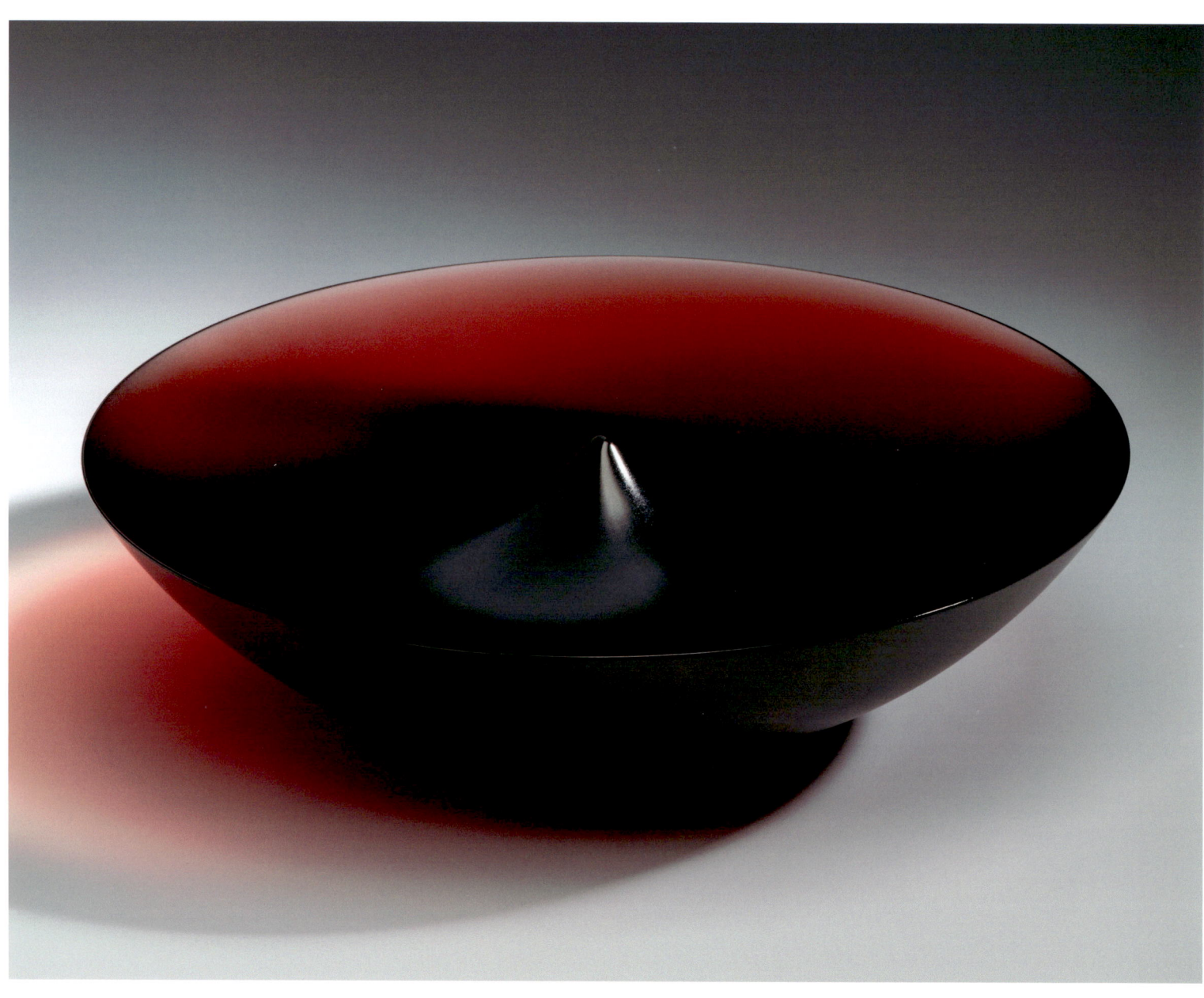

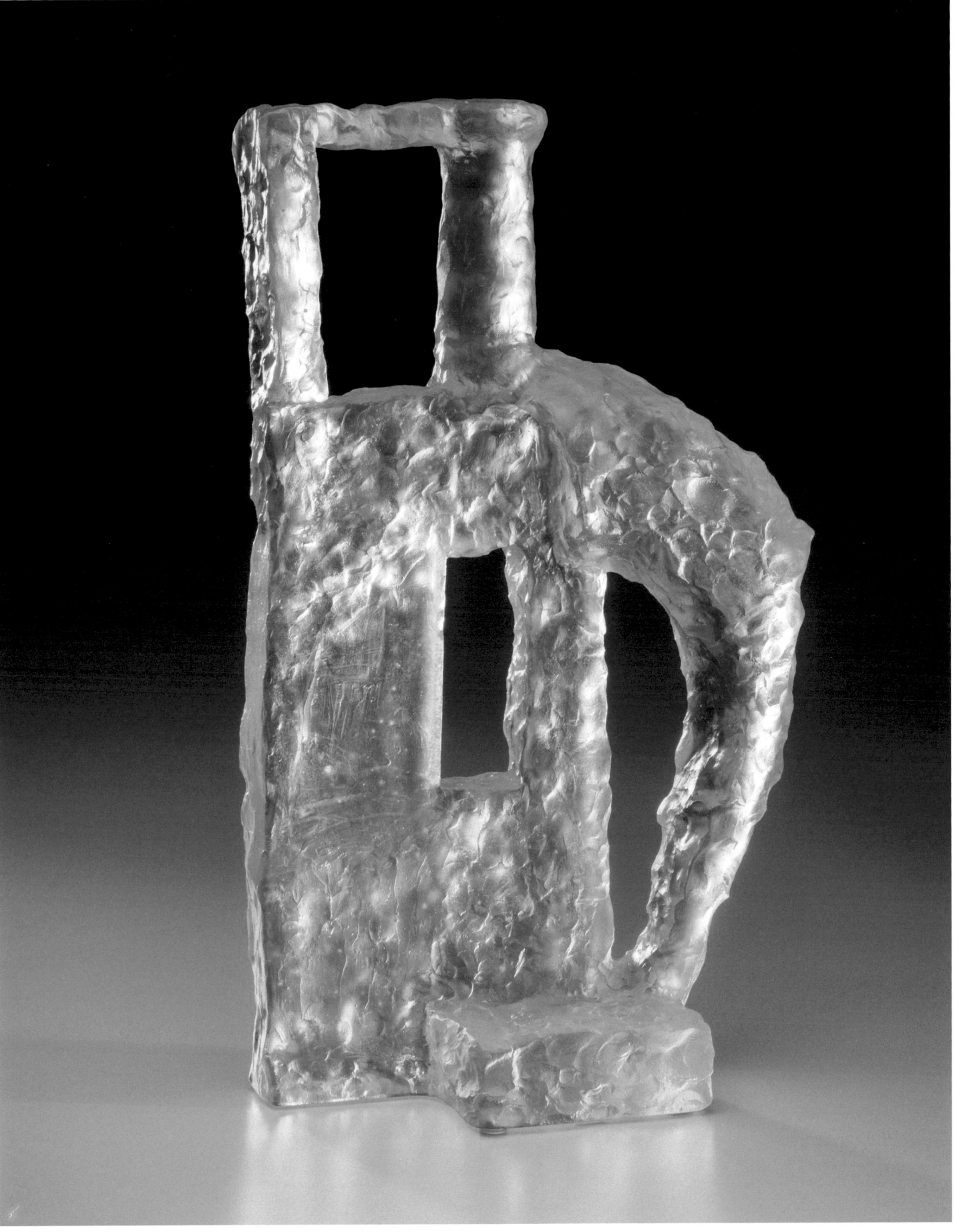

Thaddeus Wolfe

born 1979, United States

Assemblage Vessel, 2018, from the
Assemblage series, 2011–ongoing.
Cast glass, 15¼ × 8½ × 9½ in.
(38.74 × 21.59 × 24.13 cm)

Thaddeus Wolfe has made a name for himself in the contemporary art glass movement with his sculptures, vessels, and lamps, each of which are intricate explorations in richly variegated color and surface texture. His work is often compared to Brutalist architecture for the way it often cantilevers over its own sides; it also evokes the crystalline structures of mineral formations. A native of Ohio, Wolfe began studying glass while earning his BFA at the Cleveland Institute of Art. While he found it a challenging medium, his perseverance has earned him recognition as an artist who is pushing its boundaries. "I am faithful to it because its material properties provide me with inspiration and challenges," he says. "It seems to have endless possibilities, while also having many limitations."[1]

Wolfe's work begins in Styrofoam, which he calls "a material of our time."[2] He uses it to build and carve the exact form he desires, leaning into the material's ability to hold complex structure and impart unique textures. He creates a silicone and plaster mold of his sculpture, into which he blows a gob of layered glass. Once he breaks apart the mold, he spends time coldworking the resulting piece, grinding and cutting away sections of the glass to achieve polished areas. Today, Wolfe works out of a studio in Brooklyn, an environment he has cited as inspiration for his dimensional, crumbling forms. LM

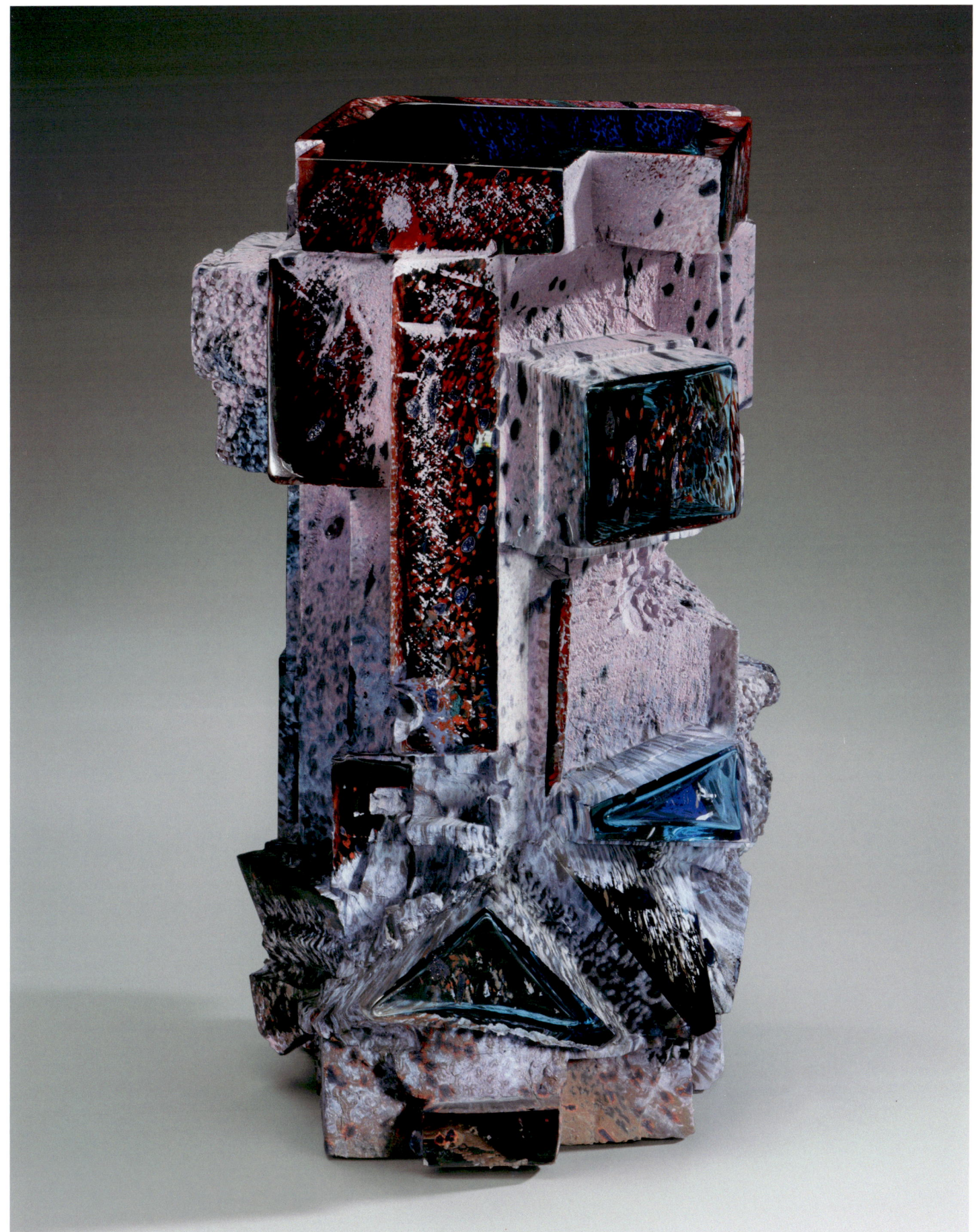

Ann Wolff

born 1937, Germany, works primarily in Sweden

Bowl, 2012.
Blown, etched, and sandblasted glass, 6 × Diam. 12 in. (15.24 × 30.48 cm)

"My glass vessels are designed to radiate light, to give shelter, to support—I would like to be sitting inside them. Glass carries my scattered thoughts into the light."[1]

Born in Germany right before WWII, Ann Wolff became one of the leaders of the International Studio Glass movement in the twentieth century. Her early education in Germany was very much informed by the principles of the Bauhaus movement, which combined fine arts with craft and design. Although Wolff first became famous for her work in glass, drawing and sculpture have also been a focus of her long, prolific career. Working in Sweden in the 1960s, first making production glass at the Swedish glasshouse Kosta Boda and later as an independent artist, Wolff was already a notable figure in European glass when she attracted the attention of Marvin Lipofsky and Dale Chihuly, who invited her to teach at the Pilchuck School of Glass as an early faculty member and one of the first teachers from Europe.

During the 1980s, Wolff created a series of blown and engraved vessels decorated with narrative scenes. As with all of her work, these bowls and cups focus deeply on the experiences of women's lives. Bowls, as objects representing domestic life, serve as a fitting form for these explorations. On this vessel, in deep purples with golden yellow highlights, Wolff's surrealist narrative scene includes depictions of a house, a woman holding on to a raven's tail, a woman giving birth to children with Mickey Mouse ears, and a large yellow teapot, all superimposed over a landscape of rolling hills.[2] SNC

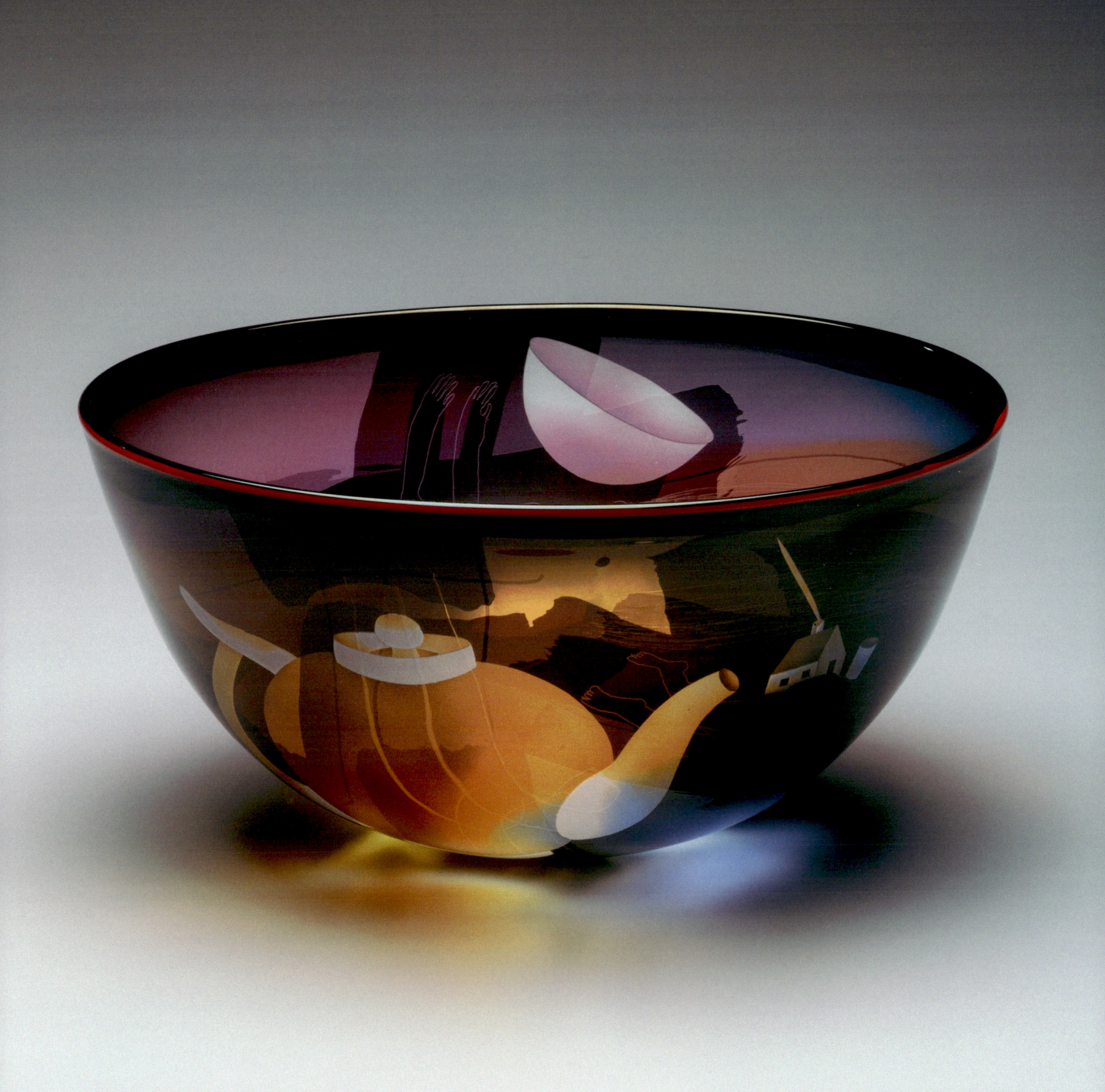

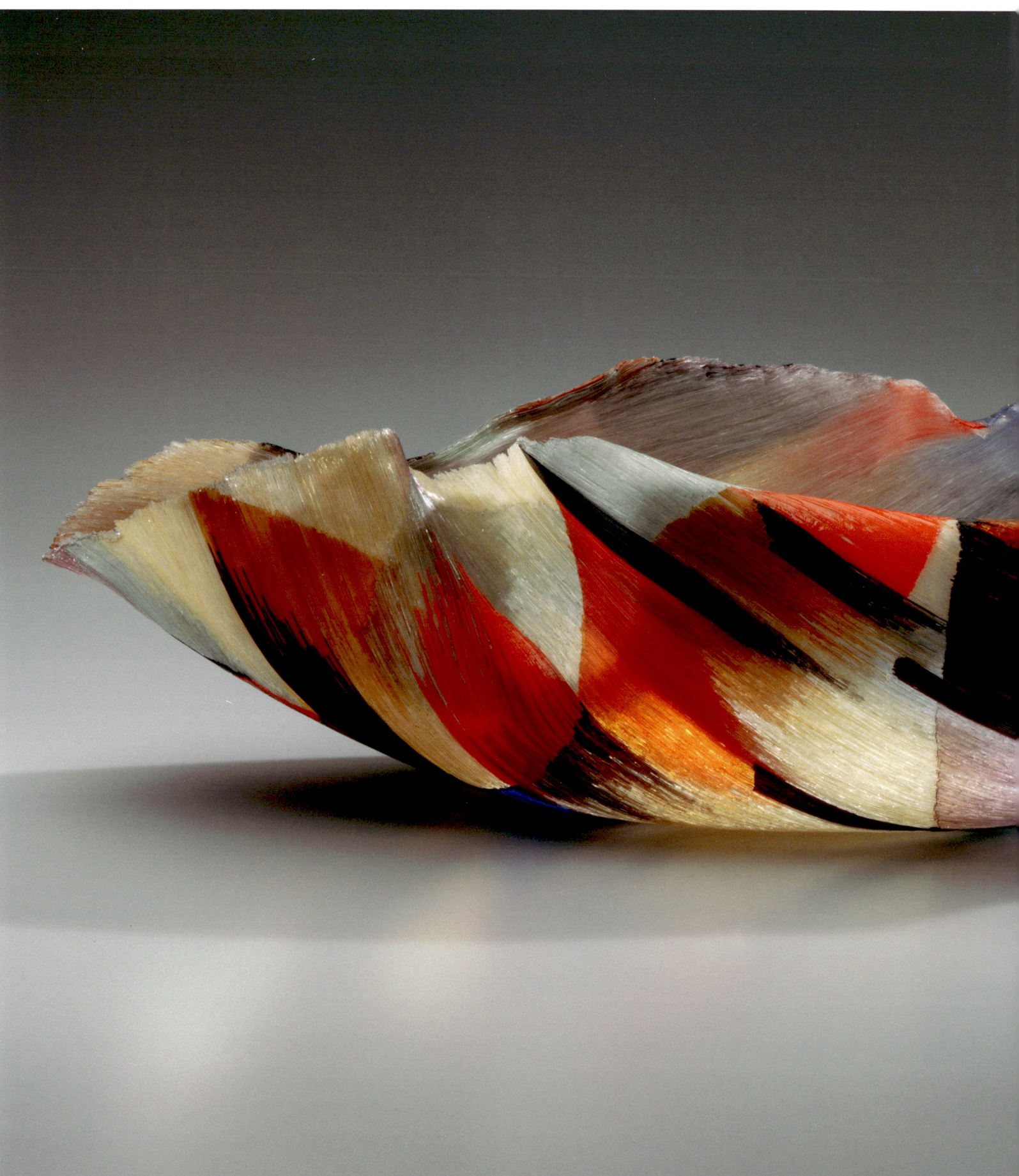

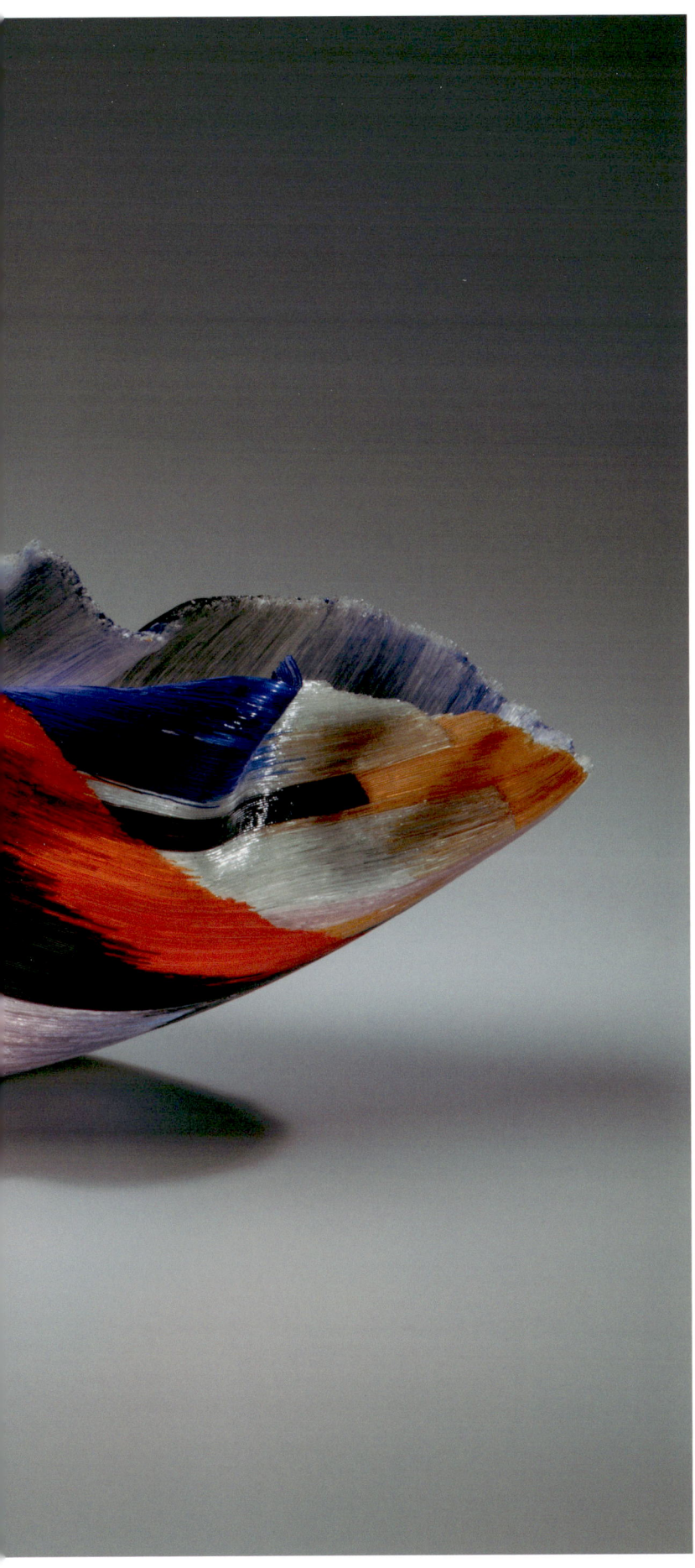

Toots Zynsky

born 1951, United States

Traffic, 1992, from the *Order and Chaos* series, 1990–99.
Filet de verre, 5½ × 18 × 6½ in.
(13.97 × 45.72 × 16.51 cm)

Toots Zynsky

born 1951, United States

Isabella, 2003.
Filet de verre, 11¼ × 22 × 16 in.
(28.58 × 55.88 × 40.64 cm)

Toots Zynsky was an early and influential leader in the Studio Glass movement in the United States. She grew up in Lynnfield on the North Shore of Massachusetts, not far from Salem, and remembers visiting the Peabody Essex Museum as a child. Her transformative introduction to Dale Chihuly's new glass program during college at the Rhode Island School of Design (RISD) in Providence spurred the beginning of her long and influential career in glass.[1] In 1980, as the new associate director of the New York Experimental Glass Workshop in New York City, Zynsky began to regularly use hand-pulled glass threads in her work. She continued to refine this technique until, in 1982, in collaboration with the Dutch artist and inventor Mathijs Teunissen van Manen, she codeveloped machinery that automated the stretching of glass rods to a universal thinness akin to "thread." She named this original technique *filet de verre* (glass thread), and it defines her iconic work.

Another artist influential to Zynsky at that pivotal time in her career was Gianni Toso, an Italian-born artist specializing in flameworking (pl. 63). Zynsky was entranced by his rich and varied use of color in his intricate compositions, and Toso's guidance led Zynsky to seek out glass rods from the firm of Moretti in Murano on her first trip to Europe in 1983.[2] The wide range of colors that Moretti had available inspired Zynsky to deeply explore dynamic color combinations in her subsequent work. Over four decades later, Zynsky still innovates, creating works that delight in their infinite variety of forms and juxtapositions of color.

Isabella was named in reference to Hurricane Isabel that hit the Atlantic coast while Zynsky was making the piece in September 2003.[3] The flashes of orange and blue across the white surface of the vessel represent a fire-and-ice color theme that Zynsky initially developed when she was commissioned to create ten torches for the 2002 Paralympic Winter Games in Salt Lake City, Utah.[4] She translated her signature *filet-de-verre* technique into torches, in shades of orange for the Olympic flame and blue for the winter theme, that evoked prosthetic limbs and symbolized strength and the achievements of the athletes.[5] SNC

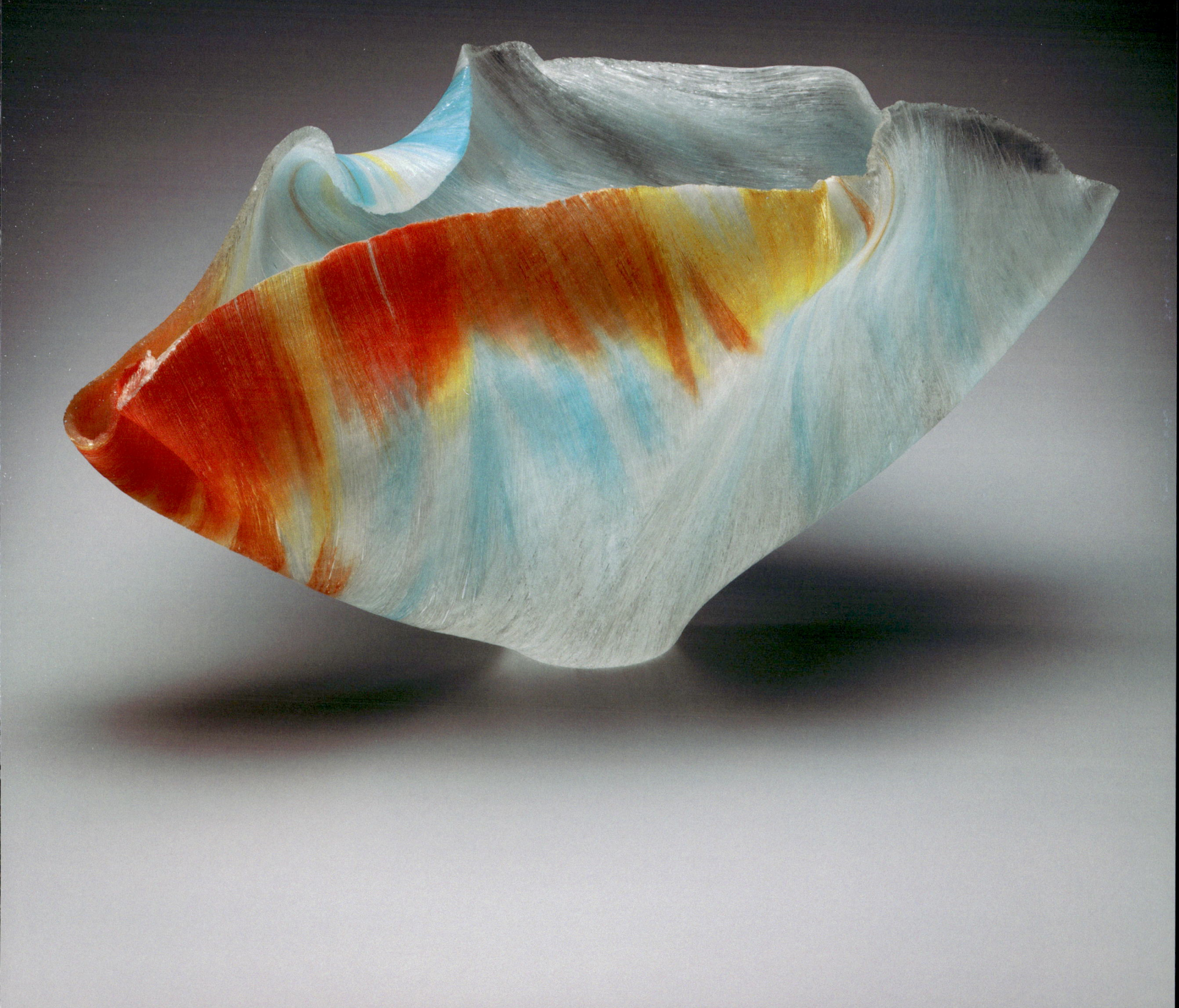

Notes and Citations

150

Plate 1

Oben Abright, "Oben Abright," Echt Gallery, accessed July 12, 2024, https://www.echtgallery.com/oben-abright-1.

Plate 4

Shawn Waggoner, "Sonja Blomdahl: Queen of Symmetry," *Glass Art* (March/April 2000), quoted on Sonja Blomdahl's website, https://www.sonjablomdahl.com/glass-art.

Plate 8

1. Stanislav Libenský and Jaroslava Brychtová began working together in 1954 in the Czech glassmaking center of Železný Brod and married in 1963.

2. Other related works from this series are in the Cleveland Museum of Art, Corning Museum of Glass, Indianapolis Museum of Art at Newfields, and Toledo Museum of Art. The Pforzheimers also acquired Libenský and Brychtová's *Laid Table*, 1990, in 2014.

3. Kate Elliott and Katya Kohoutová., *Stanislav Libenský, Jaroslava Brychtová: Paintings, Drawings, and Sculpture* (Seattle: Elliott Brown Gallery, 1995), 8.

Plate 9

Sadia Tasnim, "CONVERSATION: Nancy Callan on capturing fleeting moments in new work now on view at San Francisco's Montague Gallery," *UrbanGlass*, March 24, 2022, https://urbanglass.org/glass/detail/nancy-callans-phenomena-at-the-montague.

Plate 23

1. Corning Museum of Art, "*Pâte de Verre* with Shin-ichi and Kimiake Higuchi | Master Class Series, Volume IV," Youtube Video, May 15, 2020, https://www.youtube.com/watch?v=GouSwkT2bsE&t=568s

2. Corning Museum of Art, "*Pâte de Verre*."

Plate 24

Eric Hilton, "About," Eric Hilton Glass, accessed July 12, 2024, https://www.erichiltonglass.com/about.

Plate 29

Tahree Lane, "Dominick Labino: A giant in art and technology," *The Blade*, June 10, 2012, https://www.toledoblade.com/a-e/art/2012/06/10/Dominick-Labino-A-giant-in-art-and-technology/stories/201206100027.

Plate 30

1. Karen LaMonte, "Shaping the Invisible," Hillwood Estate, Museum, and Garden, streamed live on November 16, 2023, YouTube video, https://www.youtube.com/watch?v=mfDq9CdMEcg&t=2875s.

2. Karen LaMonte, email to author, May 16, 2024.

3. LaMonte, "Shaping the Invisible."

Plate 31

K. William LeQuier, "About," K. William LeQuier Glass, accessed July 12, 2024, https://www.kwilliamlequier.com/about.

Plate 46

1. Ann Robinson, catalogue essay for *The Cast* exhibition, accessed May 10, 2024, http://www.annrobinson.co.nz/text.html, see: "texts & reviews" section, the cast 01, Our reality is isolation.

2. Peter Simpson, article on the exhibition *Pacific Rim: Ann Robinson's Glass 2003*, Museum of New Zealand/Te Papa Tongarewa, Wellington, New Zealand, accessed May 10, 2024, http://www.annrobinson.co.nz/text.html, see: "texts & reviews" section, pacific rim 03, An act of love.

3. Ann Robinson, artist address at conference accompanying exhibition *Transparency in Glass 2001*, Victoria and Albert Museum, London, England, accessed May 10, 2024, http://www.annrobinson.co.nz/text.html, see: "texts & reviews" section, conference 01, Do it in the wax.

Plate 47

1. Erica Rosenfeld, accessed April 30, 2024, https://www.ericarosenfeld.com/about.

2. Erica Rosenfeld, email message to author, May 8, 2024.

Plate 48

1. She was inspired by his use of glass and paint in his iconic work *The Bride Stripped Bare by Her Bachelors, Even (The Large Glass)*, 1915–1923, at the Philadelphia Museum of Art, a work she encountered soon after earning her MFA in drawing and painting from the University of Georgia in 1975.

2. Ruffner worked with Hans Godo Fräbel. Oral history interview with Ginny Ruffner, September 13–14, 2006, Archives of American Art, Smithsonian Institution.

3. Art is life to Ruffner. Injured in a terrible car accident in 1991 that put her in a coma for five weeks and in a wheelchair for five years, she spent years in intense therapy to regain her abilities to walk and talk again. Art was an essential part of her recovery. Just seven months after her accident, she started working again. As she did before her accident, she worked with a team of mostly women artists to help her execute her visions for new artworks.

4. Bonnie J. Miller quoting Ginny Ruffner, *Why Not: The Art of Ginny Ruffner* (Seattle: University of Washington Press, 1995), 34.

Plate 49

1. See a work by Ruffner in the collection on page 115.

2. Kari Russell-Pool, email to author, May 8, 2024.

Plate 51

1. Formlines are curvilinear lines that outline a figure or create an abstract motif.

2. Preston Singletary, *Fusion Notes* (Seattle: Minor Matters, 2023), 30.

Plate 55

1. Bullseye Glass Co., *Lino Tagliapietra at Bullseye Glass: Masterworks from Furnace and Kiln* (Portland, OR: Bullseye Glass Co., 1999), 12.

2. Bullseye, 14.

3. Nancy Callan, email to author, May 14, 2024.

4. Carl and Betty Pforzheimer saw the panel in the Tagliapietras' home when visiting and fell in love with it.

5. As told to Carl Pforzheimer by Lino Tagliapietra.

Plate 68

1. Ariela Gittlen, "These 7 Artists Are Testing the Limits of Glassmaking," *Artsy*, accessed May 1, 2024, https://www.artsy.net/article/artsy-editorial-7-artists-testing-limits-glass-making.

2. Gittlen.

Plate 69

1. Ann Wolff cited in Tina Oldknow and Cristine Russell, *Voices of Contemporary Glass: The Heineman Collection* (Corning, NY: Corning Museum of Glass in association with Hudson Hills Press, New York, 2009), 334.

2. This birth scene relates closely to several other works by Wolff including another bowl, *Mickey's Birth*, 1982, (2012.3.48) in the Corning Museum of Glass collection, and a vitreograph, *Mickey Mouse Birthday*, 1982, (2014.10.38) in the collection of the New Britain Museum of American Art.

Plate 71

1. Zynsky's time at RISD under Chihuly's influential leadership, in the company of fellow students like Dan Dailey and Therman Statom, and the early connections to the burgeoning Studio Glass movement, led to incredible opportunities for the young artist such as participating in the building of the Pilchuck Glass School in 1971.

2. Sarah Nichols, "Toots Zynsky: Colour, the Common Thread," *The Decorative Arts Society Journal* 47 (2023):112–113.

3. Toots Zynsky Studio, email to author, November 28, 2023.

4. In addition to the torches, Zynsky also created a series of related commissions as gifts for the Paralympic Executive Committee members. Email, November 28, 2023.

5. "Toots Zynsky," Luce Artist Biography, Smithsonian American Art Museum, https://americanart.si.edu/artist/toots-zynsky-7311.

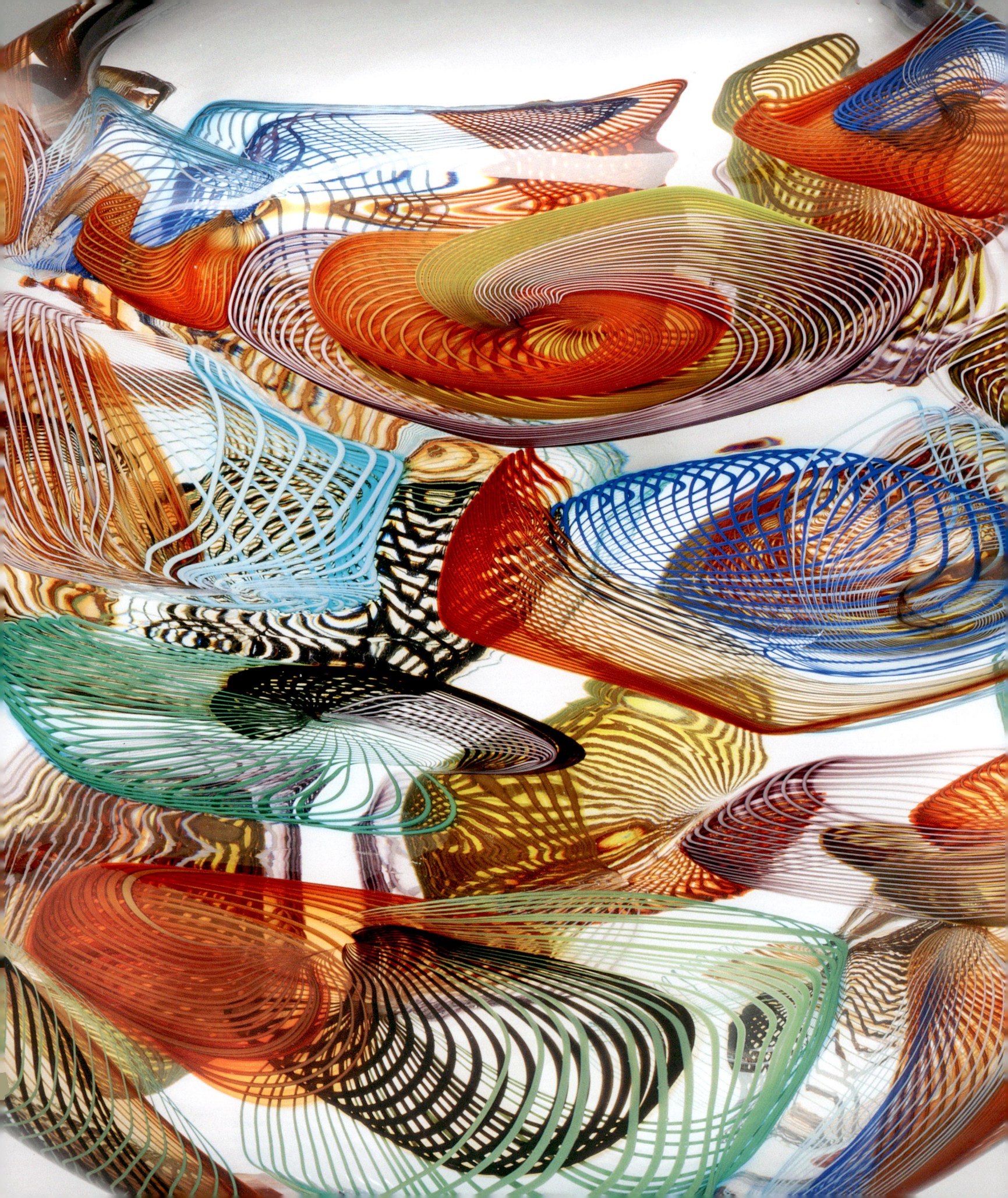

Collection Checklist

Compiled by Isabella Nadeau

All works are in the collection of the Peabody Essex Museum, gift of Carl and Betty Pforzheimer

Unknown titles of works are indicated by unitalicized descriptors

All measurements are height precedes width precedes depth

Studio Glass

Oben Abright
Born 1980, United States

Market Street Series VIII, 2007
From the *Market Street* series, 2004–14
Cast glass, oil paint, and mold-blown glass
16¼ × 10½ × 7½ in. (41.28 × 26.67 × 19.05 cm)
2022.6.1

Doug Anderson
Born 1952, United States

Leap Frog, 1987
Cast *pâte de verre*
5¼ × 5¼ × 3¼ in. (13.34 × 13.34 × 8.26 cm)
2022.6.2

Leon Applebaum
Born 1945, United States

Floral Perfume Bottle, 1981
Blown glass
5¼ × Diam. 3 in. (13.34 × 7.62 cm)
2022.6.3AB

Herb Babcock
Born 1946, United States

Vessel, 1981
Blown glass
6 × Diam. 5¾ in. (15.24 × 14.61 cm)
2022.6.4

Gary Beecham
Born 1955, United States

Textile Vessel, 1981
Blown and fused glass
5 × Diam. 10¼ in. (12.7 × 26.04 cm)
2022.6.5

Geometric Textile, 1984
Blown and fused glass
Diam. 23⅝ × 1 in. (60.01 × 2.54 cm)
2022.6.6

Howard Ben Tré
1949–2020, United States

From Benjamin G., 1980
Cast glass with copper
Diam. 17 × 9 in. (43.18 × 22.86 cm)
2022.6.7

Ricky Bernstein
Born 1952, United States

An Homage to Carl, 2006
Vitrolite glass, aluminum, and mixed media
Approximately 96 × 144 × 6 in. (243.84 × 365.76 × 15.25 cm)
2023.37.1

Giles Bettison
Born 1966, Australia

Paddock Series #52, 1999
From the *Paddock* series
Blown glass, cold-assembled and
hotworked *murrine*
15½ × Diam. 4¾ in. (39.37 × 12.07 cm)
2022.6.8

Sonja Blomdahl
Born 1952, United States

Vase, 1990
Blown glass
10½ × Diam. 9 in. (26.67 × 22.86 cm)
2023.8.1

John Brekke
Born 1955, United States

Bowl, 1988
Blown glass
8 × Diam. 10⅜ in. (20.32 × 26.35 cm)
2022.6.12

Sculpture, 2004
Blown and carved glass
9 × Diam. 9 in. (22.86 × 22.86 cm)
2022.6.11

Yellow X, 2004
Blown and carved glass
Diam. 23½ × ½ in. (59.69 × 1.27 cm)
2022.6.10

Emily Brock
Born 1945, United States

Rare Books, 1990
Flameworked, blown, and cast glass
13⅝ × 14½ × 14½ in. (34.61 × 36.83 ×
36.83 cm)
2022.6.13

Jane Bruce
Born 1947, United Kingdom

Bowl, 1987
Blown glass
5 × Diam. 5⅛ in. (12.7 × 13.02 cm)
2022.6.14

Blue Green Ball, 2004
Wheel-cut blown glass
7¾ × Diam. 6½ in. (19.69 × 16.51 cm)
2022.6.15

Bullseye Ball, 2004
Wheel-cut, kilnformed, and blown
Bullseye glass
6¾ × Diam. 6¼ in. (17.15 × 15.89 cm)
2022.6.16

Jaroslava Brychtová
1924–2020, Czech Republic, and

Stanislav Libenský
1921–2002, Czech Republic

Head VI (Queen), 1987
Cast glass
13¾ × 7¾ × 5 in. (34.93 × 19.69 ×
12.7 cm)
2023.30.1

Laid Table, 1990
Cast glass
5¾ × 10¼ × 5 in. (14.61 × 26.04 ×
12.7 cm)
2022.6.96

Moshe Bursuker
Born 1978, Israel
Works in United States

Winter Tree Platter, 2009
Blown glass, sandblasted glass, and
metal
Diam. 20¾ × ⅛ in. (52.71 × 0.32 cm)
2022.6.17

Nancy Callan
Born 1964, United States

Ice Princess, 1995
Blown glass and metal
13½ × 4⅞ × 4½ in. (34.29 × 12.38 ×
11.43 cm)
2022.6.19AB

Melon Droplet, 2019
Blown and etched glass
16½ × Diam. 14½ in. (41.91 × 36.83 cm)
2022.6.18

William Carlson
Born 1950, United States

Concursatio, 2002
Cast glass on steel plate
Cubes: 5 × 5 × 2½ in. each (12.7 ×
12.7 × 6.35 cm)
Overall: 39⅝ × 39¾ × 2¾ in. (100.65 ×
100.97 × 6.99 cm)
2022.6.20.1–27

Sydney Cash
Born 1941, United States

Sculpture, 1981
Slumped glass
8¼ × 4⅝ × 4 in. (20.96 × 11.75 ×
10.16 cm)
2022.6.21

Dale Chihuly
Born 1941, United States

Floodline Cylinder, 1974
Applied and blown glass
8¾ × Diam. 6 in. (22.23 × 15.24 cm)
2022.6.27

Blanket Cylinder, 1979
Applied and blown glass
6 × Diam. 3⅛ in. (15.24 × 7.94 cm)
2022.6.23

Blanket Cylinder, 1979
Applied and blown glass
6¾ × Diam. 4⅛ in. (17.15 × 10.48 cm)
2022.6.24

Blanket Cylinder, 1979
Applied and blown glass
8 × Diam. 4¾ in. (20.32 × 12.07 cm)
2022.6.25

Basket, 1981
Blown glass
9 × 9 × 8½ in. (22.86 × 22.86 ×
21.59 cm)
2022.6.22

Bowl, 1983
From the *Macchia* series
Blown glass
8½ × 12⅝ × 11 in. (21.59 × 32.07 ×
27.94 cm)
2022.6.29

Blanket Cylinder, 1984
Applied and blown glass
12⅞ × Diam. 8⅛ in. (32.7 × 20.64 cm)
2022.6.30

Blue and purple set, 1987
From the *Seaforms* series
Blown glass
5 × 11⅛ × 10 in. (12.7 × 28.26 ×
25.4 cm)
2022.6.32A

*Celadon, Indian Red, and Lapis Persian
Set*, 1988
From the *Persians* series
Blown glass
Overall: 9 × 23 ¼ × 22 ¼ (22.86 ×
59.06 × 56.52 cm)
2022.6.31A-H

Sculpture, 1991
From the *Seaforms* series
Blown glass
3¼ × Diam. 3½ in. (8.26 × 8.89 cm)
2022.6.26

Sculpture, 1991
From the *Seaforms* series
Blown glass
1⅞ × 10½ × 2¼ in. (4.76 × 26.67 ×
5.72 cm)
2022.6.28

Dale Chihuly
and
Lino Tagliapietra (*assistant*)
    Born 1934, Italy

Vessel, 1993
    From the *Venetians* series
    Blown glass
    21⅛ × 13½ × 13 in. (53.66 × 34.29 ×
    33.02 cm)
    2022.6.33

Tessa Clegg
    Born 1946, United Kingdom

Bowl, 1990
    Cast *pâte de verre*
    6½ × Diam. 8½ in. (16.51 × 21.59 cm)
    2022.6.34

Daniel Crichton
    1946–2002, United States
    Worked in Canada

Vessel, 1981
    Blown glass and alabaster
    5⅜ × Diam. 7 in. (13.65 × 17.78 cm)
    2022.6.35

Dan Dailey
    Born 1947, United States

Banana Woman, 1990
    From the *Face Vase* series, 1988–97
    Blown glass and applied vitreous
    enamel
    22¼ × Diam. 14½ in. (56.52 ×
    36.83 cm)
    2022.6.36

Fritz Dreisbach
    Born 1941, United States

Goblet, 1980
    Blown glass
    7¼ × 3 × 3⅝ in. (18.42 × 7.62 ×
    9.21 cm)
    2022.6.37

Mongo Bowl, 1981
    From the ongoing *Mongo* series
    Blown glass
    6⅞ × 9¼ × 8¾ in. (17.46 × 23.5 ×
    22.23 cm)
    2022.6.40

Goblet, 1984
    Blown glass
    9½ × 6½ × 3¼ in. (24.13 × 16.51 ×
    8.26 cm)
    2022.6.38

Goblet, 1984
    Blown glass
    10⅞ × 4 × 3½ in. (27.62 × 10.16 ×
    8.89 cm)
    2022.6.39

Stephen Dee Edwards
    Born 1954, United States

Sea Form #196, 1981
    From the *Sea Form* series
    Blown and carved glass
    7¾ × 8½ × 10¼ in. (19.69 × 21.59 ×
    26.04 cm)
    2022.6.41

Head, 1991
    Blown, cast, cut, and fused glass
    17⅜ × 7½ × 6½ in. (44.13 × 19.05 ×
    16.51 cm)
    2022.6.42

Kyohei Fujita
    1921–2004, Japan

Kaguya-hime 141–114, ca. 1988
    Mold-blown glass with enamel, silver,
    and gold and platinum foil
    6¼ × 4⅞ × 4⅞ in. (15.88 × 12.38 ×
    12.38 cm)
    2022.6.44.1AB

Decanter #141–224, 1992
    Blown glass
    9¾ × Diam. 6⅝ in. (24.77 × 16.83 cm)
    2022.6.43.1AB

Michael Glancy
    1950–2020, United States

Aventureen Squared, 1981
    Blown, cut, and sandblasted glass
    10 × 4¾ × 2½ in. (25.4 × 12.07 ×
    6.35 cm)
    2022.6.45

Crystal Sentinel, 1982
    Blown, engraved, and electroplated
    glass with copper, and industrial plate
    glass
    Cylinder: 9⅝ × Diam. 2⅜ in. (24.45 ×
    6.03 cm)
    Base: 12 × 12 × ¼ in. (30.48 × 30.48 ×
    0.64 cm)
    2022.6.46AB

William Gudenrath
    Born 1950, United States

Candlestick, 1986
    Blown glass
    7 × Diam. 3¾ in. (17.78 × 9.53 cm)
    2022.6.47

Candlestick, 1992
    Blown glass
    8¾ × Diam. 3⅜ in. (22.23 × 8.57 cm)
    2022.6.49

Candlestick, 1994
    Blown glass
    8⅜ × Diam. 4⅛ in. (21.27 × 10.48 cm)
    2022.6.50

Dragon-stem goblet, 1995
    Blown glass
    12¼ × Diam. 4 in. (31.12 × 10.16 cm)
    2022.6.51

Candlestick, 2000
    Blown glass and platinum leaf
    6⅞ × Diam. 3⅞ in. (17.46 × 9.84 cm)
    2022.6.48

Vase, 20th–21st century
    Blown glass
    8¼ × Diam. 4½ in. (20.96 × 11.43 cm)
    2022.6.52

Vase, 20th–21st century
    Blown glass and gold leaf
    6¾ × Diam. 5½ in. (17.15 × 13.97 cm)
    2022.6.53

Dorothy Hafner
    Born 1952, United States

Blue Cascade, 2007
    Multi-layer fused glass and metal
    24½ × 14¼ × 6 in. (62.23 × 36.2 ×
    15.24 cm)
    2022.6.54AB

Jiří Harcuba
    1928–2013, Czech Republic

Cityscape, 2006
    Cast and engraved glass
    8 × 8¼ × 1 in. (20.32 × 20.96 ×
    2.54 cm)
    2022.6.55

Sculpture, 2006
    Fused and engraved glass
    6⅛ × 6½ × 1⅝ in. (15.56 × 16.51 ×
    4.13 cm)
    2022.6.56

Jamie Harris
    Born 1975, United States

Modulated Infusion Wall Panel, 2008
    From the ongoing *Infusions* series
    Blown glass, cast glass, and metal
    24 × 19⅜ × 1⅜ in. (60.96 × 49.21 ×
    3.49 cm)
    2022.6.57

Chris Hawthorne
    Born 1953, United States, and
James Nowak
    Born 1956, United States

Vessel, 1990
    From the *Aquarium* series
    Blown glass
    18¼ × 23½ × 12½ in. (46.36 × 59.69 ×
    31.75 cm)
    2022.6.58

Kimiake Higuchi
Born 1948, Japan

Cyclamen V-3, 1995
Pâte de verre
15¾ × 14⅛ × 6 in. (40.01 × 35.88 × 15.24 cm)
2022.6.59

Eric Hilton
Born 1937, United Kingdom
For Steuben Glass Works, United States

Infinite Journey, 20th–21st century
Cast glass, sandblasted glass, and granite
5 × 9⅜ × 9⅜ in. (12.7 × 23.81 × 23.81 cm)
2022.6.60A-E

Pavel Hlava
1924–2003, Czech Republic

Nature and Autumn, 1992
Blown, cut, polished, and laminated glass
13¼ × 15¾ × 4¼ in. (33.66 × 40.01 × 10.8 cm)
2022.6.61

James A. Houston
1921–2005, Canada
Worked in United States
For Steuben Glass Works, United States

Arctic Fisherman, designed ca. 1970
Sag cast, cut, and wheel-engraved lead glass, and 18k gold
Overall: 8½ × 8 × 3¾ in. (21.59 × 20.32 × 9.53 cm)
2022.6.163AB

Dick Huss
Born 1946, United States

Turquoise blue–silver bowl, 1989–1990
Blown glass
6¾ × Diam. 15½ in. (17.15 × 39.37 cm)
2022.6.62

Sidney Hutter
Born 1954, United States

Turned Jerry Vision Vase #126, 2001
From the ongoing *Solid Vase Form* series
Cut, ground, and laminated plate glass
16½ × 9½ × 8⅜ in. (41.91 × 24.13 × 21.27 cm)
2022.6.63

David Jacobson
Born 1952, United States

Multi-colored *murrine* bowl, 2011
Blown, cut, and fused glass
2¼ × Diam. 16½ in. (5.72 × 41.91 cm)
2022.6.82

Margie Jervis
Born 1956, United States, and

Susie Krasnican
Born 1954, United States

Black and white pitcher with glasses, 1983
From the *Profiles and Silhouettes* series
Fused glass with enamel
13½ × 18⅞ × 7 in. (34.29 × 47.94 × 17.78 cm)
2022.6.83

Fred Kahl
Born 1965, United States

Vessel, 1989
Blown and cast glass
16¼ × 13½ × 11 in. (41.28 × 34.29 × 27.94 cm)
2022.6.84

Martin Kremer
Born 1947, United States

Red Ellipsis, 2005
Fused, kilnworked, and coldworked glass, and metal
4⅛ × 34 × 7⅛ in. (10.48 × 86.36 × 18.10 cm)
2022.6.85

John Kuhn
Born 1949, United States

Glass paperweight vase, 1980
Blown glass
8⅜ × 4 × 1½ in. (21.27 × 10.16 × 3.81 cm)
2022.6.87

Sculptured vessel, 1981
Blown, cut, and chemically treated glass
8¾ × 8¼ × 5¼ in. (22.23 × 20.96 × 13.34 cm)
2022.6.88

Symbiosis II, 1991
Ground and polished cut optical lead glass
12½ × 11 × 11 in. (31.75 × 27.94 × 27.94 cm)
2022.6.86

Dominick Labino
1910–1987, United States

Bottle vase, 1970
Blown glass
11⅝ × Diam. 5 in. (29.53 × 12.7 cm)
2022.6.91

Red Festoons, 1980
Blown and pulled glass
4¾ × Diam. 4¼ in. (12.07 × 10.80 cm)
2022.6.90

Sculpture, 1981
From the *Emergence* series, 1971–84
Blown, cut, and polished glass
7⅛ × Diam. 2½ in. (18.1 × 6.35 cm)
2022.6.89

Karen LaMonte
Born 1967, United States

Child's Dress, 2004
Cast glass
13¼ × 13 × 10 in. (33.66 × 33.02 × 25.4 cm)
2022.6.92

K. William LeQuier
Born 1953, United States

Sentinel #17, 1986
From the *Sentinel* series
Blown and plate glass
18¾ × 24 × 4¾ in. (47.63 × 60.96 × 12.07 cm)
2022.6.94A-E

David Levi
Born 1959, United States

Bird Bowl, 1991
Blown glass
17¼ × 20¼ × 15 in. (43.82 × 51.44 × 38.1 cm)
2022.6.95

Marvin Lipofsky
1938–2016, United States

Vase, 1966
Blown glass and copper
12¾ × 7 × 5 in. (32.39 × 17.78 × 12.7 cm)
2022.6.97

Harvey K. Littleton
1922–2013, United States

Crested Form, 1976
Blown and cut glass
16½ × 10½ × 5½ in. (41.91 × 26.67 × 13.97 cm)
2022.6.99

Geometric Sculpture #15, 1979
Blown and cut cased glass
5⅜ × 9¾ × 3½ in. (13.65 × 24.77 × 8.89 cm)
2022.6.98AB

Impact Check with Yellow, 1981
Vitreograph on paper
30¼ × 21½ (76.84 × 53.34 cm)
2022.6.100

Ruby Blue Linked Forms, 1989
Blown, cut, and polished cased glass
Overall: 13⅜ × 17½ × 12 in. (33.97 × 44.45 × 30.48 cm)
2023.8.2A-D

Kristina Logan
Born 1964, United States

Candlestick #7 and #9, 1999
Flameworked glass and bronze
10¼ × Diam. 4⅜ in. (26.04 × 11.11 cm)
2022.6.102.1
10⅛ × Diam. 4¼ in. (25.72 × 10.8 cm)
2022.6.102.2

Red Teapot #5, 2001
Pâte de verre, flameworked glass, and sterling silver
7 × 6¾ × 4 in. (17.78 × 17.15 × 10.16 cm)
2022.6.103AB

Jessica Loughlin
Born 1975, Australia

Vertical Views 18, 2003
Kilnformed glass, wheel-carved glass, and metal
2 panels, each 48 × 5⅜ × 1⅜ in. (121.92 × 13.65 × 3.49 cm)
2022.6.93AB

Lundberg Studios, United States

Paperweight, 1976
Flameworked and *millefiori* glass
2¼ × Diam. 3 in. (5.72 × 7.62 cm)
2022.6.257

Dante Marioni
Born 1964, United States

Vessel, 1986
Blown glass
30 × 8 × 6¼ in. (76.2 × 20.32 × 15.88 cm)
2022.6.105

Richard Marquis
Born 1945, United States

Crazy Quilt Teapot, 1979
From the *Crazy Quilt* series
Fused and blown *murrine* and aventurine glass
4¾ × 5¾ × 4⅞ in. (12.07 × 14.61 × 12.38 cm)
2022.6.110

Core Vessel, 1987
Blown and fused glass
4⅜ × 2¼ × 1¾ in. (11.11 × 5.72 × 4.45 cm)
2022.6.106

Crazy Quilt Teapot, 1990
From the *Crazy Quilt* series
Fused and blown *murrine* and aventurine glass
3¼ × 3½ × 3¼ in. (8.26 × 8.89 × 8.26 cm)
2022.6.107

Marquiscarpa #29, 1991
From the *Marquiscarpa* series, 1991–2011
Fused, slumped, blown, and wheel-carved *murrine*
6½ × 8½ × 3⅛ in. (16.51 × 21.59 × 7.94 cm)
2023.8.3

Teapot Goblet, 1992
Blown glass
9⅝ × 4½ × 3¾ in. (24.51 × 11.43 × 9.53 cm)
2022.6.108

Mark Matthews
Born 1954, United States

Jaguar, 2014
Blown, masked, and sandblasted glass
3 × Diam. 3 in. (7.62 × 7.62 cm)
2022.6.111

Tom McGlauchlin
1934–2011, United States

Tall Dessin de Bulle, 1980
Blown glass
11¾ × Diam. 6 in. (29.85 × 15.24 cm)
2022.6.113

Vase, 1982
From the *Prism Cut* series
Blown glass
10⅛ × 5¾ × 3¾ in. (25.72 × 14.61 × 9.53 cm)
2022.6.112

Charles Miner
Born 1947, United States

Grand Slam, 1997
Cast lead glass (crystal)
14 × Diam. 17⅞ in. (35.56 × 45.4 cm)
2022.6.114

Roswell Frogs, 2006
Cast lead glass (crystal)
10¼ × 21 × 20½ in. (26.04 × 53.34 × 52.07 cm)
2022.6.115AB

Klaus Moje
1936–2016, Germany
Worked in Australia

Bowl form, 1981
Fused, slumped, and ground glass
Diam. 10⅜ × 2 in. (26.35 × 5.08 cm)
2022.6.117

Bowl, 1997
Fused, slumped, and ground glass
2¾ × 10⅞ × 13⅞ in. (6.99 × 27.62 × 35.24 cm)
2022.6.118

Untitled #10, 1997
Fused, slumped, and ground glass
Diam. 20⅞ × 2¾ in. (53.02 × 6.99 cm)
2022.6.116

William Morris
Born 1957, United States

Black Soft Form, 1980
Blown glass
6¾ × 7½ × 3½ in. (17.15 × 19.05 × 8.89 cm)
2022.6.121

Vase, 1980
Blown glass
9½ × 9½ × 3 in. (24.13 × 24.13 × 7.62 cm)
2022.6.119

Standing Stone, 1984
Mold-blown glass
18 × 18¼ × 6 in. (45.72 × 46.36 × 15.24 cm)
2022.6.120

Jay Musler
Born 1949, United States

Cityscape, 1995
Blown, acid-etched, and painted glass
8⅛ × Diam. 18 in. (20.64 × 45.72 cm)
2022.6.122

Jean-Claude Novaro
1943–2014, France

Vase, 1988
Blown glass
7½ × 10½ × 8 in. (19.05 × 26.67 × 20.32 cm)
2022.6.123

John Nygren
Born 1940, United States

Red poison arrow frog on rock paperweight, 1983
Blown and flameworked glass
3¾ × 3 × 3 in. (9.53 × 7.62 × 7.62 cm)
2022.6.124

Orient and Flume Art Glass, United States

Paperweight, 1977
Flameworked and *millefiori* glass
2½ × Diam. 2¾ in. (6.35 × 6.99 cm)
2022.6.258

Tom Patti
Born 1943, United States

Solar Gray Soltex Riser, 1979
From the *Solar Riser* series, 1977–81
Blown, fused, and laminated glass
5¼ × 4 × 3¾ in. (13.34 × 10.16 ×
9.53 cm)
2022.6.125

Bronze Echo with Green 140, 1989–91
From the *Echo* series, 1989–91
Stacked, fused, blown, and polished
glass
2¾ × 6⅛ × 3⅞ in. (6.99 × 15.56 ×
9.84 cm)
2023.8.4

Mark Peiser
Born 1938, United States

Ascension, 1985
Uranium and cast glass
13⅝ × 6¼ × 3½ in. (34.61 × 15.88 ×
8.89 cm)
2022.6.128

Sculpture, 1985
From the *Innerspace* series, 1983–94
Cast, cut, and polished glass
9¾ × 4⅝ × 2½ in. (24.77 × 11.75 ×
6.35 cm)
2022.6.127

Clifford Rainey
Born 1948, United Kingdom

Maquette for Torso No. 2, 2000
Cast glass, maple, rock, metal, and
plastic
24 × 8 × 8⅛ in. (60.96 × 20.32 ×
20.64 cm)
2022.6.129AB

Richard Ritter
Born 1940, United States

Floral Core #22, 2002
From the *Floral Core* series, 2001–09
Cast and sandblasted glass with
murrine
3¾ × 14 × 11 in. (9.53 × 35.56 ×
27.94 cm)
2023.8.5

Ann Robinson
Born 1944, New Zealand

Neodymium Generation Bowl, 1995
Cast lead glass (crystal)
8 × Diam. 15¼ in. (20.32 × 38.74 cm)
2022.6.131

Erica Rosenfeld
Born 1975, United States

Fulton Street, 1:30 am, 2007–09
Hotworked, carved, and sewn *murrine*
on mesh
17½ × 30½ × 1 in. (44.45 × 77.47 ×
2.54 cm)
2022.6.132

White mosaic plate, 20th–21st century
Fused and cut glass
2¼ × 22¼ × 8¾ in. (5.72 × 56.52 ×
22.23 cm)
2022.6.133

Martin Rosol
Born 1956, Czech Republic
Works in United States

Relique, before 1993
Cut, laminated, and sandblasted glass
with gold leaf
9½ × 3⅝ × 3⅛ in. (24.13 × 9.21 ×
7.94 cm)
2022.6.134

Eric Rubinstein
Born 1956, United States

Vase, 2002
From the *Red Square* series
Blown, cut, and etched glass
10 × 10⅛ × 4¾ in. (25.4 × 25.72 ×
12.07 cm)
2022.6.136

Seascape Stones, 2009
From the *Seascape* series
Hotsculpted cut glass
6⅜ × 5¾ × 3¾ in. (16.19 × 14.61 ×
9.53 cm)
2022.6.135

Ginny Ruffner
1952–2025, United States

Elements of a Still Life II, 1996
From the *Conceptual Narrative* series
Flameworked and painted glass
17¾ × 20 × 12 in. (45.09 × 50.8 ×
30.48 cm)
2022.6.137

Kari Russell-Pool
Born 1967, United States

Daisy Wish Bowl, 1992
Hotsculpted and flameworked glass
7⅜ × Diam. 8¾ in. (18.73 × 22.23 cm)
2022.6.138

Kari Russell-Pool
Born 1967, United States, and

Marc Petrovic (*assistant*)
Born 1967, United States

3 Birds, Flowers, 2001
From the *Banded Vessels* series,
2001–ongoing
Blown and flameworked glass
19 × Diam. 9½ in. (48.26 × 24.13 cm)
2022.6.139

Carlo Scarpa
1906–1978, Italy
For Venini and Company, Italy

Vase, 1981, designed 1940
From the *Tessuti Battuti* series
Blown and ground glass
8⅞ × Diam. 5 in. (22.54 × 12.7 cm)
2022.6.140

Vase, 1981, designed 1940
From the *Tessuti Battuti* series
Blown and ground glass
13½ × Diam. 5 in. (34.29 × 12.7 cm)
2022.6.141

Toby Ruth Schwartz
1954–2017, United States

Lady in the Castle, 1983
Blown, etched, and sandblasted glass
4⅜ × Diam. 2½ in. (11.11 × 6.35 cm)
2022.6.143AB

Toby Ruth Schwartz
1954–2017, United States, and

Hank Schwartz
Born 1954, United States

Grapes, 1981
Blown, etched, and sandblasted glass
6½ × Diam. 5 in. (16.51 × 12.7 cm)
2022.6.142

Josh Simpson
Born 1949, United States

Vase, 1978
Blown glass
3¾ × Diam. 3¾ in. (28.26 × 9.53 cm)
2022.6.145

Iridescent Tektite, 1981
From the ongoing *Tektite* series
Tektite meteorite formula glass, iridescent silver glass, and crystal spheres
4 × 8 × 7 in. (10.16 × 20.32 × 17.78 cm)
2022.6.144

New Mexico Vase, 1981
From the ongoing *New Mexico* series
Blown glass and reactive silver
4½ × Diam. 3¾ in. (11.43 × 9.53 cm)
2022.6.146

Multi-layered flower vase, 1981 or 1995
Blown glass
5¼ × Diam. 3¾ in. (13.34 × 9.53 cm)
2022.6.147

Preston Singletary
Born 1963, United States (Tlingit)

Oystercatcher, 2006
Blown and sand-carved glass, and steel
16⅛ × 12 × 15 in. (40.96 × 30.48 × 38.1 cm)
2022.6.148.1–2

Paul Stankard
Born 1943, United States

Wild Roses, 1975
Flameworked glass
1⅞ × Diam. 2¾ in. (4.76 × 6.99 cm)
2022.6.151

Chokeberry and Blossom, 1976
Flameworked glass
2 × Diam. 3 in. (5.08 × 7.62 cm)
2022.6.159

St. Anthony's Fire, 1979
Flameworked glass
2⅜ × Diam. 3 in. (6.03 × 7.62 cm)
2022.6.153

Yellow Wildflower, 1970s
Flameworked glass
1⅞ × Diam. 2¾ in. (4.76 × 6.99 cm)
2022.6.152

White Flowers, 1980
Flameworked glass
1¾ × Diam. 2¾ in. (4.45 × 6.99 cm)
2022.6.157

Loosestrife Botanical, 1981
Flameworked glass
3½ × 2½ × 2 in. (8.89 × 6.35 × 5.08 cm)
2022.6.158

Rose Bouquet, 1982
Flameworked glass
1¾ × Diam. 3 in. (4.45 × 7.62 cm)
2022.6.156

Cactus Environment with Anthropomorphic Roots, 1985
Flameworked glass
2¼ × Diam. 3¼ in. (5.72 × 8.26 cm)
2022.6.154

Blackberry Bouquet, 1995
Flameworked glass
2⅛ × Diam. 3¼ in. (5.4 × 8.26 cm)
2022.6.150

Tap Root Bouquet and Veiled Orb, 1999
Flameworked glass
6 × 5⅛ × 3¾ in. (15.24 × 13.02 × 9.53 cm)
2022.6.155

Honeybee Swarm with Flowers and Fruit, 2012
Flameworked glass
5½ × Diam. 5½ in. (13.97 × 13.97 cm)
2022.6.149

Lino Tagliapietra
Born 1934, Italy
For Effetre International, Milano

Three Eggs, 1984
Retailed by Oggetti, United States
Blown glass
10¾ × Diam. 7 in. (27.31 × 17.78 cm)
2022.6.182

8½ × Diam. 6 in. (21.59 × 15.24 cm)
2022.6.183

6¾ × Diam. 4½ in. (17.15 × 11.43 cm)
2022.6.184

Rainbow charger, 1985
Blown glass and metal
21⅛ × 20¾ × 2½ in. (53.66 × 52.71 × 6.35 cm)
2022.6.169

Rainbow vessel, 1985
Blown glass
9¾ × Diam. 9¼ in. (24.77 × 23.5 cm)
2022.6.181

Mogambo, 1988
Blown glass
13⅛ × 8½ × 4 in. (33.34 × 21.59 × 10.16 cm)
2022.6.173

Lino Tagliapietra (*glassblower*)
Born 1934, Italy, and

Marina Angelin (*designer*)
Born mid-20th century, Italy
For Effetre International, Murano

Four Eggs, 1983
Blown and cut glass, *lattimo* (milk) glass, and *fasce* (bands) glass, A.P.
10½ × Diam. 7 in. (26.67 × 17.78 cm)
2022.6.164

9½ × Diam. 6½ in. (24.13 × 16.51 cm)
2022.6.165

7½ × Diam. 5 in. (19.05 × 12.7 cm)
2022.6.166

6½ × 4¼ × 4½ in. (16.51 × 10.8 × 11.43 cm)
2022.6.167

Vase, 1984
Blown glass
13 × Diam. 9½ in. (33.02 × 24.13 cm)
2022.6.196

Angelin vessel, 1984
Blown glass
9 × Diam. 8½ in. (22.86 × 21.59 cm)
2022.6.185

Pueblo vase, 1986
Blown glass
13¼ × Diam. 5 in. (33.66 × 12.7 cm)
2022.6.175

Incalmo vase, 1988
Blown glass
9¼ × Diam. 12¼ in. (23.5 × 31.12 cm)
2022.6.168

Incalmo, 1988
From the *Stone* series
Blown glass
14¾ × 7 × 5 in. (37.47 × 17.78 × 12.7 cm)
2022.6.174

Pueblo charger, 1989
Blown glass and metal
19½ × 19 × 1 in. (49.53 × 48.26 × 2.54 cm)
2022.6.193

Pueblo Vase, 1989
Blown glass
9⅛ × Diam. 12 in. (23.18 × 30.48 cm)
2022.6.192

Lino Tagliapietra
Born 1934, Italy

Prototype Egg Shape, 1988
Blown glass
13 × Diam. 8 in. (33.02 × 20.32 cm)
2022.6.201

Notte del Redentore, 1988
Blown glass
13 × 9½ × 9¼ in. (33.02 × 24.13 × 23.5 cm)
2022.6.209

Zebrato, 1990
Blown glass and applied glass 8¾ × 7¼ × 7½ in. (22.23 × 18.42 × 19.05 cm)
2022.6.172

Vessel, 1992
Blown glass
7¾ × Diam. 10½ in. (19.69 × 26.67 cm)
2022.6.207

Sasso di Marsiglia, 1993
Blown glass
Diam. 10 × 5 in. (25.4 × 12.7 cm)
2022.6.195

Spirale, 1996
Blown glass
25¼ × Diam. 4 in. (64.14 × 10.16 cm)
2022.6.189

Tucson, 1997
Blown and carved glass
21½ × 9 × 6 in. (54.61 × 22.86 × 15.24 cm)
2022.6.188

Vessel, 1997
Blown glass
14½ × 7½ × 5 in. (36.83 × 19.05 × 12.7 cm)
2022.6.208

Alghero, 1998
Blown and carved glass
17¼ × 8¼ × 7 in. (43.82 × 20.96 × 17.78 cm)
2022.6.187

Borneo, 1998
Blown glass
18 × 12 × 8 in. (45.72 × 30.48 × 20.32 cm)
2022.6.171

Odissea, 1998
Fused hand-pulled cane, *murrine*
70¼ × 24 × 12 in. (178.44 × 60.96 × 30.48 cm)
2022.6.170

Provenza, 1998
Blown glass
18¼ × 10½ × 6 in. (46.36 × 26.67 × 15.24 cm)
2022.6.206

Tholtico, 1998
Blown and carved glass
12½ × Diam. 9 in. (31.75 × 22.86 cm)
2022.6.200

Endeavor, ca. 2000
Blown and carved glass
13 × 71⅜ × 4¾ in. (33.02 × 181.29 × 12.07 cm)
2022.6.199

Mandara, 2004
Blown glass
17 × 17¼ × 4 in. (43.18 × 43.82 × 10.16 cm)
2022.6.203

Tampa, 2005
Blown and wheel-engraved glass
11¼ × 11 × 6 in. (28.58 × 27.94 × 15.24 cm)
2022.6.202

Canto, 2006
Blown glass
22¼ × 15 × 7 in. (56.52 × 38.1 × 17.78 cm)
2022.6.194

Stromboli, 2006
Blown and wheel-engraved glass
14⅝ × 9¼ × 5 in. (37.15 × 23.5 × 12.7 cm)
2022.6.205

Bengala, 2008
Blown and wheel-engraved glass
10½ × 9½ × 7½ in. (26.67 × 24.13 × 19.05 cm)
2022.6.204

Seattle Sunset, 2008
Blown glass
19¼ × 11½ × 6 in. (48.9 × 29.21 × 15.24 cm)
2022.6.197

Niomea, 2009
Blown glass
29¾ × 15 × 7 in. (75.57 × 38.1 × 17.78 cm)
2022.6.179

Vienna, 2009
Blown glass
40⅝ × 19 × 8½ in. (103.19 × 48.26 × 21.59 cm)
2022.6.180

Kira, 2010
Blown glass
15½ × 16½ × 6½ in. (39.37 × 41.91 × 16.51 cm)
2022.6.198

Saturno, 2010
Blown glass
69 × 17¾ × 17¾ in. (175.26 × 45.09 × 45.09 cm)
2022.6.186

Sculpture, 2010
Blown and carved glass
16½ × 15 × 6 in. (41.91 × 38.1 × 15.24 cm)
2022.6.191

Dinosaur, 2019
Blown glass
55 × 9 × 9 in. (139.7 × 22.86 × 22.86 cm)
2023.8.6.1–4

Florencia, 2019
Blown glass
25 × 10 × 8 in. (63.5 × 25.4 × 20.32 cm)
2022.6.190

Lino Tagliapietra
Born 1934, Italy, and

Thomas S. Buechner III
1926–2010, United States

Set of goblets, 1988
Blown glass
14¾ × Diam. 7½ in. (37.47 × 19.05 cm)
2022.6.176

11¾ × Diam. 3¾ in. (29.85 × 9.53 cm)
2022.6.177

10¾ × Diam. 3½ in. (27.31 × 8.89 cm)
2022.6.178

Dalibor Tichý
1950–1985, Czech Republic

Emerald Ring, 1982
Cast and hotworked glass
9¾ × 5½ × 6 in. (24.77 × 13.97 × 15.24 cm)
2022.6.211

Cesare Toffolo
Born 1961, Italy

Goblet, 20th–21st century
Filigree, blown, and flameworked glass
6⅜ × Diam. 3 in. (16.19 × 7.62 cm)
2022.6.212

Goblet, 20th–21st century
Filigree, blown, and flameworked glass
5¾ × Diam. 4¼ in. (14.61 × 10.8 cm)
2022.6.213

Gianni Toso
Born 1942, Italy
Works in the United States

Chasidim-Franciscan Chess Set, 1983
Flameworked glass and wood
10½ × 26½ × 26½ in. (26.67 × 67.31 × 67.31 cm)
2022.6.214.1–33

Simchat Torah, 1994
Flameworked glass
21¼ × 26¾ × 20 in. (53.98 × 67.95 × 50.8 cm)
2022.6.215

Midsummer Night's Dream, 2002
Flameworked glass and metal
22 × 20¼ × 18 in. (55.88 × 51.44 × 45.72 cm)
2022.6.216

Milon Townsend
Born 1956, United States

Secret Treasure, 1998
Flameworked glass
5¼ × 3¾ × 3¾ in. (13.34 × 9.53 × 9.53 cm)
2022.6.217

Karla Trinkley
Born 1956, United States

Widow's Walk, 20th–21st century
Cast glass
7 × 8½ × 8½ in. (17.78 × 21.59 × 21.59 cm)
2022.6.218

Bertil Vallien
Born 1938, Sweden

Dorian Bay, 1985
Sandcast glass
5¼ × 16¾ × 4½ in. (13.34 × 42.55 × 11.43 cm)
2022.6.219AB

Sylvia Bernice Vigiletti
1933–2020, Canada

Sculpture, 1981
Blown glass
4⅝ × 3¼ × 1½ in. (11.81 × 8.26 × 3.81 cm)
2022.6.220

František Vízner
1936–2011, Czech Republic

Red bowl with peak, 2006
Cut glass, shaped on the grindstone
3½ × Diam. 10⅝ in. (8.89 × 26.99 cm)
2022.6.222

Bowl, 2009
Cut glass, shaped on the grindstone
5 × Diam. 11¾ in. (12.7 × 29.85 cm)
2022.6.221

James Watkins
Born 1955, United States

Bottle with Window and Frame, 1991
Päte de verre
18⅜ × 10¾ × 5 in. (46.67 × 27.31 × 12.7 cm)
2022.6.224

Thaddeus Wolfe
Born 1979, United States

Assemblage Vessel, 2018
From the *Assemblage* series, 2011–ongoing
Cast glass
15¼ × 8½ × 9½ in. (38.74 × 21.59 × 24.13 cm)
2022.6.225

Ann Wolff
Born 1937, Germany
Works primarily in Sweden

Bowl, 2012
Blown, etched, and sandblasted glass
6 × Diam. 12 in. (15.24 × 30.48 cm)
2022.6.223

Rachael Woodman
Born 1957, United Kingdom

Bowl, 2006
Blown glass bowl with bevelled edge
3¾ × Diam. 5⅞ in. (9.53 × 14.92 cm)
2022.6.226

Bowl, 2006
Blown glass bowl with bevelled edge
7¾ × Diam. 5⅞ in. (19.69 × 14.92 cm)
2022.6.227

Toots Zynsky
Born 1951, United States

Untitled, 1982
Blown glass with hot-spun opaque glass thread wrap
6⅜ × Diam. 7 in. (16.19 × 17.78 cm)
2022.6.229

Sculptural vessel, 1984
Filet de verre
6 × 12½ × 11¾ in. (15.24 × 31.75 × 29.85 cm)
2022.6.233

Untitled, 1985
Filet de verre
5¾ × Diam. 12½ in. (14.61 × 31.75 × 31.75 cm)
2022.6.231

Untitled, 1988
From the *Tierra del Fuego* series, 1987–1990
Filet de verre
6½ × 13 × 8½ in. (16.51 × 33.02 × 21.59 cm)
2022.6.232

Traffic, 1992
From the *Order and Chaos* series, 1990–99
Filet de verre
5½ × 18 × 6½ in. (13.97 × 45.72 × 16.51 cm)
2022.6.228

Isabella, 2003
Filet de verre
11¼ × 22 × 16 in. (28.58 × 55.88 × 40.64 cm)
2022.6.230

Historic Glass

Artist in Rome

Cup, 4th century
Blown and cut glass
1⅞ × Diam. 3⅝ in. (4.76 × 9.21 × 9.21 cm)
2022.6.234

Frederick Carder
1863–1963, United Kingdom
For Steuben Glass Works, United States

Goblet, ca. 1915
Blown glass
6¼ × Diam. 4¼ in. (15.88 × 10.8 cm)
2022.6.161

Light blue jade bowl, 1925
Blown glass
2 × Diam. 7½ in. (5.08 × 19.05 cm)
2022.6.160

Aurene, 1920s
Blown Glass
7½ × Diam. 2¼ in. (19.05 × 5.72 cm)
2022.6.162AB

Maurice Marinot
1882–1960, France

Flacon a corps quadrangulaire en verre (rectangular bottle), 1933
Blown and etched glass
4¼ × 3 × 2½ in. (10.8 × 7.62 × 6.35 cm)
2022.6.104AB

Micromosaics

Artists in Italy

Micromosaic, 18th–19th century
Glass and copper
¾ × ⅝ × ⅛ in. (1.91 × 1.59 × 0.32 cm)
2022.6.64

Micromosaic, 18th–19th century
Glass and copper
1 × ⅝ × ⅛ in. (2.54 × 1.59 × 0.32 cm)
2022.6.65

Box, micromosaic, 18th–19th century
Glass and gold
Open: 3⅝ × Diam. 3⅛ in. (9.21 × 7.94 cm)
2022.6.66

Micromosaic, 18th-19th century
Glass and metal
1½ × 2⅛ × ⅛ in. (3.81 × 5.4 × 0.32 cm)
2022.6.67

Ring, micromosaic, 18th–19th century
Glass and gold
1¼ × 1 × 1¼ in. (3.18 × 2.54 × 3.18 cm)
2022.6.68

Micromosaic, 18th–19th century
    Glass, felt, and metal
    1¾ × 2½ × ⅛ in. (4.45 × 6.35 ×
    0.32 cm)
    2022.6.69

Micromosaic, 18th–19th century
    Glass and stone
    1½ × 1¾ × ⅛ in. (3.81 × 4.45 × 0.32 cm)
    2022.6.70

Micromosaic, 18th–19th century
    Glass and metal
    1⅞ × 2⅝ × ⅛ in. (4.76 × 6.67 ×
    0.32 cm)
    2022.6.71

Earring, micromosaic, 18th–19th century
    Glass, stone, and silver
    Resting on earring back: 1¼ × 1 × ¾ in.
    (3.18 × 2.54 × 1.91 cm)
    2022.6.72

162 Brooch, micromosaic, 18th–19th century
    Glass and gold
    1⅝ × 2⅛ × ⅝ in. (4.13 × 5.4 × 1.59 cm)
    2022.6.73

Micromosaic, 18th–19th century
    Glass and stone
    1¼ × 1½ × ⅛ in. (3.18 × 3.81 × 0.32 cm)
    2022.6.74

Micromosaic, 18th–19th century
    Glass and stone
    1½ × 1¼ × ¼ in. (3.81 × 3.18 × 0.64 cm)
    2022.6.75

Micromosaic, 18th–19th century
    Glass and stone
    1¼ × 1⅝ × ¼ in. (3.18 × 4.13 × 0.64 cm)
    2022.6.76

Sculpture, micromosaic, 18th–19th
    century
    Glass, stone, lapis
    4¼ × 2¾ × ⅝ in. (10.8 × 6.99 × 1.59 cm)
    2022.6.77

Micromosaic, 18th–19th century
    Glass and felt
    1¼ × 1 × ⅛ in. (3.18 × 2.54 × 0.32 cm)
    2022.6.78

Ring, micromosaic, 18th–19th century
    Glass and gold
    Diam. 1 × 1¼ in. (2.54 × 3.18 cm)
    2022.6.79

Plaque, micromosaic, 18th–19th century
    Glass and marble
    Framed: 14¾ × 14¾ × 1¾ in. (37.47 ×
    37.47 × 4.45 cm)
    2022.6.80

Micromosaic, 18th–19th century
    Glass and metal
    Framed: 16 × 12 × 1¾ in. (40.64 ×
    30.48 × 4.45 cm)
    2022.6.81

Paperweights

Attributed to Baccarat, France

Paperweight, 19th century
    Cane fragments
    2⅛ × Diam. 2¾ in. (5.4 × 6.99 cm)
    2022.6.251

Baccarat, France

Paperweight, 1848
    Millefiori glass
    2 × Diam. 3 in. (5.08 × 7.62 cm)
    2022.6.242

Paperweight, 1849
    Millefiori glass
    2¼ × Diam. 3 in. (5.72 × 7.62 cm)
    2022.6.244

Prancing horse paperweight, ca.
    1845–1855
    Millefiori and engraved lead glass
    2⅛ × Diam. 3¼ in. (5.4 × 8.26 cm)
    2022.6.241

Commemorative signed and dated
    paperweight, 1858
    Millefiori glass
    2 × Diam. 2¾ in. (5.08 × 6.99 cm)
    2022.6.235

Paperweight, 19th century
    Flameworked glass
    2⅛ × Diam. 2¾ in. (5.4 × 6.99 cm)
    2022.6.250

Paperweight, 19th century
    Millefiori glass
    2¼ × Diam. 3 in. (5.72 × 7.62 cm)
    2022.6.255

Paperweight, 19th century
    Flameworked glass
    1¾ × Diam. 2½ in. (4.45 × 6.35 cm)
    2022.6.252

Paperweight, 19th century
    Millefiori glass
    2 × Diam. 3 in. (5.08 × 7.62 cm)
    2022.6.256

Paperweight, 19th century
    Millefiori glass
    2 × Diam. 2½ in. (5.08 × 6.35 cm)
    2022.6.254

Eastern Rosella, 1996
    Millefiori glass
    2¼ × Diam. 3½ in. (5.72 × 8.89 cm)
    2022.6.240

Poisson Papillon (Butterfly Fish), 1996
    Flameworked and *millefiori* glass
    2¼ × Diam. 3¼ in. (5.72 × 8.26 cm)
    2022.6.237

Paperweight, 1997
    Flameworked and *millefiori* glass
    2½ × Diam. 3½ in. (6.35 × 8.89 cm)
    2022.6.239

Cashmere, 1998
    Millefiori glass
    2¼ × Diam. 3¼ in. (5.72 × 8.26 cm)
    2022.6.243

Sur un Fil (On a Wire), 1998
    Flameworked and *millefiori* glass
    2⅜ × Diam. 3½ in. (6.03 × 8.89 cm)
    2022.6.236

Paperweight, 1999
    Flameworked and *millefiori* glass
    2¼ × Diam. 3¼ in. (5.72 × 8.26 cm)
    2022.6.238

Clichy Glasshouse, France

Paperweight, 19th century
    Millefiori glass
    1¾ × Diam. 2½ in. (4.45 × 6.35 cm)
    2022.6.245

Paperweight, 19th century
    Millefiori glass
    2¼ × Diam. 3 in. (5.72 × 7.62 cm)
    2022.6.249

Paperweight, 19th century
    Millefiori glass
    1⅞ × Diam. 3 in. (4.76 × 7.62 cm)
    2022.6.248

Cristalleries de Saint-Louis, France

Paperweight, 19th century
    Millefiori glass
    1¾ × Diam. 2¾ in. (4.45 × 6.99 cm)
    2022.6.246

Paperweight, 19th century
    Millefiori and aventurine glass
    2 × Diam. 3 in. (5.08 × 7.62 cm)
    2022.6.247

St. Louis Raspberry, 19th century
    Flameworked glass
    2 × Diam. 3 in. (5.08 × 7.62 cm)
    2022.6.253

Further Reading

164 Adamson, Glenn, and Henry Adams. *Lino Tagliapietra: Sculptor in Glass*. New York, NY: Monacelli, 2023.

Anderson, Nola. *Glass: The Life and Art of Klaus Moje*. Sydney, NSW: NewSouth Publishing, 2021.

Baizerman, Suzanne, ed. *Marvin Lipofsky: A Glass Odyssey*, exh cat. Oakland: Oakland Museum of California, 2003.

Bard Graduate Center. *Voices in Studio Glass History: Art and Craft, Maker and Place, and the Critical Writings and Photography of Paul Hollister*. https://exhibitions.bgc.bard.edu/studioglasshistory/.

Belarde-Lewis, Miranda Shkík, and John Drury. *Preston Singletary: Raven and the Box of Daylight*, exh cat. Tacoma, WA: Museum of Glass, 2019.

Buckingham, Katie, Gayle Clemans, and Kim Harty, eds. *Nancy Callan: Forces at Play*, exh cat. Tacoma, WA: Museum of Glass, 2024.

Chihuly, Dale. *Venetians: Dale Chihuly*. Altadena, CA: Twin Palms Publishers, 1989.

Dietz, Ulysses G., and John Bigelow Taylor. *Paul J. Stankard : Homage to Nature*. New York: Harry N. Abrams, 1996.

Fairbanks, Jonathan L., and Pat Warner. *Glass Today by American Studio Artists*, exh cat. Boston: Museum of Fine Arts, 1997.

Frantz, Susanne K. *Lino Tagliapietra in Retrospect: A Modern Renaissance in Italian Glass*. Tacoma, WA: Museum of Glass, 2008.

Frantz, Susanne K., ed. *Stanislav Libenský, Jaroslava Brychtová, A 40-year Collaboration in Glass*. Munich and NY: Prestel, 1994.

Gordon, John Stuart. *American Glass: The Collections at Yale*. New Haven, CT: Yale University Art Gallery, 2018.

Halper, Vicki. *Richard Marquis: Keepers*, exh cat. Tacoma, WA: Museum of Glass, 2019.

Kriele, Dorothea, ed. *Ann Wolff: Observations and Reflections*. Berlin: DCV, Dr. Cantz'sche Verlagsgesellschaft, 2003.

Lippard, Lucy R., Steven A. Nash, Brett Littman, Arthur C. Danto, Laura Addison, and Tina Oldknow. *Karen LaMonte*. New York, NY: Rizzoli Electa, 2020.

Miller, Bonnie J. *Why Not? The Art of Ginny Ruffner*. Tacoma, WA: Tacoma Art Museum, 1995.

Osborne, Margot, and Giles Bettison. *Giles Bettison: Pattern and Perception*. Mile End, South Australia: Wakefield Press, 2015.

Oldknow, Tina. *Collecting Contemporary Glass: Art and Design After 1990 from the Corning Museum of Glass*. Corning, NY: Corning Museum of Glass, 2014.

Oldknow, Tina, and Cristine Russell. *Voices of Contemporary Glass: The Heineman Collection*. Corning, NY: Corning Museum of Glass, 2009.

Oldknow, Tina, and Roger Schreiber. *Dante Marioni: Blown Glass*. New York: Hudson Hills Press, 2000.

Page, Jutta-Annette, Peter Morrin, and Robert Bell. *Color Ignited: Glass 1962-2012*, exh cat. Toledo, OH: Toledo Museum of Art, 2012.

Singletary, Preston. *Fusion Notes*. Seattle, WA: Minor Matters, 2023.

Warmus, William, Tina Oldknow, Nezka Pfeifer, et al. *Josh Simpson: 50 Years of Visionary Glass*. Atglen, PA: Schiffer Publishing, 2022.

Warmus, William, and Donald Kuspit. *Tom Patti: Illuminating the Invisible*. Tacoma, WA: Museum of Glass: International Center for Contemporary Art, 2005.

Whitehouse, David, et al. *Reflecting Antiquity: Modern Glass Inspired by Ancient Rome*, exh cat. Corning, NY: Corning Museum of Glass, 2007.

Wright, Diane C., ed. *Glass: Masterworks from the Chrysler Museum of Art*. Norfolk, VA: Chrysler Museum of Art, 2017.

Yelle, Richard Wilfred. *Glass Art from UrbanGlass*. Atglen, PA: Schiffer, 2000.

Index

This book is published in conjunction with the donation of the Pforzheimer collection to the Peabody Essex Museum, Salem, Massachusetts, in May 2022, and the installation of *Studio Glass* in the Pforzheimer Gallery, an ongoing presentation opened in May 2024.

Library of Congress Cataloging-in-Publication Data

Names: Peabody Essex Museum, author. | Chasse, Sarah, editor.
Title: Gathering : the Carl and Betty Pforzheimer collection of studio glass / edited by Sarah N. Chasse, with Lan Morgan.
Description: Salem, Massachusetts : Peabody Essex Museum, [2025] | "Gathering: The Carl and Betty Pforzheimer Studio Glass Collection contextualizes the Pforzheimers' collection of twentieth- and twenty-first-century studio glass within the 225-year trajectory of Peabody Essex Museum's glass collection and the international and American glass movements. It includes essays by Sarah Chasse and Lan Morgan and a catalogue of collection highlights and entries"— Provided by publisher.
Identifiers: LCCN 2024048620 | ISBN 9798987929384 (hardcover)
Subjects: LCSH: Studio glass—Catalogs. | Pforzheimer, Carl H., III—Art collections—Catalogs. | Pforzheimer, Betty— Art collections—Catalogs. | Studio glass—Private collections— Massachusetts—Salem—Catalogs. | Peabody Essex Museum— Catalogs.
Classification: LCC NK5110 .P43 2025 | DDC 748—dc23 eng/20241214
LC record available at https://lccn.loc.gov/2024048620

Published in 2025 by the Peabody Essex Museum

Peabody Essex Museum
East India Square
Salem, Massachusetts 01970
pem.org

Distributed by University of Washington Press
uwapress.uw.edu

Produced by Marquand Books, Seattle
marquandbooks.com

Edited by Kathleen Garrett
Designed by Ryan Polich
Typeset in Aktiv Grotesk by Tina Henderson, Miko McGinty Inc.
Proofread by Ivy Long
Color management by I/O Color, Seattle
Printed and bound in China by Artron Art Group

Credits

All photographs by Richard P. Goodbody unless otherwise indicated
All works © the artists unless otherwise indicated

Covers

Harvey K. Littleton, *Ruby Blue Linked Forms* (pl. 34)

Front Matter

Frontispiece: Detail of K. William LeQuier, *Sentinel #17* (pl. 31)
Page 4: Detail of Paul Stankard, *Honeybee Swarm with Flowers and Fruit* (pl. 52)
Page 6: Detail of Jamie Harris, *Modulated Infusion Wall Panel* (pl. 21)

Introduction

Page 10 (fig. 1): Photo by Peter Vanderwarker
Page 12 (figs. 2, 3): Photos by Kathy Tarantola/PEM; (fig. 4): Photo by Peabody Essex Museum
Page 13 (fig. 5): Photo by Kathy Tarantola/PEM
Page 14 (fig. 6): Photo by Kathy Tarantola/PEM; (fig. 7): Photo by Peabody Essex Museum
Page 15 (fig 8): Photo by Walter Silver/PEM
Page 16 (fig. 9): Photo by Mark Sexton/PEM
Page 17 (fig. 10): Photo by Walter Silver/PEM; (fig. 11): Photo by Peabody Essex Museum
Page 18 (fig. 12): Image Courtesy of the Japanese Society of America. Photo by John Bigelow Taylor; (fig. 13): Photo by Mel Taing/PEM
Pages 20–21 (fig. 14): Photo by Mel Taing/PEM

Crafting a Legacy

Page 22: Detail of Lino Tagliapietra, *Vienna* (pl. 57)
Page 24 (fig. 2): Photo by Buck Ennis
Page 25 (fig. 3): Photo by Jacqueline Quint/PEM
Page 31 (fig. 11): Courtesy of Carl and Betty Pforzheimer
Page 32 (fig. 12): Photo by Kathy Tarantola/PEM
Page 37: Detail of Richard Marquis, *Crazy Quilt Teapot* (pl. 37)

Plates

Plate 6: Detail of Emily Brock, *Rare Books*: Photo by Jacqueline Quint/PEM
Plates 12–14: © 2024 Chihuly Studio / Artists Rights Society (ARS), New York
Plate 49: Photo by Kathy Tarantola/PEM

Collection Checklist

Page 152: Detail of Lino Tagliapietra, *Kira* (pl. 58)